200 35204

SOCIETY FOR NEW TESTAMENT STUDIE

MONOGRAPH SERIES

General Editor: R. McL. Wilson, F.B.A.

Associate Editor: M. E. Thrall

36

HEBREWS AND HERMENEUTICS

Hebrews and Hermeneutics

The Epistle to the Hebrews as a New Testament
example of biblical interpretation

GRAHAM HUGHES
Lecturer in Biblical Studies
United Theological College, Sydney

CAMBRIDGE UNIVERSITY PRESS

CAMBRIDGE

LONDON NEW YORK NEW ROCHELLE

MELBOURNE SYDNEY

PUBLISHED BY THE PRESS SYNDICATE OF THE UNIVERSITY OF CAMBRIDGE
The Pitt Building, Trumpington Street, Cambridge, United Kingdom

CAMBRIDGE UNIVERSITY PRESS
The Edinburgh Building, Cambridge CB2 2RU, UK
40 West 20th Street, New York NY 10011–4211, USA
477 Williamstown Road, Port Melbourne, VIC 3207, Australia
Ruiz de Alarcón 13, 28014 Madrid, Spain
Dock House, The Waterfront, Cape Town 8001, South Africa

http://www.cambridge.org

First published 1979
First paperback edition 2004

A catalogue record for this book is available from the British Library

Library of Congress Cataloguing in Publication Data

Hughes, Graham, 1937–
Hebrews and Hermeneutics.
(Monograph series – Society for New Testament Studies; 36)
Bibliography: p.
Includes index.
1. Bible. N. T. Hebrews – Criticism, and interpretation, etc.
2. Bible – Hermeneutics. I. Title. II. Series: Studiorum Novi
Testamenti Societas.
Monograph series; 36.
BS2775.2.H8   227´.87´063   77-84806

ISBN 0 521 21858 6 hardback
ISBN 0 521 60937 2 paperback

For Agathe Thornton

CONTENTS

PREFACE

The ensuing work represents the modification of a dissertation presented to the University of Cambridge in 1971 for the degree of Ph.D. The revision has been made after a number of years in a small but lively country parish in New Zealand, so that in some sense it gathers up three stages of activity: the original exegetical labour, practical Christian involvement, and further theological reflection.

Presumably every author senses the limitations of his work as he is about to send it off to be fixed in print. That is especially so in this case. Up until my appointment as a lecturer in biblical studies (subsequent to the completion of the typescript for this book) I had always regarded myself essentially as a practising parish minister who had had some lucky breaks in which to indulge in his favourite hobby! That meant, however, a sense of being exposed on several flanks. The suggestions of the fourth chapter, which really required an expertise in church history, philosophy and linguistic theory, as well as some knowledge of the bible and theology, have been made especially tentatively.

At every stage of the work I have incurred a deep indebtedness to many people. As do all his students, I owe to Professor C. F. D. Moule an especial tribute for his insights and skill in the supervision of the original work. I am similarly under obligation to Professor Erich Grässer, with whom I spent one semester in 1970, and who listened very patiently to my ideas. In making certain criticisms of their points of view at some places in the following work, I have occasionally been conscious of a sort of betrayal of the friendship shown me by both these men; such criticisms are offered, therefore, in respect, gratitude and affection.

The research was made possible, initially, by the granting to me of the Begg Travelling Scholarship by the Theological Education Committee of the Presbyterian Church of New Zealand and by the generosity of the electors for the Lewis and Gibson Scholarship at Westminster College, Cambridge. The most recent stage of the work was facilitated by a Post-Doctoral Fellowship from the University of Otago, New Zealand.

Agathe Thornton, to whom the work is offered, rescued me when I first came to the University as a student for the ministry and, together with her husband, Harry Thornton, has been a good friend and counsellor ever since.

I have been appreciative of the care and skill of Mrs Noela Pollard in typing the final draft; Professor Evan Pollard checked the typescript with a sharp eye for detail; and Professor Ian Breward made valued criticisms and suggestions for the last chapter.

In all this my dear wife and children, in amazing patience, have borne with an absent or otherwise preoccupied husband and father. To them belongs my deepest gratitude. Perhaps at last we shall now have time to 'do things', together!

ABBREVIATIONS

AngTheolRev	*Anglican Theological Review*
BA	*Biblical Archaeologist*
BZ	*Biblische Zeitschrift*
CanJTheol	*Canadian Journal of Theology*
CBQ	*Catholic Biblical Quarterly*
EQ	*Evangelical Quarterly*
ExT	*Expository Times*
EvTh	*Evangelische Theologie*
HTR	*Harvard Theological Review*
HUCA	*Hebrew Union College Annual*
IEJ	*Israel Exploration Journal*
JBL	*Journal of Biblical Literature*
JES	*Journal of Ecumenical Studies*
JJS	*Journal of Jewish Studies*
JQR	*Jewish Quarterly Review*
JTS	*Journal of Theological Studies*
NEB	*New English Bible*
NovT	*Novum Testamentum*
NTS	*New Testament Studies*
RGG[3]	*Die Religion in Geschichte und Gegenwart,* vols. I–VI and Index, ed. K. Galling (Tübingen, 1957[3]-1965[3])
RSV	*Revised Standard Version*
SJT	*Scottish Journal of Theology*
TDNT	*Theological Dictionary of the New Testament,* vols. I–IX, ed. G. Kittel and G. Friedrich (Grand Rapids, Mich., 1964-74)
TEV	*Today's English Version* ('Good News for Modern Man')
ThBl	*Theologische Blätter*
ThLz	*Theologische Literaturzeitung*
ThR	*Theologisches Rundschau*
ThZ	*Theologische Zeitschrift*

TSK	*Theologische Studien und Kritiken*
VuF	*Verkündigung und Forschung*
ZNW	*Zeitschrift für die Neutestamentliche Wissenschaft*
ZSTh	*Zeitschrift für Systematische Theologie*
ZThK	*Zeitschrift für Theologie und Kirche*

INTRODUCTION

The inclination to introduce any study on the Epistle to the Hebrews by
remarking in some way or another on the enigma which attends this
important letter of our New Testament canon seems almost irresistible.[1]
The tendency is not difficult to account for. On one hand the letter's
significance as an early source for, and continuing influence upon, the
devotional piety and understanding of Christians is unquestionable. Attention is frequently drawn, for instance, to its important statements about
the nature of worship.[2] It is the source of profoundly important Christian
conceptions such as the highpriesthood of Christ, or of Christian life as
an ongoing pilgrimage. Over many centuries Christian theologians have
allowed themselves to be guided in Christological explorations by the
heavy emphases the letter places on both the humanity of Jesus and also
his dignity as Son of God.[3] Some passages, for example the 'definition of
faith' at the head of chapter 11 or the carefully written opening statement
about the Word of God which culminates in Jesus the Son, have regularly
served as models for the expression of these ideas.

But on the whole these contributions made by the unknown author of
our letter function in isolation from their context. As a document, the
letter attracts only minimal attention either from scholars,[4] or from those
who read for more devotional or homiletical purposes.

Apart from the 'anonymity' of the letter (by which I mean not just the
fact that the writer's name is unknown, but rather the isolation in which
he seems to exist even among the other New Testament writers) the first
reason for this is no doubt the great distance which twentieth-century
readers find between themselves and the complicated cultic ideas which
play such a major role in the letter. The conception of Jesus as faithful
highpriest interceding for his hard-pressed followers is a reasonably
manageable one. But the ancillary ideas of sacrifice, atonement and ritual
purification which undergird so much of the argument are considerably
less so. This sense of distance, moreover, coincides with more scholarly
suspicions that the whole construction may be misconceived, that to cast

1

Jesus' meaning into Old Testament forms is a backward step, theologically speaking.[5]

In a slightly different direction lies the problem of identifying at any depth with the concerns which have apparently motivated the letter. Though present-day readers can grasp the point of much of the author's 'pilgrimage' language,[6] the need to spell out in such meticulous detail the points of comparison and contrast between Jesus and the Jewish institutions must now seem to be totally nonexistent.

There is the further difficulty of knowing how his arguments are supposed to 'work', at least in some places. This is not something which is unique to this writer among the others of the New Testament, of course. Most of them simply adopted, exactly as one would expect, at least some of the techniques of deduction operating at their time, especially in the field of scripture exegesis. Nevertheless the writer of Hebrews manages to pose some especial difficulties.[7]

We could mention, too, the difficulties which exegetes have experienced in determining how the letter hangs together: what is the organising thread which allows the various themes to relate to each other in any coherent and obvious way? Such is the profusion and mutual incompatibility of attempts at structure analysis[8] that one might despair of the whole enterprise as an altogether subjective adventure.[9] Yet the structure of the letter is undoubtedly an important clue as to its intentions[10] and in this book we too shall give a good deal of attention to the question.

But underlying all these problematic issues, and in some ways providing the reason for them, is the most basic question: what is the real point and purpose of this letter? What is the occasion in which it first takes its form and the situation to which it is addressed?

Though of course such generalisations are always too wide and are made at the expense of the significant exceptions, one might still risk the judgement that the interpretations of the 'life-situation' question have fallen into two broadly defined groups.[11] On one hand the more traditional view is based on what may be called the 'relapse interpretation'. In other words, the author, presumably himself a Hellenistic-Jewish Christian convert, is writing to a community of Jewish Christians who, because of impending persecution or for some other reason, are seriously contemplating the abandonment of their more recently acquired faith and reverting to the faith of their fathers. The letter is accordingly seen as intending a polemical confrontation with Judaism, arguing the impossibility of returning to the forms of worship so totally outmoded by the advent of Jesus, and earnestly encouraging a persevering allegiance to the Christian confession. This is the interpretation which has prevailed over most of the history of the exegesis and is still widely held especially among Anglo-Saxon scholars.[12]

During this century, however, an alternative viewpoint has been promoted which takes the primary intention of the letter not to be an engagement, hand to hand, with Judaism but rather sees the letter much more generally as a summons to Gentile Christians for a more spiritualised conception of faith. From this point of view the Jewish motifs are employed simply as examples or symbols of an unworthily materialistic form of faith, basically incompatible with that to which Christ calls his followers and for which he has shown the way. Whereas the older view, with its interest in the confrontation between Jesus and Judaism, had attended more carefully to the dogmatic or Christological elements of the letter, the newer view urges that since theology regularly functions as the motive for exhortation in the letter, this scheme must be allowed to regulate our understanding of its overall intentions. Its character as a 'word of exhortation' (13.22) must be regarded as more significant, exegetically, than its dogmatic or theological statements.[13]

We shall need to pay careful attention to the claims of each of these viewpoints, but we may state in advance that one of the central theses offered in this book is that neither of the major alternative interpretations of the 'life-setting' of the letter altogether satisfactorily explains certain of its features; and that there is another way of looking at it which not only offers us new insights into the author's interests and intentions, but allows him to speak with an unexpected proximity and freshness across the centuries to matters which are of intense interest to present-day Christian theologians. The thesis which is offered is that the writer of Hebrews is the theologian who, more diligently and successfully than any other of the New Testament writers, has worked at what we now describe as hermeneutics. The question which has preoccupied him more deeply than any other, we shall argue, has been that of saying how we may conceive the Word of God (or to use the term he chooses in his opening statement, God's 'Address') as being subject to historical processes and yet remaining, recognisably, God's Word.[14] In contemporary theological discourse the term 'hermeneutics' usually refers to the interpretative interaction set up by reason of the historical distance which intervenes between ourselves and the originating events on which Christian faith depends.[15] But it has also been recognised that the difficulties inherent in this interpretative process are brought to their sharpest focus precisely in the interrelationship between the Old and the New Testaments of the Christian scriptures.[16] The writer of the letter to the Hebrews is a Christian who stands in very close proximity to that junction point and therefore has had to work in a pioneering way with all the questions which at our distance and with our collective resources must seem only mildly difficult by comparison.

In any such attempt to allow an ancient text such as the one we have before us to speak in the context of contemporary discussions, we too have clearly already become engaged in the hermeneutical process. Since the questions which are asked are manifestly ours, the answers cannot possibly be exactly the ones given by our first-century writer. That, I would hope, should not be allowed to thwart us before we had started; otherwise there would be no possibility of learning from any cultural setting other than our own,[17] and since interpretation may be held to play a definitive role in any meaningful interchange it might even raise a question as to whether learning of any kind is possible.[18] In my own interaction with the text of this ancient theologian I have tried to allow two questions to be regulative: if he were here, would he recognise and give assent to the inferences we have drawn from his work? And, in drawing up the formulations we have, could we have arrived at these quite independently of the text, or did it provide the indispensable starting point for our own reflections?[19]

Obviously, because interpretation is not a 'pure' science but depends heavily on more aesthetic and literary judgements, even these questions have a degree of openness about them. But that we should attempt to converse across the centuries with theologians of the past, especially with those who stand close in time to the decisive events of Christian origins, rather than simply talk among ourselves, seems to me axiomatic. And that we need some sort of principles to preserve us from the subjectivism of George Tyrrell's famous 'dark deep well'[20] seems equally obvious. After as careful thought as I can give the matter, these are the principles I have formulated and by which I have tried to work.

It remains, perhaps, to be said that since approximately the mid 1960s – in some theological circles – 'hermeneutics' has enjoyed a vogue-like popularity as 'a way of doing theology'. That the present work comes too late to catch that particular wave of interest does not greatly concern me. While many statements of undoubted value have emerged from that movement, I am much more interested in the more regular business of the interpretation of ancient documents, in particular the ancient documents of Christian faith. This task, while it presents an especial urgency in the times in which we live, is larger and more important than any passing 'fashion' in theology. It is this, the perennial responsibility laid on Christian faith to understand and interpret the documents on which it so largely depends, which I hope might be helped by my reflections upon it.

1

THE SON

1 The Son as the new form of God's 'Address'

There are few more striking or more carefully written sentences in the
New Testament than that with which the Epistle to the Hebrews begins.
These succinct, economical words describing God's self-disclosure through
many generations but as having now taken place finally and fully in the
person of his Son, are regularly referred to as a model statement of this
Christian conception of revelation. And yet it is precisely the care with
which the sentence has been put together which raises certain difficulties
about it. For such a carefully written statement asks that care is taken
that it be understood.[1] But herein is our problem. For not only does the
all-but-explicit 'Logos-doctrine'[2] appear quite unrelated, either literally
or theologically, to the highpriestly Christology – or for that matter to
any of the other major Christological expressions of the letter – but where
the term 'Word of God' does appear it bears no obviously Christological
significance.[3]

We might be excused, therefore, in regarding it as a polished but essentially unrelated headpiece to the body of the work.[4] But in this case the
question may be asked whether we have fulfilled our responsibility to
understand the statement or whether we have not simply abdicated from it.

Our investigation, as has been hinted, must run at two levels. We must
attempt in the first place to understand the literary connections which run
between the prologue and the body of the letter. But then we shall be
engaged theologically insofar as we attempt to give an account of its meaning in the light of those relationships.[5]

(a) Hebrews 1.1–4

Though we cannot properly understand any relationship which the
prologue bears to the rest of the work, and therefore perhaps not its
meaning either, before we have attempted to analyse the main interests
of the letter, we may nevertheless begin with a preliminary attempt to set
out some of the conceptions it (the prologue) contains.

The letter begins with an unambiguous interest in 'revelation'. The subject of the opening sentence is 'God' and both the main and subordinate verbs are forms of λαλέω, 'to speak'. Though the description πολυτρόπως possibly includes visions and other manifestations,[6] God's self-disclosure is therefore primarily understood as given in audible, as over against visual, terms. Within this overall setting, a complex pattern of relationships is defined. There is certainly a conception of a longitudinal 'revelation history', in which earlier and more fragmentary forms of God's Address have been overtaken and replaced by a perfected form of the same thing. There is thus established between the various moments of the revelation history a recognisable continuity which allows them, in spite of their discontinuity, to be construed as parts of a single process. This continuity is not something which the moments, or the forms taken on itself by the Word of God (to use this more convenient though possibly anachronistic term), contain within themselves, so much as that they function as the bearers of God's Address. In themselves they remain πολυμερῶς καὶ πολυτρόπως, 'partial and piecemeal',[7] certainly as far as the earlier forms of the process are concerned. This means that it is the Speaking of God itself which contains the real continuity and which allows the historical (or empirical) forms which it takes to itself to be recognisably moments in an ongoing process.[8]

But there is also a strong *dis*continuity insofar as the perfected form of this Speaking stands over against the preliminary forms. As the goal, or the end term, of any process of development is recognisably something different from the process itself (perhaps as a building is something different to the process of construction – building – by which it became *a* building), so the Word in the Son stands over against the Word in the prophets. The process *has* reached its end term and has therefore achieved perfection because the Word in the Son is the eschatological form of what God has to say (ἐπ' ἐσχάτου τῶν ἡμερῶν).[9] The Son, as bearer of the perfected form of God's Address, accordingly stands – as their fulfilment – over against the earlier, anticipatory forms mediated through the prophets.

Though we are unquestionably in touch with both the thoughts and words of the writer of the letter in these opening phrases, there is a great deal less certainty about this with respect to the succeeding statements of the prologue (i.e., from verse 2, ὃν ἔθηκεν . . .). For though the letter contains considerably fewer hymnic statements than some scholars have believed,[10] there is wide consensus that here in the prologue, material from older and different sources has been incorporated.[11] There is disagreement about the extent and the previous forms of such traditional material, E. Grässer arguing that everything apart from verse 3 can be attributed to

the pen of our writer,[12] while R. Deichgräber believes that though
verses 2 and 4 came from sources different to verse 3, they still very
possibly contain older formulations.[13] While recognition must be taken
therefore of the possibility and probability that there are words and forms
present which the writer would not have used himself, the reasonably
simple observation remains that he *has* incorporated such ideas into his
text and therefore *agrees* with them, and presumably chose such statements as saying as well or better than he could himself, things which he
wanted to say.

We may note therefore that this piling up of words and phrases, all of
which are in themselves of heightened or exalted language, is by way of
establishing the title (ὄνομα) or dignity of the Son who is the bearer of the
eschatological Word. But do they do more than that? Should we attempt
to find connections linking these detailed references to points of discussion
in the wider letter?[14] The fact that in verse 3 at least, in which most of
these exalted titles or accomplishments are listed, we have almost certainly
to do with material not the author's own suggests that too narrow an
analysis is not in order. It is rather more important to see what the writer
wants to achieve through enlisting these titles of dignity. And that, as we
have said, is to confirm the finality, and the dignity, of the Son in whom
has come the eschatological form of God's Address. The prologue as a
whole, therefore, is pre-eminently about the Word in the Son.

(b) Hebrews 1.5-2.4

Turning to inquire into the relationship between this statement and the
wider thought of the letter, it is therefore crucial to notice the importance
attached to the term 'Son' in terms of this transition. Apart from the fact
that this is the term which allows the hymnic statements of verses 2b to 4
to be introduced (ἐν Υἱῷ, ὃν ἔθηκεν κληρονόμον - - -), more importantly for
our purposes here, it is precisely this term (ὄνομα, verse 4) which is explored
and exploited in the comparison-contrast of the Son with the angels in this
first major section of the letter.

What is the purpose of this comparison of the Son and the angels?
Various answers have been forthcoming. One guess is that the community
to whom the letter is written has been in danger of confusing Jesus as the
Son of God with some angelic personage.[15] A different, quite brilliant,
thesis has been offered by E. Käsemann, namely that the angels here
stand representatively for the eschatological community already present
at the heavenly enthronement of the Son.[16] Each of these suggestions,
however, ignores the interpretation put on his work by the author himself
as given in 2.1-4. The whole comparison of the Son with angels is that the

Word, already identified in the prologue as having reached definitive form in the Son, may be compared and contrasted with the form of the λόγος mediated by angels (ὁ δι'ἀγγέλων λαληθεὶς λόγος, 2.2).[17]

That the λόγος mediated through the angels means the Torah of the old covenant can hardly be doubted. It is true that the confident assertion of many scholars that 'it was a common belief in first-century Judaism that the Law was given through angelic mediators'[18] is more difficult to document than the scholars in question seem to allow. With only one or two exceptions the rabbinic sources usually cited do not go beyond asserting the *presence* of angels at the giving of the Law, not that they were the intermediaries.[19] But the idea is certainly known in the New Testament,[20] and one or two non-New Testament references do occur in which it seems to be present.[21] The angels, in comparison with Jesus, thus stand representatively as the mediators of the Law and then for the covenant of which the Law forms such a central part. This must be conclusive. As we said above, to see it otherwise is to ignore the author's own interpretation of his work.

But in this case we cannot fail to notice the material continuity of the angel-comparison with the prologue statement. For here, as there, the issue under discussion is how the previous dispensation of God's Word stands in relation to the new dispensation. Again, here as there, the importance and finality of the newest Word of God is made to depend upon the dignity of the Son. At the same time, the dialectic of continuity–discontinuity which we found in the prologue is also continued here. For it is not the case that a simple antithesis is set up between the angel-mediated Torah and the Word in the Son. On the contrary both bear about them an identical demand for response (2.2). The differences in this claim are matters of dignity and degree, not in terms of its essential quality. It is not too much to say that it is in either case the same Word making the same kinds of demand upon those who are its recipients.[22]

Having begun so confidently in declaring that Jesus is the eschatological form of God's Word (1.1, 2.3f) the author can scarcely any longer avoid the questions being faced with urgency everywhere in the New Testament communities, and not least by the group to whom he is writing. That is the problem of how the πειρασμοί experienced in this world seem to have continued, unabated, past the 'turn of the ages'. At 2.5, therefore, he checks himself in the midst of his discussion to acknowledge the reality both of the sufferings and the theological questions which they entail, and introduces in a passing way the theme which will come to play such an important role further on in his letter precisely in response to this question – namely the eschatological highpriesthood of Jesus. The passage 2.5–18 therefore represents something of an interruption to the development of his argument, which is taken up again at 3.1ff. We, too, shall return to the issues opened up in this preliminary way, but at a more appropriate place.[23]

(c) Hebrews 3.1–4.13

The setting up of a comparison between Jesus and Moses is fairly certainly to be regarded as an extension of the theme enunciated in the prologue statement and opened out in the section on angels, i.e. as a comparison of the *revelations* given in the old and the new covenants respectively.[24] Certainly it cannot be without significance that the Old Testament reference around which the whole comparison is built (Num. 12.6–8) has to do with Moses' superlative quality as the bearer of revelation. Over against the other prophets who hear and see in dreams and visions, with Moses God speaks 'mouth to mouth, clearly and not in dark speech' (Num. 12.8). Moses is there already spoken of as servant ($\vartheta\epsilon\rho\acute{\alpha}\pi\omega\nu$), and in Hebrews this is reinforced as the 'servant who bears witness of the things which shall be spoken' ($\vartheta\epsilon\rho\acute{\alpha}\pi\omega\nu$ $\epsilon\grave{\iota}\varsigma$ $\mu\alpha\rho\tau\acute{\upsilon}\rho\iota\omega\nu$ $\tau\tilde{\omega}\nu$ $\lambda\alpha\lambda\eta\vartheta\eta\sigma\omega\mu\acute{\epsilon}\nu\omega\nu$, 3.5).

But the word 'servant' also allows the writer to set the two mediators, Moses and Jesus, in their correct relationship. For this characterises the subservient order of Moses in comparison with Jesus the Son, just as the angels are witnessed to as 'ministering spirits' (1.14). Accordingly we see how this comparison also turns upon the hinge of Jesus' divine sonship: 'Moses was faithful in the whole house as servant ... but Christ was faithful over the house as son' (3.5f). The twin themes of 'revelation' and the importance of the sonship of Jesus with respect to the superiority of the new dispensation indicate that we are still within the context of the prologue statement. The passage presently before us may be explored and understood accordingly.

For example it is this continuity with ideas already opened up which interprets the exact relationship within which Moses and Jesus stand to one another. It is neither an absolute confrontation in which the honour and integrity of Moses have been eclipsed by the dignity of Jesus, as some have read it on the assumption that a simple polemic is intended against Judaism,[25] or against some primitive equation between Moses and Jesus,[26] or against an early prophet-Christology.[27] But nor, of course, are they simply equals.[28] Their status in the 'house', and the relative weight of $\delta\acute{o}\xi\alpha$ borne by each, makes this clear. In other words the relationship between the two mediators of revelation is a dialectical one and it is determined by the continuity–discontinuity dialectic already implicit in the relationship between the covenants themselves.

It is this setting which makes best sense of the 'house' image also. Though there are certainly some puzzling allusions intertwined with this conception, probably most simply explained as imaginative developments of the writer around the reference to 'house' in Numbers 12.7,[29] the most basic line of thought is clear: Moses is a servant *in* the house, or household;[30] Jesus, as Son, is *over* it. This suggests that the household, God's people, has its own continuity at once independently of, and yet also obviously dependent upon, the mediators of the divine revelation.

Seeing the comparison of Jesus and Moses in terms of the two dispensations of revelation is also the clue to the description, unique in the New Testament, of Jesus as 'Apostle' (3.1). Scholars have from time to time been fascinated by the suggestive conjunction of this term with that of highpriest apparently under the rubric 'of our confession'. Sensing the possibility of an actual confessional formula underlying the phrase, they have attempted to deduce the author's own interests by critical analysis of his reworking of the original.[31] Apart from the troublesomely high degree of conjecture in such attempts, however, it has long been pointed out that the writer of the letter nowhere suggests that 'to hold fast the confession' means anything more than the maintenance of Christian faith.[32] In a rather different direction, the close proximity here of the term Apostle with the discussion about Moses, coupled with the strong interests in the epistle as a whole in the 'pilgrimage' motif, said to be a mark of the New Moses speculation,[33] and, further, that in the letter we shall read of a πρώτη διαθήκη (itself the equivalent of the Law of Moses, 9.19) being replaced by καινὴ διαθήκη (9.15), all combine to suggest to some that here Jesus, as Apostle of the new covenant, is to be thought of as the New Moses.[34] Again, the association of ideas remains speculative and inconclusive.[35]

The most natural associations to be made with Jesus' designation as ἀπόστολος are, on one hand, the readers' designation as κλήσεως ἐπουρανίου μέτοχοι, those who 'share in a heavenly call' (3.1), and, on the other, the affirmation of his faithfulness 'to him who appointed him' (3.2). Jesus' significance as Apostle, then, consists quite simply in his being the mediator of the divine call. Not only does this set the pattern for the pilgrimage motif which will run throughout the letter and which culminates in the vision of the heavenly πόλις whither the faithful of all ages are bound (11.16, 12.22) but, more specifically, it prepares the way for the extensive comparison of the Christian readers with those of the wilderness generation who were similarly called to pilgrimage, but by Moses and with the more limited goal before them of the promised land of Canaan (3.16ff).

Again, therefore, we have to do with this dialectical relationship between the old and new dispensations, and the former and latter recipients, of the

Word of God. It is therefore not accidental that the Word motif should be so much in evidence throughout the comparison of the two communities; it *is* the Word which establishes the relationship between them. That is why Psalm 95.7-11 suits the author's purposes so happily. For the psalm not only speaks of the people of old who were called to pilgrimage but it locates the point at issue - obedience or disobedience, faith or unbelief - precisely in terms of response to the Word of God. That is why the psalm phrase 'Hear today his voice ...' is twice taken up and underlined in the writer's own text (3.15, 4.7) and why the exegesis of the psalm begins so significantly with the question τίνες γὰρ ἀκούσαντες ...;(3.16). That the passage concludes with the 'poem on the Word of God'[36] (4.12f) can hardly be insignificant either.[37]

That it is the same Word which has come equally to Christians as to the wilderness generation, though through their respective mediators, is made clear by the facts that it makes exactly the same kind of demand - namely of belief and consequently to faithful pilgrimage[38] - and that the former generation therefore functions directly for the Christians as a warning example of unbelief and disobedience (ἀπιστία, 3.12, 19; ἀπείθεια, 4.6, 11). This becomes especially clear in the concluding words of the section: σπουδάσωμεν ... ἵνα μὴ ἐν τῷ αὐτῷ τις ὑποδείγματι πέσῃ τῆς ἀπειθείας. Ζῶν γὰρ ὁ λόγος τοῦ θεοῦ ... (4.11f).[39] This, it will be remembered, was how the continuity between the dispensations of the Word was established in the comparison between Jesus and the angels at 2.1-4.

It is because the Word of God makes these demands for response and obedience, wheresoever and by whomsoever it is heard, that the Christian readers must not be found wanting in their time, 'while it is still called "today" ' (3.13). They must therefore: pay attention (κατανοήσατε, 3.1), hold on (κατάσχωμεν, 3.6, 14), exhort one another (παρακαλεῖτε, 3.13), fear (φοβηθῶμεν, 4.1) and hasten (σπουδάσωμεν, 4.11). For it is a serious business to be caught dallying with this Word of God which calls not only for a person's obedience, but also penetrates and discerns the inner recesses of his heart or mind (4.12f).[40] He to whom the Word has been given shall be required to give a word in return (πρὸς ὃν ἡμῖν ὁ λόγος, 4.13).

Both Moses and Jesus have been attested to as faithful mediators of this Word. Wherefore (δίο, 3.7) both communities stand responsible for their attitudes toward it. If not syntactically, at least in the thrust of the argument the δίο of 3.7 connects with the βλέπετε of 3.12.[41] The motif of the Word therefore not only connects the comparison of Moses and Jesus to the rest of the passage, but in fact interprets that comparison to us.

It is nevertheless a mistake to see the Word of God, as it is conceived by the author, only in these sombre, responsibility-establishing terms.[42] Its threatening quality is only for those who fail to accept its positive content. Those who do receive it believingly are the partakers of a heavenly call (3.1), and are even now in process of entering the eschatological Rest (4.3). Neither was the call to the Israelites without its aspect of grace (as can be seen from the changes the writer has made to the psalm text. We shall take this up in more detail: pp. 49 and 162 n. 57). For them, as for the Christians, the Word initially took the form of gospel (4.2, 6) and of promise (4.1).

In these several ways, therefore, the revelation of the Word of God is seen as a continuous activity, stretching right across the boundaries of its various economies, and binding the members of the covenants into a single history of salvation. At the same time it is abundantly clear that in its dispensation through the Son it has achieved a clarity and finality not possible for those who received it through Moses; for he was a servant, not the Son of the household, and he spoke with reference to future things (3.5), not in end of days (1.2). We may say, therefore, that in the comparison of Jesus with Moses we are still in touch with ideas laid down in the prologue statement.

(d) Hebrews 4.14–5.10, 7.1–28

At 4.14 we come to speak more continuously of the highpriesthood of Jesus, that which is probably the major theme of the letter, but which has so far been mentioned only fleetingly. The question is: does this have an organic relationship with that which has gone before or do the comparisons of Jesus with Moses and the angels serve simply as prolegomena to this the central theme?[43] Our argument, perhaps by now predictable, will be that the comparison of Jesus with the Aaronite Priesthood is the third in a carefully prepared sequence and that the motif which binds it to the previous two comparisons continues to be the idea of God's new revelation in the Son.[44]

Our initial task must be to establish how far this comparison runs in the letter. Though every interpreter of Hebrews has reason to hesitate before what must seem to be a high degree of subjectivity in these matters (see the remarks on p. 2 above), there do appear to be good material and formal indications that the author saw a break in his thought at the end of chapter 7, and that 4.14–7.28 was intended to represent a fairly continuous and cohesive section, interrupted only by the obvious digression at 5.11–6.20.

Materially, we may notice the change in setting which takes place after chapter 7; from here on the discussion is predominantly given over to the details of the heavenly sanctuary and what is transacted there, whereas up until this point the subject was mainly concerned with the Son and how he related to his various predecessors. In fact it is striking that this term, Son, of such importance in the first seven chapters and occurring eleven times in them, occurs only once more in the letter after chapter 7 (9.29). Chapters 1-7 contain, we may say then, a series of comparisons of Jesus, personally, in his capacity as Son, with persons or groups of persons figuring in the old covenant. This does not happen again nearly so clearly after 7.28.

There seem to be formal indications that support this. Apart from the κεφάλαιον δὲ ἐπὶ τοῖς λεγομένοις ... with which chapter 8 opens, fairly clearly suggesting a transition in the thought,[45] there can be found a heavy concentration in the closing verses of chapter 7 of important words or themes occurring between 4.14 and 7.28, indicating that these verses are intended to form a summing-up of what has preceded. We may notice that (*a*) Jesus' exaltation 'through the heavens' of 4.14 recurs at 7.28; (*b*) the two important scripture testimonies of the passage, Psalms 2.7 and 110.4, are conflated in the closing line Υἱόν . . . εἰς τὸν αἰῶνα (7.28); (*c*) Jesus' 'perfection' in terms of God's approval of his priesthood, mentioned in 5.9f, is caught up at 7.28; (*d*) his sinlessness, referred to at 4.15, is again emphasised at 7.26; (*e*) a high proportion of verbal similarities link the descriptions of the levitical Priesthood at 5.1-3 and 7.27f; (*f*) Jesus' ability to save 'those who come' (τοὺς προσερχομένους, 7.25) reflects the summons 'let us come' (προσερχώμεθα) of 4.16; (*g*) God's Oath which establishes the new order over against the old (7.18-22) again comes up in the closing words of the passage (7.28).

This section, 4.14-5.10, 7.1-28, consists then, we may say, in a third comparison of Jesus the Son, this time with Aaron and his successors in the levitical Priesthood. We may note in passing that even here, where the differences between the two economies will be drawn in so sharply, the dialectical continuity between them is nevertheless present. This is clearly the intention of the passage near the head of the section which establishes the characteristics of priesthood in general (5.1-10) and shows how, as priest, Jesus qualifies pre-eminently. In view of all that will be said in chapter 7, the direct comparison of Jesus and Aaron (. . . καθώσπερ καὶ 'Ααρών. Οὕτως καὶ ὁ Χριστός . . ., 5.4f) must be seen as especially striking, and should be set alongside the similar statement concerning Moses (. . . 'Ιησοῦν, πιστὸν ὄντα. . .ὡς καὶ Μωϋσῆς, 3.2) and the not dissimilar one with respect to the angels (εἰ γὰρ ὁ δι' ἀγγέλων λαληθεὶς λόγος ἐγένετο βέβαιος . . . πῶς ἡμεῖς ἐκφευξόμεθα, 2.2).

Perhaps of more clear importance for the sequence of the comparisons is the continued interest in Jesus' sonship which here, as in the previous cases, provides the contrast with Jesus' predecessors of the earlier dispensation. Reference to sonship is introduced as early as 5.5f where the key Old Testament testimony, Psalm 2.7, which has already been used at 1.5, is now used to interpret Jesus' priesthood εἰς τὸν αἰῶνα κατὰ τὴν τάξιν Μελχισεδεκ (Psalm 110.4). As we have noticed, these two scriptures are brought together at the close of the section, 7.28, and may be said to be regulative within it (Psalm 110.4, so important in this passage, occurs nowhere else in the letter!). This, in fact, is Melchizedek's importance to the writer, as we see at 7.3 where he concludes his brief midrash on Genesis 14.17ff with the words ἀφωμοιωμένος δὲ τῷ Υἱῷ τοῦ θεοῦ.[46] This does not mean that he saw some kind of identification of the priest of Salem with the second person of the Trinity,[47] but that he is adopting the biblical statements about Melchizedek and his kind of priesthood as a way of stating his own conception of the priesthood of Jesus. This can be seen from the way Melchizedek drops out of sight halfway through the chapter; the true alternative to the levitical structures is the permanent priesthood of the Son.[48] The Son terminology is therefore again the hinge on which the comparison of Jesus with the Old Testament institutions is made to turn.

But are we any longer in touch with the revelation theme which, we have said, is the underlying concern in this series of comparisons?

The key term in the biblical description of Melchizedek, for our author, is the psalmist's phrase εἰς τὸν αἰῶνα. This is already made clear in the first sentence of chapter 7, which, in spite of the proliferation of parenthetical phrases and subordinate clauses drawn from Genesis 14, is basically an extension of, and comment on, the last sentence of chapter 6: Ἰησοῦς, κατὰ τὴν τάξιν Μελχισεδεκ ἀρχιερεὺς γενόμενος εἰς τὸν αἰῶνα. This means that the main terms of the comparison of the Jesus/Melchizedek type of priesthood with that of the Levites will be that of permanence (εἰς τὸν αἰῶνα) as against transience. This is confirmed, in fact, by the selectivity exercised by the writer over the data offered in Genesis 14 - the etymological explanations of the names of Melchizedek and Salem are passed over without further mention, and details of the gifts of wine and bread, exploited by Philo (*Leg. Alleg.* 3.25f),[49] are not mentioned. What does interest the writer is the fact that Genesis is conspicuously (for him and his contemporaries) silent about Melchizedek's origins, and being thus 'without genealogy' he must be, as the psalmist states, 'priest for ever'.[50]

It might be supposed that the details about Abraham's giving of the tithes and his receiving a blessing (verses 4-10) are told for their own sake, and so here at any rate the author is thinking in more comprehensive terms than the specific 'transient-permanent' ones we have suggested. In fact what is most interesting about these is precisely the way in which they are subordinated to this latter motif. For the key to these verses lies in the antithesis οἱ μὲν ἐκ τῶν υἱῶν Λευει... ὁ δὲ μὴ γενεαλογούμενος ἐξ αὐτῶν...(verses 5, 6; the first of several μὲν-δέ antitheses in this carefully written chapter). Here, of course, the ἀγενεαλόγητος of verse 3 has been picked up and the contrast between the multiplicity (and therefore impermanence) of the levitical priests and the singularity of the Melchizedek-type priesthood, left implicit there, is now made explicit. This is underlined by the phrase τὴν ἱερατείαν λαμβάνοντες (verse 5). Not only does that order of priesthood demand a plurality of officiants but it is also an office (or rather function; see on ἱερατεία in n. 51) which has to be acquired by every succeeding occupant.[51]

It is at verse 8, however, that the issue is brought to its sharpest expression. Here there is condensed into one statement both the fundamental cause for, and the sharpest definition of, the impermanence that pervades the whole levitical structure – it is operated by 'men who are subject to death' (ἀποθνήσκοντες ἄνθρωποι). It is this which necessitates the clumsy mechanics of hereditary succession for its survival and validity. That on which the old Priesthood prided itself most[52] is thus exposed as its innermost weakness. By contrast the scripture testifies only to the life of Melchizedek; the fact that no reference to his birth, death or descent can be found exactly corroborates the psalmist's statement that *his* priesthood endures for ever. Person and office coalesce in a way impossible in the old order.

Nothing could be of much greater significance for our present study than the fact that the question of the nature and function of the Law, which question is to play a crucial role throughout the chapter, should be introduced in this context in which the relative qualifications of the Levites and of the Jesus/Melchizedek order of priesthood are under discussion (verse 5). The importance of this fact lies not just in that the question here is of the passing and the permanent priesthoods, but that it is also a question about authority. In addition to the fragility of the old institution, as witnessed to by the genealogical tables, the authority by which the succeeding occupants exercise their office is one deputed *to* them, i.e., by the Law. We shall see, in fact, that the exact relationship between Law and Priesthood, in terms of logical precedence, is not always spelled out particularly clearly. But here, when the Law is first mentioned within the present discussion, there can be no such ambiguity. The Law *bestows* the right of Levites to tithe their brethren. It is not a personal dignity: ultimately not even levitical birth carries its own sanctions. These are established and maintained from outside by the legal decree. It is this impersonal and derived quality of priesthood to which that of Melchizedek stands in contrast. For unlike his levitical counterpart, Melchizedek requires no external qualifications for his priesthood, but bears it in the strength of his personal dignity.[53]

Not only does the Law confer this dignity, however. It also defines its boundaries and delimits the area of its validity. Precedence it gives, but only over fellow Israelites who like the priests themselves are 'descended from the loins of Abraham'. This is why the designation of Abraham as 'patriach' (verse 4) is so pointed.[54] The whole complex of Law-Priesthood-tithes is designed to work, and does work, within the boundaries of Abraham's people. But the entire scheme is relativised by the spectacle of Abraham (the father of them all, no less!) giving tithes to one who stood completely outside the system. And this, not on the basis of legal obligation, but out of his free recognition of one who stood superior to himself. Herein lies the greatness of Melchizedek ($\vartheta\epsilon\omega\rho\epsilon\hat{\imath}\tau\epsilon$ $\delta\grave{\epsilon}$ $\pi\eta\lambda\acute{\iota}\kappa\sigma$ $\sigma\hat{\upsilon}\tau\sigma$, verse 4); he is one who stands quite above the entire structure of Law and Priesthood, dependent on neither legal authorisation nor levitical descent and yet acknowledged as superior by none other than Father Abraham.

The issue is finally clinched with the argument from Hebraic solidarity principles (verses 9f). Because Levi can, according to this mode of thinking, be identified in principle with his great-grandfather, Abraham's action and attitude stand representatively for those of his offspring including Levi and his priestly clan. Here the thrust of the argument which began in verse 4 in specifying Abraham as 'patriarch' is brought to its conclusion. In that it was the patriarch himself who offered tithes, it follows that the whole institution including the Levites, is at one stroke relativised by the order of priesthood represented by Melchizedek.

We may profitably pause here to review our position. Our overarching question is whether the structure of the prologue statement, with its interest in a prior and latter form of revelation and its identification of the one with the Old Testament institutions and the other with Jesus as God's Son, is still operative. We have seen that it is Jesus' dignity as Son which constitutes his new dimension of priesthood over against the levitical order. But it is also beginning to emerge that the issues of chapter 7 crystallise around questions concerning *transience-permanency* and about the relationship between the levitical Priesthood and the Mosaic *Torah*. Here are important ingredients in the prologue definition. For there the eschatological form of the Word of God is set in relationship to its anticipatory forms; and we have seen how these forms are, by means of the subsequent comparisons with the angels and with Moses, identified with the Torah of the old covenant. With this position plotted on our wider chart, we may continue the investigation of the Law-Priesthood theme in chapter 7.

Verse 11 marks an obvious, if unannounced, development of the thought. Here the historical incident of Melchizedek's encounter with Abraham is left behind. From now on interest is wholly centred in *the* priest for whom Melchizedek served merely as a type. We see now, if we had ever lost sight of it, that Melchizedek has no more than a derived importance for our author. The real interest has always been in Christ and it is *his* figure and *his* priesthood which has been controlling the discussion throughout.

We see immediately how the two themes enunciated in verses 4-10 continue to dominate. (*a*) The *interrelationship of the Law and the Priesthood* under the old order is spoken of straight away - ὁ λαὸς γὰρ ἐπ' αὐτῆς (i.e., ἱερωσύνης) νενομοθέτηται (verse 11) - and is spelled out more explicitly as the argument proceeds: a change in the Priesthood involves changing the Law (verse 12); the Law never authorised a priest from the tribe of Judah (verse 14); so that it was *not* the Law, a 'fleshly command-ment', by which Jesus' priesthood was established (verse 16). Similarly (*b*) the *transience-permanence* motif is carried through, presenting itself already in verse 11 in the comment that the old institutions could not achieve 'perfection', and emerging again in verse 16 where Jesus' 'power of an indestructible life' stands in such radical contrast to the 'transformation' (μετάθεσις) to which both Law and Priesthood have been subjected. We notice also the recurrence of the leitmotiv 'priest for ever' (verse 17).

In greater detail, we may take first that which we have designated (*a*) the Law-Priesthood relationship. The parenthetical way in which the statement ὁ λαὸς γὰρ ἐπ' αὐτῆς νενομοθέτηται is thrown out almost as an aside, in verse 11, can only mean that a question about the Law is assumed to underlie the whole discussion. That is to say, the writer apparently anticipates the possibility that the Law might be appealed to as the guarantee for the eternal validity of the Priesthood,[55] and here joins them closely together so that both can be seen to be transcended in the advent of a new order of priesthood (verse 12).[56]

The phrase ἐπ' αὐτῆς, however, does create a problem,[57] for by its most natural meaning this suggests that the Priesthood has logical precedence over the Law.[58] This would involve an inversion of the writer's thought, since, as we saw, he has already affirmed the dependence of the Priesthood on the Law. How can Priesthood depend upon the Law if the Law depends on Priesthood?

Were we then wrong to take κατὰ τὸν νόμον of verse 5 in this way? That we correctly grasped the point there is confirmed by the recurrence of the same idea in the present context. One of the linchpins in the argument of this section is the fact that Jesus belonged not to the tribe of Levi but to that of Judah. The significance of this is spelled out as 'of which tribe Moses said nothing with respect to priests' (verse 14). That must mean that the revolutionary qualities of Jesus' priesthood are seen not least in that this priest, unlike every other in Israel's history, was authorised not by Mosaic Law but by a radically different principle, delineated further in verse 16 as 'the power of an indestructible life' as over against a 'fleshly commandment'.

So the thesis advanced in verse 5 is sustained and confirmed: the Priesthood owes its existence and authority to the Law. What then of the two places where the reverse seems to be implied, i.e., in verse 11 where the Law is apparently said to be given 'on the basis of' the Priesthood and in verse 12 where the abolition of the levitical order is said to involve that of the Torah?

In the first place, $\dot{\epsilon}\pi$' $\alpha\dot{\upsilon}\tau\hat{\eta}\varsigma$ need not mean exactly 'on the basis of'; it is also capable of 'in relationship with'.[59] In this case we are not driven to see a logical contradiction, a complete reversal of the previous statement, but may understand the phrase as asserting the inextricable interrelationship between the two parts of the Old Testament dispensation.

Nevertheless in the $\gamma\dot{\alpha}\rho$, by which this parenthetic phrase is fastened in its context, we are given new information – as it were, a suppressed premise. For here there is asserted an integral relationship between the failure of the levitical Priesthood to achieve perfection ($\tau\epsilon\lambda\epsilon\dot{\iota}\omega\sigma\iota\varsigma$), and the relationship of this Priesthood to the Law. In fact the required premise is supplied at verse 19 and at 10.1: it was *also* the (unfulfilled) intention of the *Law* that it should accomplish 'perfection' for the people of God. So in fact both Law and Priesthood are identified in this common, but unfulfilled, end purpose. Formerly he had said: the Priesthood depends on the Law for its validity. Now we are to go further and say that it is also true that if the Law is to attain the end for which it was given ($\tau\epsilon\lambda\epsilon\dot{\iota}\omega\sigma\iota\varsigma$) it requires an authentic Priesthood for its implementation.[60]

If this premise did not also underlie verse 12, albeit suppressed, we should be faced with a logical *non sequitur*. For the proposition that a change in the Priesthood necessitated a change in the Law does not emerge immediately from the premise that the Law establishes the Priesthood. But given the prior assumption that the Law depends upon the Priesthood for its implementation, it then follows that an inadequate Priesthood renders the Law inoperative. That the levitical Priesthood *is* inadequate is demonstrable by the fact that it fails to achieve 'perfection', and this, in turn, can be shown by the fact that another has been conceived which is superior.[61]

The interrelationship and interdependence of these two elements of the Old Testament machinery for salvation are thus established precisely in their mutual failure to attain their goal.

We have already alluded in passing to the author's observation that the Mosaic Torah made no provision for the authorisation of priests from tribes other than that of Levi (verse 14). With this goes the equally demonstrable premise that Jesus was descended from Judah.

The conclusion, to which not only these immediately preceding statements about Jesus' priestly appointment, but the argument of the whole chapter has been moving, is now trenchantly stated in verse 16. It was not according to a Law of 'fleshly commandment' that Jesus was appointed to his priestly office, but in virtue of an indestructible life. The direct implication is that the levitical Priesthood *was* based on a law of this character. The expression is a striking, almost audacious, one.[62] If it is true that the harshness of the expression is a contrived one, and its point is to show up the 'fleshly' constitution of the Law and the levitical Priesthood, the phrase will have reference both backwards and forwards. Looking backwards it will represent the culmination of that characterisation of the old order which has been gathering momentum throughout the chapter, namely that the levitical Priesthood is irrevocably constituted of ἀποθνήσκοντες ἄνθρωποι, whose authority is dependent on their belonging to a well-defined line of descent, and whose order of priesthood is already outmoded in that it has failed to achieve 'perfection'. But this failure indicates another aspect of its fleshly constitution, and in this the expression points forward to the chapters that lie ahead. It is fleshly in that its ministration is capable only of external, physical or levitical purity; it touches only the body not the conscience.[63] This thrusting through to inner spiritual or moral categories on the part of the new order reveals *why* the old could not achieve 'perfection' (9.9f). The characterisation σάρκινος thus exposes its radical weakness both in constitution and capacity.

(*b*) In speaking of the joint failure of the Law and Priesthood to achieve 'perfection' for the members of the first covenant, we have already touched on the other theme which we said forms one of the main elements of the comparison between the two orders of priesthood, namely the contrast between the *transience* of the one and the *finality* of the other. We have noted above that this failure (to achieve 'perfection') appears on the charge sheet against both institutions (verse 11), and the theme is developed through the chapter, and indeed through the letter, as one of the clear signs of the inadequacy of the old order and therefore its impermanence in face of the finality of the new.[64] Both in his personal 'perfection' (2.10, 5.9, 7.28) and also in his capacity to lead others to this (ἀρχηγός, 2.10; αἴτιος σωτηρίας, 5.10; τελειωτὴς πίστεως, 12.2) Jesus has accomplished in one definitive action the functions that were intended both of the Law and the Priesthood but in which they have equally failed.

This inadequacy and therefore impermanence (unfinality) of both these elements of the old order is clarified at verse 12 in the double use of the μετατίθημι root: μετατιθεμένης γὰρ τῆς ἱερωσύνης ἐξ ἀνάγκης καὶ νόμου μετάθεσις γίνεται. Both their impermanence and their interrelatedness are underlined.

By verse 18 the comparatively moderate μετάθεσις language has given way to the much more radical term ἀθέτησις to describe that which has overtaken the 'previous commandment' because of its 'weakness' (τὸ ἀσθενές) and 'uselessness' (ἀνωφελές); and also, we note again, because the Law achieved no degree of 'perfection' (οὐδὲν γὰρ ἐτελείωσεν ὁ νόμος).

The reference to the 'Law comprised of fleshly commandment' (νόμος ἐντολῆς σαρκίνης) and to the Priesthood it supports, in comparison with that which is grounded in 'the strength of an indestructible life' at verse 16, catches up the motif first mentioned in the description of the priests as 'men subject to death' in verse 8 and which we shall find again in verses 23f. We need not elaborate further except to remark on the powerful expression of permanency achieved in the concentration in verse 16 of the words δύναμις, ζωή, ἀκατάλυτος. We have been presented with the interrelatedness of the Law and Priesthood in their μετάθεσις; to this Christ's stands as ἀκατάλυτος. That old priesthood was operated by men chiefly distinguished as ἀποθνήσκοντες; Jesus' priesthood is validated by his indestructible ζωή. The old combination was unable to achieve that for which it was given; his is κατὰ δύναμιν. The whole theme is welded together under the sign of the leitmotiv 'You are a priest for ever, according to the order of Melchizedek' (verse 17).

The importance of verses 18-21 for our present study lies not simply in their making yet more explicit the themes we have been handling, but in their introducing a new element to the discussion not previously obvious, at least in this context. This is the matter of God's Oath, and the importance it has as a foundation for Christian hope. Several scholars have discerned verbal and other connections between this passage and the concluding verses of chapter 6 where the discussion also centres on God's Oath and its significance as a ground for hope (6.13-20).[65] There a different occasion and therefore different Oath is being referred to, namely the Promise–Oath given to Abraham (Gen. 22. 16-17), but the following list of verbal and other similarities between that passage and the present one indicates that the essential interest is in the phenomenon of the Oath itself, and its meaning in terms of Christian hope, rather than in the specific reference points of the Oath. By way of demonstrating the continuity between the passages we can list, for example:[66]

ἐμεσίτευσεν ὅρκῳ, 6.17

οὐ χωρὶς ὁρκωμοσίας, 7.20

ἰσχυρὰν παράκλησιν ἔχωμεν … κρατῆσαι τῆς προκειμένης ἐλπίδος, 6.18
ἐπεισαγωγὴ δὲ κρείττονος ἐλπίδος, 7.19

τὸ ἀμετάθετον τῆς βουλῆς αὐτοῦ … δύο πράγματα ἀμετάθετα, 6.17f
μετατιθεμένης γὰρ τῆς ἱερωσύνης … καὶ νόμου μετάθεσις γίνεται …
ἀθέτησις … προαγούσης ἐντολῆς, 7.12, 18

(ἐλπὶς) εἰς τὸ ἐσώτερον τοῦ καταπετάσματος, 6.19
ἐλπὶς, δι' ἧς ἐγγίζομεν τῷ θεῷ, 7.20

πρόδρομος ὑπὲρ ἡμῶν … Ἰησοῦς, 6.20
διαθήκης γέγονεν ἔγγυος … Ἰησοῦς, 7.22

ἀρχιερεὺς γενόμενος εἰς τὸν αἰῶνα, 6.20
Σὺ ἱερεὺς εἰς τὸν αἰῶνα, 7.21

The factor which allows these two passages to be brought into line is that in each, Jesus' definitive act of self-sacrifice, through which he creates the way of access for Christians, constitutes in itself the reason for hope. In both cases this 'better hope' is grounded in and confirmed by an utterance, that is to say, a Word, of God – the promise which is strengthened by his Oath. Certainly in each case the way Jesus' action relates to the Oath is different, but that is because in each case the Old Testament material is being used differently (a fact to which we must address ourselves more carefully in chapter 2; see n. 67). In the first case Jesus' entry into the sanctuary is regarded essentially as a *continuation* of that which was given to Abraham, namely the solemn assurance of God which enables and encourages 'hope'. To the Christians has been given a similar, though much greater, encouragement: namely, that which is constituted by Jesus' eschatological entry into the sanctuary. In the case of his comparison with the levitical priests, the relationship between Jesus and the Old Testament is not continuous but *antithetical* (though of course the actual words of the text from Psalm 110.4 are themselves drawn from the Old Testament; the point is rather their assumed reference here to Jesus).[67] The Oath, therefore, confirms and supports the new order *as over against* the old, and again becomes the ground for Christian 'hope' which, because of the Oath, is in fact a 'better hope'. What we must see very clearly is that in both these places the *action* of Jesus has in some way become a *Word* of God, and transcends or replaces earlier forms of that Word. Whereas it was the promise (ἐπαγγελία) and Oath (ὅρκος) which called forth 'hope' (ἐλπίς) and indeed 'faith' (πίστις) and 'perseverance' (μακροθυμία) in the earlier dispensation (6.12ff), for Christians it is the entry of Jesus beyond the curtain which becomes for them the 'hope which is held out' (6.13-20). At 7.18-22 it is the Oath *and* the act which constitute the reason for 'hope', which act of priesthood, we have seen, has been compared in great detail with the Law-Priesthood combination of the old order in demonstration of the replacement of the one by the other.

This reference back from the discussion in chapter 7 to the exhortatory section which precedes it (6.13-20, but more comprehensively, 5.11-6.20) is further illuminating, however, in that it shows that the writer's preoccupation with 'hope' is not an idle, slightly academic exercise, but is his anxious response to the advanced degree of spiritual torpor which has begun to characterise this community (5.11-6.8). It is to this situation of sluggishness that the example of the patriarchs is offered, they who did not lose hope but 'through faith and perseverance, apprehended the promise' (6.12). Now the way in which this exhortatory section – with its plea that the readers really 'hear' what is to be said – both sets out from (5.10) and returns to (6.20) the point at which the writer wishes to speak about the Melchizedek-quality of Jesus' priesthood, means that for these Christian readers who have begun to lose hope, the new form of God's *Promise-Oath* is subsumed precisely in that *Priesthood*. That is why, for the Christians, the promise resolves into the fact of Jesus' entry beyond the veil (6.19f), and the replacement of the earlier, inadequate Priesthood by Jesus' form of priesthood can be similarly described as 'the introduction of a better hope' (ἐπεισαγωγὴ κρείττονος ἐλπίδος, 7.19).

It is the case that we have considerable difficulty in grasping how a *deed* can be a *word*, though that interrelationship seems to have been more easily achieved for the Hebraic and early Christian mind.[68] The consistency of the conjunction in our epistle, however, puts it beyond doubt that this in fact is what is happening: Jesus' definitive *act* of priesthood is the definitive form of God's *Word*. If that were not demonstrated in these two particular passages in chapters 6 and 7, then it must certainly be recognized as controlling the highly schematic prologue statement where, as we saw, the 'Word' terminology, under which the whole prologue is set, in fact flows over into a statement of what Jesus has *done*. And this, in turn, becomes characteristic of the movement throughout the letter as a whole. The author's express intention in writing about what the Christians' high-priest has achieved is to encourage his readers to a more confident Christian hope and perseverance. That act is somehow in itself a 'word of encouragement'.[69]

The verses 22–4 of chapter 7 pick up, largely by way of recapitulation, some further aspects of the permanency of Jesus' priesthood as over against the multiplicity and therefore impermanence of the levitical tenure of office. Verse 22 is notable in that we meet there for the first time in the letter the concept of the new or 'better' covenant ($\kappa\rho\epsilon\acute{\iota}\tau\tau\omega\nu\ \delta\iota\alpha\vartheta\acute{\eta}\kappa\eta$).

The concluding verses of the chapter, as we have already noticed (above, p. 13), are studded with phrases or themes which have played an important role throughout this section in which Jesus has been compared with the Old Testament order of priests (from 4.14 onwards); which fact, we have argued, suggests that these verses (7.26–8 or perhaps 25–8) represent a summing up of all that this long comparison has been about and, indeed, since this is the third such comparison in the series, of the main theme which connects the comparisons together. From this point of view it is altogether striking that the very last verse of chapter 7 should state in unambiguously antithetical terms a relationship between the $\nu\acute{o}\mu o\varsigma$ of the old dispensation – the $\nu\acute{o}\mu o\varsigma$ which undergirded the institution of priests (or, indeed, highpriests) who were $\overset{\backprime}{\alpha}\nu\vartheta\rho\omega\pi o\iota$ (with all that that means) and characterised by their 'weakness' ($\overset{\backprime}{\alpha}\sigma\vartheta\acute{\epsilon}\nu\epsilon\iota\alpha$) – and the divine $\lambda\acute{o}\gamma o\varsigma$ by which the validity of Jesus' priesthood has been guaranteed for eternity.

It is certainly true that the writer has considerably more to say by way of comparing the priestly institutions and ordinances of the two orders, so that most exegetes see the passage of the ideas sweeping on until 10.18 without any decisive break. It is also true that several of the important issues which have been introduced prior to chapter 8 are elaborated beyond that point (for example: the $\overset{\backprime}{\epsilon}\pi\alpha\gamma\gamma\epsilon\lambda\acute{\iota}\alpha$ which the ministry of Jesus constitutes for Christians is discussed again at 8.6 and 9.15; the 'better' covenant or 'new' covenant at 8.16ff and 9.15ff; Jesus' highpriestly entry into the sanctuary at 9.12, 24; *et al.*). Further, the comparison of the two orders continues the salvation-historical nature of the inquiry as indicated in the fact that the two covenants are the 'first' and the 'new' (see below, pp. 45f). An interest in the $\nu\acute{o}\mu o\varsigma$ which underlies the old order continues (8.4; 9.19, 22; 10.1, 8).

For all this it is nevertheless hard to believe that there has not been a shift in the discussion, as the $\kappa\epsilon\varphi\acute{\alpha}\lambda\alpha\iota o\nu\ \delta\acute{\epsilon}$ of 8.1 leads us to expect. We have already noticed that the sonship of Jesus no longer plays any significant role in the argument. As a consequence the comparison between old and new orders is not nearly so personalised in terms of the respective merits of the mediators or participants in the way which has characterised the discussion up to the end of chapter 7. After that point the interest shifts discernibly to the actions and ordinances by which the two covenants can be compared in their dialectical relationship. We may therefore assume with reasonable security that 7.28 represents at least an intermediate break in the flow of the ideas. The series of comparisons prior to that is intended as a developing pattern in which the writer moves from his opening statement about God's 'Address' in his Son to an elaboration of how that Word comes to us in Jesus' highpriestly act.

We set out from the question as to how the opening statement about God's Speaking could be related to the major interests of the letter, both on literary and theological grounds (above, p. 5). Since then we have seen how that prologue statement has been developed through three elaborate, descending convolute circles of comparison in each of which Jesus, as Son of God, is compared with one or other of the different agents of revelation-redemption in the old dispensation. But the way in which the various persons or agencies have been selected for comparison cannot be without its own clear significance. For we have seen how they progress from the angelic mediators of the Law, to the human agent in that revelation, to the priestly organisation based on that Law. Over against each of these, in very different ways, but always including that dialectical quality of continuity even in their discontinuity which we noticed as present in the prologue statement, Jesus is consistently portrayed as a new form, and an eschatologically superior form, of God's 'Word'. We have been enabled to see therefore not just how the opening statement about God's Word relates to the epistle as a whole but how it is that, within the terms of the letter, God's action in Jesus can be described as his 'Address'.

2 The theological presuppositions of the 'Word in the Son' formula

If our analysis of the letter is right, what are its implications for the longstanding problem of the 'life-situation' in which the Epistle to the Hebrews took its form?

In putting the question this way and in raising it at this place, certain methodological assumptions manifest themselves. It is a fundamental canon of contemporary literary-critical investigation that the theology of a writer can only properly be assessed when we know the context in which he is writing.[70] But are we not also to say that the kind of theology which any writer sets down is an important clue, perhaps the most important clue, in determining the life-situation in which his particular theological expression has come to birth? In fact these two ways into a writer's thought-world are inseparable, and we are therefore shut up to a degree of circularity in every hermeneutical attempt.[71] On the other hand, though interrelated, these two methods are separate and identifiable, and the literary-critical process can quickly become invalidated when an *undue* circularity is allowed to develop between them.[72]

The fact that our inquiry into the Epistle to the Hebrews initially took the shape of an analysis of its theological patterns indicates that here preference has been given to the latter approach. That is, rather than attempting to set up a hypothetical life-situation, against which to understand the writer's theology, we have entered in immediately on the task of interpreting his thought; hopefully the analysis of these patterns will indicate something of the presuppositions out of which he writes and perhaps, therefore, also something of the situation to which he writes.

The priority of this method is dictated not merely by personal preference, but simply by the pragmatic observation, encapsulated in Origen's famous remark,[73] that attempts to isolate the historical setting from literary and other criteria remain hopelessly hypothetical and ambiguous.[74]

We have already sketched in outline the two major lines along which the letter has usually been interpreted (in the Introduction, above). These are on one hand the more traditional view which we called the 'relapse interpretation', and on the other hand the more recent view which sees the 'Jewishness' of the letter simply as the product of its using the Old Testament institutions as a 'foil'[75] for what the author wishes to say about Christ, or as 'the most convenient example of the material (*kosmisch*) character of all sacral institutions of this world'.[76]

From the perspectives gained in the analysis we have now undertaken, however, both these points of view must appear unduly extreme.

On the one side several aspects have emerged which both individually and, even more so, collectively tell against the old covenant-new covenant scheme standing simply symbolically for a materialistic–spiritual division. For one thing, the sheer scale and detail of the comparison must strongly suggest in itself that what has been of quite paramount interest here has been the *relationship* between the old and the new. No other explanation can fully do justice to the meticulously formulated opening statement which is then drawn out into the elaborate three-stage comparison between Jesus and his predecessors. The intense theological labour which has been invested in working out the complex dialectical relationship between the covenants must say as clearly as anything could that it is this, the actual (concrete) relationship between the two forms of religious experience, which is constantly under scrutiny.

That it is the relationship which is as important to the writer as the finality and superiority of Jesus is confirmed by the observation, clear to all, that in spite of the sweeping condemnations made of certain aspects of the old order, it is by no means a blanket condemnation. One of the signs of the inadequacy of the newer interpretation lies, accordingly, in its failure to appreciate the organic connections which are seen in the letter to bind the old covenant to the new, or which pass right across the boundaries between them and allow them to be seen as stages in a single, ongoing 'salvation-history'. To describe, for instance, the previous order as 'the most convenient example'[77] or as a 'method' for affirming the finality of Christian faith,[78] is quite to fail to understand that in the letter it is *the same Word* which summons both communities toward their eschatological destination (chapter 11) and which also stands in judgement over both (2.1–4 etc.). In other words that which is seen as the initiating, controlling, directive energy within the first dispensation is understood as identical with that which applies in the second. If the one community functions for the other as 'example', that can only be because both stand within the same historical process, which is seen from the outset to be the process of the Word of God in history.[79]

Thirdly, as we have already noticed, whatever echoes of Platonic ideas we may find in the author's conception of heavenly archetype and earthly copy,[80] the fact is quite undeniable that the two covenants, in their inferiority and superiority, also stand in sequential or horizontal relationship as earlier and latter. As every exegete of the letter knows, one of the centres of controversy in its interpretation lies just here with respect to the priority in importance between these two thought-patterns. This is therefore a question to which we shall necessarily return (pp. 42f below). For the moment, perhaps, enough evidence has been produced to make it clear that the historical connection between the covenants is certainly among the more important questions, if not *the* question (as we shall argue), for this writer. We simply may not reduce the massive interest shown in these connections by the writer to a desire for an 'example' or 'method'.

On the other hand the advocates for this more recent view have exposed certain weaknesses in the older 'relapse theory'. Interestingly, one of the points which they have been keen to press is one we have suggested can also count against them; namely the fact that the disapproval of the old institutions is not a blanket one, which is what we should expect, they say, if the letter had been written to, or in, a polemical situation.[81]

A second point they press quite consistently is the clear fact that overriding all the theological interests of the writer is his ever-present anxiety for the spiritual welfare of the friends whom he addresses. This recognition is urged against a particular form of the older interpretation which tended to focus upon the dogmatic statements of the letter, especially what it has to say about both Jesus' humanity and his dignity as Son, with a consequent failure to appreciate sufficiently its subordination of theology to paraenesis. Against this view it is urged that the letter is rather an urgent plea from the heart of a friend than an exercise in dogmatic theology.[82] But this point can be made to count as much in favour of one view as the other. For the most urgent exhortations have as much, if not more, relevance to a hand-to-hand combat situation (theologically speaking) than to the more detached, philosophical setting envisaged by the newer exegesis.[83]

Of more serious difficulty seems to be the virtually total absence of any reference to the supposed Jewish 'seducers'.[84] The 'various and strange teachings' of 13.9 refer, presumably, to Jewish dogmas, since the passage clearly refers to food laws of some kind and sounds reminiscent of the passage which speaks of the offerings 'which cannot attain perfection for the conscience of those who worship, but have to do only with food and drink . . .' (9.9f). Even so, 'various' (ποικίλαι) and 'strange' (ξέναι) must seem odd ways to describe teachings to which these (supposedly) Jewish-Christian converts are being enticed *back*.

C. F. D. Moule has urged that the 'we have' of 'we have an altar from which they have no right to eat who serve the tent' (13.10) implies a directly polemical situation:[85] 'Christians are the people who possess the real thing'[86] as opposed to the Jews who do not. Against this, however, it might be reasonably argued that the phrase should be bracketed with the other ἔχομεν phrase in its close vicinity, 13.14. Certainly there it is a negative: οὐ γὰρ ἔχομεν ὧδε μένουσαν πόλιν. But the sense runs on immediately to the city Christians *do* have, at least in prospect: ἀλλὰ τὴν μέλλουσαν ἐπιζητοῦμεν. A connection is not too hard to make between the two: 'We have an *altar* which is of an eschatological kind (they who serve the tent here on earth have no access to it)' and 'We have a *city* of eschatological quality, not passing but permanent.'[87] As we shall see in due course, the words 'we have' (ἔχομεν) do seem to bear an especial importance (below, pp. 72f), but it is not obvious that they have polemical overtones; rather they function as a reminder to the Christians of their good reasons for perseverance in their day-to-day Christian profession.[88]

A second important problem with the 'relapse theory' is that if the letter really was written to Christians in order 'to arm them with arguments against non-Christian Jews',[89] the arguments seem to work so *badly*. In this whole area, of course, we are obliged to reckon with the very wide differences between methods of persuasion in that century and ours. For all that, the problems are not negligible and seem strongly to suggest that, for the moment at least, the questions are of a more 'internal' kind, in which 'the author is urged by a practical necessity to think out his faith, or rather to state the full content of his faith, for the benefit of his readers'.[90] Some such setting, in which a reasonable agreement on the basic premises of faith can be taken for granted, relieves the seemingly intractable problems which become associated with the writer's 'arguments' on the assumption that they have to persuade the unpersuaded.[91]

If neither of the two major lines of approach satisfactorily explains all the aspects of our letter, what *is* the setting in which this document comes into being - a document in which such massive interest in the interrelationship between the dispensations of the divine revelation is brought to bear on a concrete situation of friends in trouble?[92] Some of the familiar details can be sketched in quickly: we know that the readers were a small group with whom the writer was well acquainted. They had tended to remain theologically backward and now were incapable of resolving, in any practically or theologically satisfactory manner, the threat of persecution which constantly appeared more imminent. The author, in his concern, sits down to write them his 'word of exhortation'. He enjoins them to constancy, to faithfulness and to hope with respect to the Word of God they have received in Christ. This Word has largely the character of promise, and it is constituted by the proleptic, eschatological entry of Jesus the forerunner into the very presence of God where, as their faithful highpriest, he now intercedes on their behalf.

So we can account for some of the features of his letter. But herein lies the central methodological question of our study: why should such a 'word of exhortation', written to a concrete situation of urgency, demand *such* a massive structuring and working out of the salvation-historical purposes of God? And why *this particular structure*?

It is difficult, if not impossible, to resist the impression that behind this letter of the moment there lie deep resources of sustained theological reflection. It is this which, when called upon, rises up to shape and inform so distinctively the letter the author must write to his friends. And it is this which betrays to us the man and his history.[93]

The facts which we have observed about his work, from his carefully articulated opening statement about the previous and latter forms of the Word of God, through the equally carefully controlled sequence of comparisons in which this statement is drawn out, mean that this has been a major problem, not simply for the immediate letter, but upon which this man's deepest theological reflection has been centred. For the shape his letter assumes (almost instinctively?) is that of working out the relationship of the old to the new; in knowing how to say that previous forms of God's Word were and remain God's Word and yet can now be obsolete; in knowing how the self-disclosure of him 'whose years have no end' (1.12) is itself subject to the contingencies of historical process.

What is the spiritual history of the man for whom this has been the deepest theological question of all? His work shows clear signs of association with an Alexandrian or Hellenistic type of Judaism,[94] or at least much more clearly so than with Palestinian forms. We may posit, therefore, that in his letter we encounter a man, a Hellenistic Jew of great theological acumen,[95] who has been confronted by and converted to Christian faith. Just as Paul's conversion experience issued in his theology of Law and Grace (if we may use that particular form of shorthand), so this man's conversion has set the programme for his continuing theological work. It will be the question of the historical structures of God's revelation.

His attempt to portray Jesus' meaning in terms of sacrifice and priesthood does not, therefore, represent an attempt to pour his newfound faith into worn-out wineskins,[96] nor necessarily the result of despair at the delay of the parousia,[97] but to say how Jesus' work represents the end term of his own Jewish institutions of life-long familiarity.

But must we not pause here to inquire whether his conception of Jesus as eschatological highpriest is in fact derived from his own theological reflection? Do we not have to reckon on the possibility of his having come across the idea either from other, non-Christian, sources or from within some other strands of Christian reflection?

Earlier voices of protest or caution notwithstanding,[98] we are now probably obliged to recognise the fact that a priestly messiah had been conceived of prior to our author and of which he could quite well have been aware.[99] That he *could* have come in contact with this idea nevertheless remains a long way short of demonstration that he was drawing on, or reacting to, these sources. Claims that the priestly Christ of the epistle represents an attempt to show that Jesus combines both the messianic (royal) and priestly functions of the two messiahs at Qumran[100] may be judged as misconceived on at least two grounds. (*a*) Contrary to the assumption involved, the writer is not at all interested in 'proving' Jesus' (kingly) messiahship.[101] As we have ourselves noticed (above, p. 14) the 'royal' qualities of Melchizedek (βασιλεὺς δικαιοσύνης, βασιλεὺς εἰρήνης) are all but passed over in silence.[102] Nor is it the case that Χριστός is used in a titular sense in Hebrews.[103] We can compare 4.14 and 5.5 where Ἰησοῦς and Χριστός are virtually interchangeable.[104] If it is not a concern of the author to demonstrate Jesus' messiahship in the normal sense it can hardly be his intention *also* to show him as 'combining in his personality both the kingly and priestly Messiahs; i.e., a royal priest'.[105] (*b*) But of even more significance must be the fact that, so far as we know, there was never anywhere, other than in Christian writings, the suggestion that the eschatological priest would be of other than levitical or Aaronic descent.[106] This means that if the author of Hebrews was consciously shaping his proclamation to the Qumran expectation he would have been bound to treat at *very much greater depth* the question which would thereby have been raised, namely that of Jesus' non-levitical descent.[107] It is simply question-begging to assume that he could have satisfied himself with the single reference at 7.14,[108] or that he could short-circuit this serious difficulty with the Melchizedek story, showing that 'the Messianic priest...is not of Aaron but of another and higher order',[109] because it can be shown[110] that the Melchizedek references were capable of more than one interpretation and were already in use in Qumran circles (Jubilees XIII.25f) to *support* the claims of the Aaronites.[111]

Nor is there any real likelihood that the writer's Christology has been deduced from the Philonic Logos–highpriestly terminology.[112]

Although precedent for the priestly Christology of Hebrews has sometimes been sought in other Christian writers,[113] these attempts generally succeed in showing no more than the *possibility* of the writer of Hebrews' highpriestly formulation being inherent in the sacrificial language of other New Testament writers. The nearest anyone else in the New Testament comes to the author of Hebrews is Paul in his Epistle to the Romans, 8.34. But this is not otherwise worked out or built into anything like the impressive structure in Hebrews.[114] Until there is a more clear demonstration of the writer's dependence on other sources than has so far been produced we may continue in the assumption, therefore, that the conception of Jesus as eschatological priest, as he presents it in his letter, arises pretty well spontaneously out of his own theological preoccupations with the relationship between the covenants.[115]

That this distinctive Christological expression has been worked out so elaborately, and especially the fact that the wider context in which it has been set is concerned not at all with priesthood but with the agencies of revelation, leads us to reaffirm that the deepest question for the writer has not been that concerning the means of atonement, nor that of how to encourage others to a more elevated life, but that of the historical elongation of the divine self-disclosure.[116] The portrait of Jesus as priest, with its cluster of associated ideas, is the product of his reflection on the history of the Word, rather than vice versa. But this in turn means that contrary to his being the most enigmatic of the New Testament writers, and the one most distant from us, he is the New Testament theologian who has grappled most consistently, and not unsuccessfully, with the discipline we now call hermeneutics.[117]

Of course it was a preoccupation of virtually every writer in the New Testament to say how the church stood to Israel. But we ought not to forget, as we nearly always do,[118] that it was this writer more than any other in the New Testament[119] who seems to have caught up the suggestions of the prophecies of Jeremiah and, perhaps, of the Eucharistic cup-word,[120] not only to forge the definitive structures but also to provide the terminology by which we continue to divide the dispensations of God's revelatory activity.[121]

In attending carefully to his own introduction, therefore, and attempting to find its lines of connection with the body of the letter which follows, we seem to have discovered not only a new insight into this writer's objectives and interests but have also stumbled on to an unexpected proximity between these interests and some of those with which we in the latter twentieth century continue to be engaged.

EXCURSUS 1

'PERFECTION' IN THE EPISTLE

The concept 'perfection' (τελείωσις) is as important as it is difficult in the theology of the writer of Hebrews. The difficulties are occasioned as much by the diversity of ways in which he employs the group of words associated with this idea as by the complexity of the idea itself in contemporary religious usage.[1]

Fairly predictably, E. Käsemann sees in the extensive use of the word-group in Hebrews evidence of early gnostic influences; so that the picture of Jesus coming down to earth (2.18), his full participation in the lot of men (2.17 etc.), and his procuring of τελείωσις for men in a proleptic way, with a consequent exhortation to the 'enlightened' (6.4), or those who are τέλειοι (5.14), to press on to τελειότης by means of 'strong food' are all reflections in which 'one recognises the myth of the Primal Man, in which the Redeemer, as leader to Heaven and Home (*Seelenheimat*), returns himself and thus becomes the "redeemed Redeemer", equally τελειωτής and τελειωθείς'.[2]

The coincidences in terminology which Käsemann is able to adduce make the case for parallels between Hebrews and some form of primitive gnostic thought, if not convincing, at least difficult to disprove. So that, in spite of his own strong tendencies in the opposite direction,[3] O. Michel can write: 'All attempts, philologically or from the history of religions, to dislodge . . . τελειοῦν (Heb. 2.10) from its Hellenistic context, and to look for a Palestinian, Aramaic origin, have not so far met with success.'[4]

This opinion notwithstanding, others have seen connections between the New Testament interest in τελείωσις and that of Qumran.[5]

Still others have located the underlying interest in the 'perfection' language of the epistle in the eschatological perspectives adopted by author, with their range of ideas 'from a philosophical *summum bonum* to an eschatological identification with death as the ultimate "perfection" '.[6]

We may also include here the suggestion of C. F. D. Moule:[7] 'This Epistle is particularly concerned with the *incompleteness* of the Jewish Law, and it may be this theme, rather than mere stylistic factors, that has determined the use of τελεῖν, τελειοῦν, "to finish" '[8] and 'for this theme a termination-word is more appropriate than a completion-word'.[9]

Since whatever content the author was putting into this word-group is inescapably bound up with his conception of Jesus' advent as an eschatological phenomenon, the right starting point for our inquiry must be with its usage in relation to him and what he has accomplished. At 2.10 the writer has brought together three important interpretative statements about Jesus' 'perfection': his personal status as Son, his paradoxical suffering, and his (consequent?) capacity as 'leader' (ἀρχηγός). It is this paradox of a Son who suffers which gives us a first clue toward understanding his τελείωσις: that his suffering was endured *in spite of* his proper status is the reason for his having been accounted 'perfect'. That is, τελείωσις is the perfection of a communion of wills, as exemplified in Jesus' total filial obedience (as expressed, though in different terms, at 10.5ff). This, we may note, is in fact the basic usage of the term in the LXX: '...of the heart which is "undivided" πρὸς κύριον or μετὰ κυρίου in exclusive worship, without idolatry, wholly obedient to God's will'.[10] So whatever ideas the author found circulating in his contemporary world, it is a reasonable guess that this Old Testament (LXX) conception of the 'undivided heart' is the operative one.[11]

Many exegetes have also detected a connection between the τελειοῦν terminology of Hebrews and the semi-technical term in the Old Testament for the consecration of priests: מִלֵּא יַד, τελειοῦν τὰς χεῖρας (Exod. 28.41 and many other examples[12]).[13] The significance for us here is that if this thesis can be sustained, the writer must be understood as making Jesus' priestly qualifications to be dependent upon, or emergent from, his obedient relationship with God – 'God has qualified Jesus, the υἱός, "to come before him" in priestly action. He has done so by the suffering in which Jesus confirmed his obedience. As the One qualified (τελειωθείς) for priestly ministry before God, as the One eternally qualified (εἰς τὸν αἰῶνα τετελειωμένος, 7.28), He is the absolute Highpriest.'[14]

This is confirmed in the difficult passage 5.7-10. J. Jeremias has argued in a short but important article[15] that the best sense is yielded by taking the three aorist participles of the passage together (εἰσακουσθείς, τελειωθείς, προσαγορευθείς) so that the hearing of Jesus' prayer *consists in* his being 'consecrated' and designated priest, with the *reason* for his being heard given in the parenthetical phrase ἔμαθεν ἀφ' ὧν ἔπαθεν τὴν ὑπακοήν ('he learned obedience through his sufferings'). Even if the grammatical criticisms of F. Scheidweiler and E. Brandenburger[16] can be sustained, the essential point for us, namely that Jesus' τελείωσις depends upon his prior obedience, is not seriously affected.[17]

There is, however, another element in both these passages (2.10, 5.7-10) which needs drawing out. In both, Jesus' stature as 'perfected' priest includes his capacity to secure the same status, proleptically, for those who follow him. This is a fundamental notion in the epistle, and includes the whole complex of terms in which Jesus is designated 'leader' (ἀρχηγός),[18] 'forerunner' (πρόδρομος), 'the source of salvation' (αἴτιος σωτηρίας) etc.[19] It is on this count, and this alone, that Christians can already be designated τέλειοι: 'Their perfection depends altogether . . . for the moment upon their relationship with the ἀγιάζων'.[20]

Not, as is quickly clear, that this cancels any need for obedient perseverance on their own part, however. Indeed, the whole burden of the letter is to encourage them to this end. As we have already seen in the preceding chapter, *Jesus*' exaltation ('perfection') is organised in such a way by the writer as to be the motive and stimulus for the *Christians*' perseverance.

In the 'perfection' idea of the Epistle to the Hebrews, therefore, we are to discern the eschatological ambivalence which runs throughout the document. The fundamental conception is in terms of a 'perfection' of relationships, not the ontological ones of a flesh/spirit dualism. Certainly the writer regarded this as an 'end' (eschatological) possibility, which has been realised in the earthly life and ministry of Jesus, thus distinguishing the new covenant radically from the old, in which this quality of relationship had not, and never could have, been achieved. In his own 'perfection' Jesus has proleptically attained this for 'many sons' (2.1). But only proleptically. They too must persevere in their following after. The 'perfection' which attends the Christian forms, and marks them off from the forms of the previous covenant, therefore reflects, and itself shares in, the dialectic of all eschatological existence in history.

2

HISTORY

The most immediately obvious expression of the hermeneutical question lying behind the epistle is contained in the use made by the writer of the Old Testament in his quotations. That is why almost invariably studies of the hermeneutical principles of the author have been confined to this particular field of investigation.[1]

Attention has regularly been given to the singularly dynamic way in which the scriptures function for this Christian writer: 'When he uses any word to introduce a quotation he employs words expressing diction ... The *present* tense is preferred to the past tense, *active* forms to passive.' 'What *has* been said is also *being* said.'[2] In fact this observation simply raises in an especially clear and precise form the dialectic which we have said is the distinguishing mark of the relationship between the covenants. In this particular case the question takes the form: how in one context can the scriptures of the Old Testament function so immediately as a vehicle for the Word of God while in other contexts the covenant which those same scriptures enshrine is unceremoniously dismissed as outmoded?

It is true that we have to do here with the web of problems raised by the writer's citations from, and exegesis of, the Old Testament. But the inverse proportion of satisfactory answers to the expenditure of scholarly industry spent on these questions[3] warns that the most fruitful approach may not be through those avenues already well worn, that is to say by analysis of the techniques of exegesis employed, but in examination of the structures within which his theology of revelation works and which enable him to achieve what he has.[4]

Our present inquiry (into the writer's use of the Old Testament texts) therefore represents a continuation, though now in a new direction and with a more specific form of the question before us, of that undertaken in our first chapter.

Accordingly it is no accident that the writer's prologue statement about the earlier and latter forms of God's Address should continue to be our main guideline. To ask: what is our (Christian) relationship to the forms of the Word which were mediated to the fathers through the prophets? is again to receive the answer: it is an *historical* one. Whatever uses will be made of the 'Platonic' category of ideas later in the letter, we must see with complete clarity that here in the opening statement the relationship between the two forms of revelation - the imperfect and perfect - is given not as between an imperfect human or earthly form and a spiritual and heavenly form, but as earlier and later forms. The disclosure of the Word of God takes its shape as a history, a history which has a past and a present (and, indeed, a future).

But of course we cannot overlook the fact that that history is also seen as having reached its goal and that Christians are considered as standing within that culmination: ἐπ' ἐσχάτου τῶν ἡμερῶν τούτων.

Interestingly and perhaps significantly therefore, our inquiry into the use made of the Old Testament texts by the writer takes as its horizon that complex of questions with which many modern theologians are pre-occupied, i.e., those which have to do with the interrelationship of history, eschatology and revelation.[5] Our first task, therefore, is to inquire as closely as we can into the writer's conception of history and the relation-ship between history and the Word of God (section 1 below); from within this context we shall address ourselves more directly to the questions raised by the Old Testament citations (section 2); and finally we shall try to analyse the nature and importance of the eschatological implications raised by the fact that the form of the Word which has come to Christians is in or through the Son (section 3).

1 History, the form of existence in which the Word is heard as promise

The initial problem here is in knowing how or whether we can find a point of contact with the thought-structures of this first-century writer. We have already affirmed, on the basis of his opening statement, that historical perspectives perform a basic function in his understanding of the processes of revelation. He has no word for 'history', however, and perhaps only a slight idea of what we should include within that term.[6] The scale of the problem is possibly indicated by the difficulty we have ourselves in achieving agreement as to the meaning of the term. Can we nevertheless find some recognisable points of contact?

At 1.10-12 the writer incorporates into his catena of scripture 'testi-monies' the statement from Psalm 102.25-7 which affirms the radical distinction between God's mode of existence and that which is the only form known to ourselves - the difference between God's 'eternity' and our own temporality. Fortunately we need not be distracted here by the notorious problems these verses create in their simple transference of this divine dignity to Christ.[7] It is sufficient to note that the 'heavens and earth', which from the point of view of non-faith must certainly seem to be the most stable forms of reality imaginable, are in fact (understood from the perspective of faith) in constant process of change or, alternatively expressed, constantly moving toward their own dismantling by him who is their Creator. Over against this transitory form of existence, God is 'always the same', σὺ δὲ διαμένεις, σὺ δὲ ὁ αὐτὸς εἶ. Of course we must be aware of the fine but probably important distinction between 'unendingness' and 'endlessness'[8] or in other words the recognisable though disputed differences between the biblical, Hebrew way of understanding God's eternity and the more distinctly Greek or Ideal conceptions of eternity as static timelessness.[9] We are reminded of this immediately: καὶ τὰ ἔτη σου οὐκ ἐκλείψουσιν (verse 12).

Is it possible to find in the psalm text so used by the writer some foothold towards a common understanding of 'history'? We have been warned of the dangers of depending too heavily on hymnic expressions for close theological analysis.[10] On the other hand we may perhaps take some encouragement from the fact that quite a wide spectrum of contemporary Christian theologians are finding in concepts such as 'goal', 'purpose', 'movement', 'hope', 'direction' and 'decision' constituent elements of an historical understanding of the world.[11] This is by no means to claim, of course, that all these conceptions are to be found in the psalm phrases or in the writer's employment of them. It is to say that the structure of the world's existence is seen in some way as telic; that it is not without meaning but, in that it proceeds from a beginning to an end, is purposive; and that in this purpose being given to it by its creation and its dissolution there is a sense of time, a pastness and a futurity.

It would be precarious to rest too heavily on this quotation, which after all is here adduced by the writer for quite different reasons, if similar ideas could not be found in his own writing. It is therefore interesting and in our case helpful to notice that numerous exegetes have seen material links between these verses and the 'apocalyptic' passage towards the end of the letter, 12.18-29, especially verses 26-8.[12]

Here too, heaven and earth - 'the Israelite summing up of both parts of the world'[13] - are seen as destined for change or indeed for removal. Here it emerges that the distinction is not simply an ontological one - as between increate and created forms of existence, since at least some parts of creation, the members of the βασιλεία ἀσάλευτος will be (ἐπήγγελται, verse 26), or have been already (παραλαμβάνοντες, verse 28), removed from the sphere of τὰ σαλευόμενα to that of τὰ μὴ σαλευόμενα. That this is something which they have received (παραλαμβάνοντες) eliminates any possibility of its having been inherently theirs from the beginning (as some sort of divine kinship).

Here, again, then, a form of existence characterised by its flux and instability ($\mu\epsilon\tau\acute{\alpha}\vartheta\epsilon\sigma\iota\varsigma$) and described in terms of 'heaven and earth', the most comprehensive and stable forms of existence we have yet experienced, is to give way to a different order not so characterised. The present structures of existence, 'heaven and earth', are seen, then, as having definite boundaries or a terminus towards which they are already under way. There is a sense of temporal direction which accords not altogether unfavourably with what we know as a sense of history.[14]

The question remains, no doubt, as to whether a sense of the passage of time in itself constitutes an awareness of 'history', or whether it can at best be called 'an approximation of history'.[15] Are the tangential contacts established between the narrowly defined band of the saving events and world history at large only at the points of creation and eschaton sufficient to enable us to speak of an historical awareness?[16]

To this it must be said that there is in the letter to the Hebrews considerably more than an awareness of simple chronological pastness, presentness and futurity. Rather these are seen as interlocking meaningfully with one another and indeed, at some points at least, with their wider contexts of world events.

If we consider, for instance, the significance of the present for the writer it is immediately apparent that there is behind the letter a deeply brooding sense of the solemnity and urgency which attaches to the present 'maintenance of the confession' for the Christians to whom it is addressed, and this precisely because of their interaction with the historical and political forces of the age. In the dark hints which lie behind the references to suffering (2.18), or to the fact that not yet are all things brought into submission (2.5-9) - which hints take on more precision in the call to resistance even to the point of shedding blood (12.4), to strengthen the drooping arms and sagging knees (12.12) in the struggle against sin (12.4) or sinners (12.3 and cf. 10.32-4) - it is difficult not to catch allusions to some gathering political force which the Christians must necessarily contemplate with foreboding. That the maintenance of Christian faith can be so closely linked with this threatening fate (cf. the relationship between 10.32-4 and 35f) means that in some sense the decision to be a Christian is a political decision - at least to the extent that the decision not to persevere with the confession would absolve one from the political threat. The least which can be said is that in the letter to the Hebrews there is a high consciousness of the larger historical and political context in which faith is confessed.

The present moment therefore takes on decisive importance within the presuppositions of the letter insofar as the decisions made in it (the present) determine in a quite radical way the future for the individual. That this is the motive behind the urgency of the exhortations should hardly require documentation. It is the overriding concern of the letter as a whole that the readers should be galvanised out of their lethargy and that the correct decisions should be made and acted upon.[17] Though in some sense, therefore, history as a whole may be proceeding toward its goal under the sovereign direction of the Creator (1.12, 12.26), the individual is nevertheless confronted by the enormous responsibility of deciding which sphere of reality he shall join himself to: the βασιλεία ἀσάλευτος or that of τὰ σαλευόμενα.[18] To that extent, therefore, the future stands open and ambivalent before the decision of the Christian. He decides it for himself.

But from another direction, too, the confidence which may be derived from God's sovereignty over the world's history must be modified and history thus rendered more open and precarious. That is the consideration that as yet the Christian grasps the truth of God's lordship only from *within* history and therefore only with the certainty of faith which is virtually approximate to hope (11.1).[19] Quite apart from the decision as to whether or not to press on with the confession, the future contains a considerable ambiguity and uncertainty. It is precisely the tension between the uncertainty of what may happen to him in history and the confidence to which he is called by the lordship of the Creator over the world's history that constitutes faith, hope, endurance and so on as the definitive modes of Christian existence in our letter.

Not only do the present and future interact upon each other in this way but the present also relates to the past in a way which throws up its implications for the Christian. Even if we do not subscribe totally to the 'relapse theory' as providing the 'life-situation' of the letter, it is clear that a great deal of the argumentation is intended to show that the past is past and that there is no question of its supplying solutions for the present (other than in the limited form of example or corrective). This, too, would seem to be so clearly present as scarcely to need detailed documentation.[20]

The possibility of our being able to find within the letter to the Hebrews a conception of world history which is not hopelessly anachronistic therefore seems a reasonable one. History is conceived of as that order of existence which, being bound by temporal limits, is measurable and thus definable. Its finitude and direction define it over against God and his unbounded mode of existence by being what he is not and not being what he is.[21] In that it has a beginning and an end it has the nature of movement and thereby of flux and change. But in that its goals are established from outside or above history itself, the movement is not a random or meaning-less one, but purposive, it has not just movement but direction. It is this directedness, the chronological sequence in which the past inevitably stands to the present as pastness and which renders the future as open and ambivalent for any given present moment, yet in such a way that these interact upon one another, which creates the peculiarities of history and the tensions of historical existence.

The question concerning history first arose out of our observations concerning the historical perspectives of the Speaking of God as depicted in the prologue statement. We are now therefore bound to inquire more deeply concerning this relationship between God's Word and history. Two theses may be set out concerning the relationship, both of which may be allowed to take their origin from the passage most recently under review (12.18-29) but which also have wider reference within the letter.

(a) The Word of God in history necessarily takes the form of promise
The end-events spoken of in chapter 12 serve in a dual capacity. It is true, as we have just noticed, that they mark the limits of temporal existence and therefore the goal towards which world history is moving. But we cannot overlook the fact that these events also indicate the goal towards which Christian faith in particular is orientated, namely the gathering up out of history of God's people on earth or, in the writer's language, the eschatological establishment of the βασιλεία ἀσάλευτος.[22] This coincidence of the points at which world history and salvation history reach their goals means that the goal towards which the salvation history is directed is at, or beyond, but certainly not before, the boundary of world history: that is to say it is not properly a *part of* history.

That God, and then consequently that mode of existence (βασιλεία, 12.28, or πόλις, 11.10, 13.14, or again, πατρίς, 11.14) which characterises his stability in contradistinction to the flux and mutability of historical existence, is set before Christians as a future hope and expectation is that which gives rise to the 'pilgrimage' conception of Christian life.[23] That is why there can be no legitimate 'resting place' for Christians within his-torical existence (13.14) and why they are committed, so long as they will maintain the confession, to futurity and hope.

As E. Grässer has shown in great detail, the stability which distinguishes God's mode of existence is extended to, or seen as being desirable in, the character of his people in the midst of their earthly (historical) pilgrimage (by way of a curious blending of metaphysical and moral categories: faith-fulness = stability).[24] But in an even more direct way God's *Word* bears his *character*. Thus in the epistle at large we keep running into affirmations of the trustworthiness of his call or promise, which dependability is grounded in the character of him from whom it issues,[25] as, for instance, at 10.23: 'Let us hold fast without wavering, for he who promised is faithful' (similarly at 11.11). At 6.13ff this occurs in an especially graphic expression in which God is pictured as stepping in as witness to the veracity of his own promise and this on the premise ἀδύνατον ψεύσασθαι θεόν (6.18).[26]

That God's Word bears about it (not unnaturally) the character of him whose Word it is, implies that it belongs not properly in history but to that order of existence which is beyond the mutability of historical existence. This seems to be confirmed by its description as 'the heavenly call' (3.1) and in its being linked with 'the powers of the age to come' (6.5) or, again, with the 'eternal inheritance' (9.15).[27] The essential location of the Word of God is not in history but beyond it, and its function is to summon men from within history towards the meta-historical 'Rest' of God (4.1ff).[28]

But this means, of course, that for the community in history the Word of God and that of which it speaks can never be apprehended other than as promise.[29]

It is not surprising, accordingly, that even in the apocalyptically conceived passage in chapter 12, where the Christians are envisaged as already standing (προσεληλύθατε, verse 22) before Mt Zion, the eternal πόλις, the Word which speaks of the end of history and the bringing to finality of the salvation history is still reckoned as promise (ἐπήγγελται, verse 26). What is more surprising to us is that included among those end-events should be the sprinkled blood of Jesus through which is founded the new covenant. This comes as a surprise in that both within the epistle itself and also in terms of our own assessment, the death of Jesus seems to be an event in our past and therefore to be conceived 'historically'. That it should be listed here among the eschatological events suggests that it too - in conjunction with the Word with which we said it has become interchangeable (chapter 1 above) - has an essential futurity about it, or in other words that it cannot properly be understood as an element of history but more fundamentally as an eschatological event. Even the death of Jesus and his covenant, as seen from within history, are not fully revelatory but point toward their future meaning and thus still stand as promise.

The fundamental distinction between 'history' as a form of existence and that form characterised as God's βασιλεία, is what establishes the continuity between Christians and members of the old covenant. It is certainly true, from one point of view, that the Christian conceives of himself as standing within 'the last days' (1.2). But that really must not be allowed to obscure from us that that in itself is something of a paradox, occasioned by the yet greater paradox that somehow the 'end-events' of

Jesus' death and the establishing of the new covenant have been dislodged from the actual end of world history and salvation history where they essentially belong, and have taken their place 'within' but not properly as 'part of' history. The division between history and eternity properly comes at the end of history, no matter how complicated this basic fact has become by the Christians' conviction that somehow they already participate in eschatological realities. And the fact that we share, with Old Testament man, 'history' as the envelope of our existence is what gives us our sense of continuity with him.

It is this observation which tells so seriously against those studies which see the letter to the Hebrews operating with a fundamentally Alexandrian two-world concept according to which heavenly, spiritual realities are disposed over against the material world of sense experience.[30] In this reading of the letter, the Christian forms of worship, sanctuary and priesthood are contrasted with Old Testament forms; of course (as our own study has shown, above) a good deal of evidence can be collected to link the Old Testament forms with fleshly, transitory categories and to establish the Christian forms as their antitheses. But the question must be put as to whether this arrangement is not far too simplistic for what we have seen to be in fact a complex, dialectically conceived relationship.

For in the first place, one *cannot* divide the Old Testament community from that of the New Testament as though one had, and the other did not have, the Word of God. We have already seen how *the same Word* makes its uniform demands upon both communities though with different reference points (see the early parts of chapter 1 above).

Moreover the Alexandrian dualistic framework, though undoubtedly useful to the author in his attempt to express the eternal shape and dimensions of Christian existence, has been modified so considerably that it is more than questionable whether we can usefully speak any longer of 'an anthropological flesh-spirit dualism'[31] or say that the 'Anthropos-myth supplies the basis for the Christology of the letter'.[32] For example, on one side the simple flesh–spirit dualism suffers damage by the writer's repeated insistence that it is the 'conscience' of man that requires purification (9.9, 14; 10.2, 22; 13.18). The implication is *not* that one part of him is good, the other evil, but that he is in every way involved in sin.[33] But if the conscience or 'spiritual' part of man is not wholly good, even less can it be said that his flesh is wholly evil. E. Käsemann's nimble distinctions between 'Leib' and 'Fleisch'[34] hardly meet the point made by U. Luck that in the letter Jesus specifically takes to himself 'the seed of Abraham' so that 'the world as the realm of the flesh is no longer seen as totally alienated from God, even though the demonic powers are still active in it. It cannot be wholly alienated because in it are to be found the descendants of Abraham, that is a people whose διαθήκη and λατρεία point toward the perfected worship of God.'[35]

The actual continuity which Christians share with their Old Testament predecessors in terms of their historical existence thus comes to expression at several points in the letter. For example, contrary to any attempt to show otherwise,[36] there is no material distinction between the call to the wilderness community to occupy Canaan and the call to Christians to press forward to the eschatological Rest (3.7–4.13). In fact the two are conflated in such a way as to make it appear that the attainment of Canaan would indeed have represented for the wilderness pilgrims a kind of proleptic entry into that other, eschatological form of the Rest: 'We see that they were not able to enter because of unbelief. Therefore let us be anxious, while the promise of entering his Rest remains, lest someone among you should be judged to have failed to attain it' (3.19f). In fact the promise (ἐπαγγελία, 4.1) or gospel (εὐαγγέλιον, 4.2) are regarded as being identical for both communities.[37] One can only speak of a 'neue Heilssituation'[38] in the very limited sense that the *renewal* of the promise (i.e., the same one) in the time of David testifies that it is still intact. As we have seen so frequently, it is the same Word with which men of every age have to do. The issues are always in terms of faith or unfaith, obedience or disobedience.

This emerges even more clearly in the case of the Old Testament heroes of faith in chapter 11. *Those men and women looked for exactly the same heavenly city as the Christians do* (11.10, 13–16; 13.14). They were therefore aliens and strangers in history no less than the Christians (11.9, 13, 38). In this sense they may be described as an 'eschatological' community,[39] one might even call them 'Old Testament Christians'.[40] Certainly they saw the promised inheritance only 'from afar' (11.13f) and did not live to see it attained even in the partial and proleptic way in which Christians have seen it (11.39f). Yet for both Christians and patriarchs that promised future must remain invisible,[41] and in their longing for the future they, no less than any Christian, indicate that they have heard and responded to that Word of which the content must, so long as history remains, be future and therefore take the form of promise.

(b) The Word of God in history is itself a history of promise

The end-events spoken of in chapter 12, we have noticed, function in a dual capacity: they signify the end of history and at the same time signify the fulfilment of the eschatological βασιλεία. This duality of function means that God's self-disclosure, no less than the history of the world, has achieved a finality, a predetermined goal, and has therefore been involved in the same, or similar, kind of historical process as world history itself. It is certainly true that they cannot be regarded as being the same thing, for the terminus of one is its elimination; of the other, its fulfilment and perfection.

According to our thesis it is this historicising of the Word of God which has preoccupied our author at a fundamental level and which is responsible for his prologue formulation and the entire scheme of two covenants in dialectical relationship.

This pattern of historical development emerges particularly clearly from our passage in chapter 12, in the setting up of a relationship between the revelation on Mt Sinai and the fulfilment of the process on Mt Zion (verses 18-21, 22-4). These two events are set over against each other in the peculiar relationship of continuity and discontinuity within which the covenants stand at every turning in the epistle.[42] Here the discontinuity is written large: the one was terrifying, the other sublime (verses 18, 19, 21 and 22-4); the right picture for one is of blinding darkness and raging storm, for the other, of a festal banquet; one was on earth, the other is in heaven (verse 25). In contrast, the continuity element is reduced almost to the single fact that it *is* God who speaks within each covenant. Slender as this thread may seem, however, it proves to be the very factor which binds these two events into relationship and allows that relationship to become apparent. God speaks in different forms and on different occasions, but for all the outward dissimilarity his Word on *every* occasion demands response (verses 25, 28). The possibility of setting up a relationship between Sinai and Zion on the basis of the Word of God means that the one stands to the other as the imperfect to the perfected form, that the one anticipates the other, that the revelation effected in the end-events stands as the goal and culmination of this particular history of revelatory acts as well as that of history in general.[43]

In this passage the relationship between the historically mediated events of revelation and their climax in the end-events is set down in terms of Sinai and Zion. But in the wider epistle this history is expanded to include the whole succession of God's revelatory activity. It is this which is already referred to in the opening prologue statement, where God's Word is seen as the central thread along which a historical, developmental process takes place. There the whole history of God's Speaking prior to the incarnation of Jesus is comprehended within the phrase τοῖς πατράσιν ἐν τοῖς προφήταις. In chapters 6 and 11 this history is pushed back beyond Sinai to the promissory Word given to the patriarchs. In chapter 3 it is extended forward from Sinai to include the wilderness generation and the conquest of Canaan. In chapters 5ff it includes the whole history of the partial and anticipatory relationship achieved within the framework of Old Testament cultus and Priesthood.

Returning to chapter 12, however, the writer mentions there a detail
that especially catches our attention. That is his remarking on the fact
that the one covenant was instituted on earth (ἐπὶ γῆς) and the other
from heaven (ἀπ᾽ οὐρανῶν) (verse 25). This has not unnaturally been
seized upon as evidence for the Alexandrian disposition of our author and
of his organisation of the two covenants into an (inferior) earthly form
and a (superior) spiritual or heavenly form.[44] We neither can, nor need,
dispute that throughout the epistle the qualities of earthly, fleshly, copied,
temporal and mutable hang together as characteristics of the early form of
revelation and that the heavenly, the eternal and the archetypal represent
the perfection of these anticipatory forms. *But the point is*: they *are* earlier
and later forms, they are a πρωτή and καινὴ διαθήκη; the one stands to
the other as anticipation to achievement and therefore in horizontal or
historical relationship.[45]

We are therefore bound to say that a certain ambivalence attends the
word 'earth' in the epistle. On one hand the earth (and the 'empirical'
heavens) stands, we have said, for that order of existence which we designate
as 'history'. But we may not proceed from there without further inspection
to say that the cosmology envisaged is that of the heaven/earth dualism. For
'earth' just as certainly also stands as the sphere of the *first* or anticipatory
forms of God's Word, which throws the whole structure not into vertical
or spatial categories but horizontal, historical ones.[46] As we have remarked
from time to time, it becomes a matter of exegetical judgement as to which
of the two schemes – the historical or the spatial – is fundamental to the
writer's thought-structures, and which has been introduced in a secondary
capacity. But that both are present and that the terms 'heaven' and 'earth'
therefore bear about them an ambivalence requires to be noted.[47] The
interpretation followed in this study, as has become obvious, is that the
basic consideration has been to work out the historical relationship between
the first and the second covenants, which would mean that the Alexandrian
motifs find their place as the author's attempt to define the ultimate (and
therefore eternal) qualities of the second covenant in distinction to the
first.

When due recognition is given to the association between the *'earthly'*
group of ideas and the *first* covenant, an unmistakeable pattern of movement and development appears throughout the epistle, in which the
anticipatory forms of the old covenant are perfected and find their fulfilment in the heavenly, eternal, new covenant. Surprisingly the identification
of God's Word with his immutability (e.g., 1.10–12) does not result in
a conception of static, eternal truth. Within the history of the world, the
Word of God creates its own history, a history indeed which is not exempt

from μετάθεσις (7.12; cf. 7.18ff, 8.13, 10.9), that property most characteristic of world history (12.27). The inner life and movement of this
genuinely historical process is attested to by its own admission of inadequacy,
its conscious demand for fulfilment in the future.[48]

Historical process though this is, it must be affirmed yet again that from
our perspective in history this remains a history of promises. Certainly it is
true that the new covenant under which Christians live stands as perfection
to the preparatory character of the old covenant. But the new covenant
itself is only known now in a proleptical way, for, as we have seen, its true
locus is in the βασιλεία and is not properly known till the end of history. It
is this, the futurity of the Word of God, which constitutes not only its
character as promise, then, but also invests it with the forms of history.

These two theses, which themselves share something of the dialectic
we have observed as between the two covenants, help us to isolate the distinctive pattern of relationships seen by our author as existing between
history and revelation. In doing so, they prepare for us a way toward an
understanding of the role of the Old Testament in his theology.

To summarise, we have seen that from one point of view it is the
Christian's participation in history that provides the basis for his solidarity
with the Old Testament community. Because from within our historical
existence the Word of God is never grasped other than as Promise, he (the
Christian) stands in the same existential situation as they did. Faith, for
one as for the other, must be that peculiar state of trust without tangible,
visible evidence. Response, for one as for the other, must be in terms of
obedient faithfulness though the temptations to fall away into doubt and
despair may assail on every side. Failure or sin, for one as for the other,
will then be to relax one's hold on the futurity of the promise and cease
from identification with the pilgrim people. For the Christian, we have
seen, the 'content' of the promise has become 'Jesus' exaltation'. Both the
promise and the response demanded are at an infinitely higher level than
for the members of the previous covenant community. But the inner structures and tensions have not changed.

For these reasons, as we read the pages of the Old Testament, those of
whom it tells, though they are dead, *yet speak* (11.4). They address us in
our situation, for, when reduced to its essentials, it is as theirs was.[49] They
speak to us both negatively (chapters 3 and 4) and positively (chs. 6.13ff, 11).

But history enables us to hear God's Word in the Old Testament in a
different way. Because God's Word has its own history, we can enter into
that history, recognise it for what it is, and recognise ourselves as standing
within it. That is to say, because it is *God* who speaks within the old
covenant as well as the new there are recognisable points of continuity

throughout the history of his revelatory activity.[50] Here, of course, we
return to the prologue statement which, we have argued, is the hermeneutical key to the whole theology of the two covenants.

From these two perspectives, what really emerges is a 'theology of revelation', or perhaps even more exactly, a 'theology of the Word of God'.[51] For
the starting point and internal dynamic of this theology - we might say, more
than any other in the New Testament, including the Fourth Gospel - is the
conviction that God speaks. This means that in his handling of the Old
Testament this author does not rest on the contrived notions of fulfilled
prophecy,[52] or even of the inspiration of the documents.[53] Rather, the
continuity which binds Christians to the Old Testament scriptures and
them to the Christians is for the writer grounded in his conception of
God.[54] Because God is wholly consistent, his Word is discernible in the
Old Testament to those who also have the New Testament, in spite of the
external differences within the old and new modes of address.

It is from this perspective then, that we now come to deal more closely
with this author's use of the Old Testament.

2 The Word of God in the past and its meaning for the present: the writer's use of the Old Testament

Here the method outlined above is continued; that is, the use of the Old
Testament citations is approached from within the overall perspectives of
the author's theology of revelation. This means, first, that we shall be more
interested in the way the scriptures function as the vehicle of revelation,
and only in his techniques of exegesis insofar as they further our understanding in this direction; and, secondly, that what our author himself *says*
about the Old Testament will be taken as definitive for an understanding of
his use of the Old Testament texts.

(a) How one hears the Word of God in the Old Testament — Hebrews 5.11–6.20

The location of this passage indicates immediately that its fundamental
concern is with the way the Old Testament - in this case with specific
reference to one text, Psalm 110.4 - can function in revelation-bearing
capacity for Christians.[55] The parenthetic nature of the passage, taking
the Old Testament psalm text as its formal points both of departure and
return (5.10, 6.20), indicates that it serves as preparation for the author's
own Christological treatment of this text in chapter 7. As such, it provides
the clearest expression of the author's understanding of the role of the
Old Testament for Christians. Here we discover that the principle for understanding the inner relationship between the dispensations of the Word of

God is formally expounded by the writer precisely along the lines we have already deduced from more general considerations of his work, namely in terms of the history of development in God's Promise-Word.

The passage itself divides internally into two strongly antithetical parts, the first characterised by the severity of its warning, the other (beginning with the greeting ἀγαπητοί, 6.9, only found here in Hebrews!) by the warmth of its encouragement. That the antitheses are deliberately balanced is quite clear: νωθροὶ γεγόνατε ταῖς ἀκοαῖς, 5.11; ἵνα μὴ νωθροὶ γένησθε, 6.12. The second section stands to the first as the corrective prescription for the malady just diagnosed.

The fact that the corrective to these Christians' present sluggishness is specified in terms of a desired 'zeal in achieving the assurance of hope' and in their becoming 'imitators of those who in faith and perseverance inherited the promises' means that by 'sluggish' (νωθρός) we are to understand that rather more is involved than a simple intellectual problem of understanding the Old Testament text or its exegesis. 'Sluggishness in hearing' in fact seems to mirror a deep sluggishness in spiritual matters generally.[56] The relationship between 'hearing' and an advancement in Christian confidence is confirmed toward the end of the passage by the close conjunction drawn between the certainty of God's Promise-Oath (6.17f) and the 'strong encouragement to hope' (ἰσχυρὰν παράκλησιν . . . τῆς προκειμένης ἐλπίδος) contained therein for Christians. Faith, hope and hearing are therefore the central issues in this passage. That such reflections should intrude themselves just as the author stands poised for his Christological treatment of Psalm 110.4 indicates that the 'difficult word' (λόγος δυσερμήνευτος, 5.11) refers to the task of hermeneutics.

The exhortation to faith and hope is not, of course, confined in any way to this passage but characterises the epistle as a whole; in the author's own estimation his letter takes the form of a λόγος παρακλήσεως (13.22). But the somewhat general way in which the phrase is there used (παρακαλῶ δὲ ὑμᾶς, ἀδελφοί, ἀνέχεσθε τοῦ λόγου τῆς παρακλήσεως) suggests that though indeed his letter bears this quality (ἐπέστειλα ὑμῖν) the task of παράκλησις is not something to which he claims exclusive rights but is something wider than his own particular expression of it in his letter.

In fact the essentially *congregational* setting of the λόγος παρακλήσεως is indicated at 3.13ff and 10.19ff, both of which passages bear important resemblances to 5.11ff. At 3.13 the charge is that Christians should 'exhort one another daily' (παρακαλεῖτε ἑαυτοὺς καθ' ἑκάστην ἡμέραν). This charge emerges out of the message of the Old Testament text concerning the wilderness generation (Ps. 45) and has as its object that none of the Christian community should fall into a similar disobedience (4.11). The same kind of collective responsibility for each other is expressed at 10.25: 'Do not leave off gathering yourselves together ... but encouraging one another ... (μὴ ἐγκαταλείποντες τὴν ἐπισυναγωγὴν ἑαυτῶν ... ἀλλὰ παρακαλοῦντες ...).

The similarities with 5.11ff are clear. This passage also has as its urgent concern that some of the Christians are in danger of falling away into apostasy, here expressed as the re-enactment of the crucifixion of Jesus (6.6) but coinciding exactly in meaning with the example of unfaith of the Israelites after God's gracious dealing with them throughout their wilderness sojourn[57] or the deliberate act of sin after enlightenment spoken of at 10.26ff.

There is one difference, however. At those two places the corrective word was hopefully to be administered by one member of the congregation to the others. Here, at 5.11ff, the word of exhortation must be that of the author to his readers: ἐπιθυμοῦμεν δέ ... ἵνα μὴ νωθροὶ γένησθε, 6.11f. This means that in his letter the author sees himself not as performing any specialist role but simply that of any Christian about his business within the fellowship.[58] It also means that the content of his 'difficult word' (λόγος δυσερμήνευτος) will coincide with that of the more general 'word of exhortation' (λόγος παρακλήσεως). Both have as their first intention the promotion of faith and hope, the health-giving antitheses to νωθρεία, the sluggishness which is equivalent to the 'hardness of heart' of the Israelites (3.8, 13 etc.) or which has led to the 'deliberate sin' of some erstwhile Christians (10.26).

Since the 'difficult word' coincides in intention with the 'word of exhortation', and since this is the character borne by the epistle as a whole, it follows that we have only to look *at* the epistle to see the form that such a *logos* should take. This, it is clear, is a word which both reflects and reflects on the primary form of God's Address to the people ἐπ᾽ ἐσχάτου τῶν ἡμερῶν τούτων - namely the Word in the Son, the Word of which Jesus' sacrificial death, his exaltation and present, priestly intercession for his people are the content.

We may say, then, that the 'word of exhortation' (the λόγος παρακλήσεως which in the case of this congregation is unfortunately also a λόγος δυσερμήνευτος) is fundamentally not other than a making present, through the instrumentality of one of the members of the congregation for his fellows, of the λόγος τοῦ θεοῦ.[59] Alternatively expressed, we might say it is a daily *re-calling* to each other in newer and deeper ways[60] of those verities wherein we first hear God's *call*: namely, in the life and death and exaltation of Jesus.[61]

This then is the gravity of the charge that the members of this congregation manifest no aspiration to be teachers (5.12).[62] The very fact that they need someone to write to them in this way indicates they have not attained the level of Christian maturity at which deep and sustained reflection on the meaning of the Word of God takes place. It is only where such reflection and mutual sharing do take place that God's Word continues to be present. Where this has ceased to be so, feet are already set on the slope that bends down ever more steeply toward the terrifying prospect of apostasy.[63]

The whole discussion is deepened and brought nearer to the central issue of the section (the function of the Old Testament for Christians) with the introduction of the Hellenistic immaturity-milk/maturity-meat motif.[64] Here, the point already made with the 'call-recall' ($κλῆσις$-$παράκλησις$) group of ideas is made again, but differently, with 'word' themes ($λόγια$ $τοῦ$ $θεοῦ$ - $λόγος$ $δικαιοσύνης$).

What precisely is understood by the expression 'oracles of God' ($τὰ$ $λόγια$ $τοῦ$ $θεοῦ$, 5.12) is left indeterminate, probably just because the concept was so familiar both to writer and readers. Certainly it must have included the Old Testament scriptures, not only because of the established meaning of the phrase in the New Testament world,[65] but also by the present context. The fact that the discussion comes at the brink of the full-scale investigation of the text from Psalm 110.4 makes the conclusion all but inevitable that this is the $λόγιον$ pre-eminently in mind here.

$Τὰ$ $λόγια$ includes the oracles contained in the Old Testament scriptures: but the context also indicates that for the Word of God to be heard through these there is demanded an environment of Christian preparedness, an openness or receptivity toward that Word. The absence of such an openness is now stated in another way (5.13) as 'unfamiliarity with the word of righteousness' or, as we might render it, 'the word of right response'.[66] So, as we have already noted, the apathy which threatens to make the task of Old Testament interpretation so difficult for the writer is a larger thing than simple lack of interest in, or disenchantment with, the text and its interpretation. It is primarily because it is a bad *Christian* situation that attitudes to the *Old Testament* are so sluggish. That is why the two can be brought so closely together in describing the one as immaturity in the most elementary understanding of the divine oracles ($τὰ$ $στοιχεῖα$ $τῆς$ $ἀρχῆς$ $τῶν$ $λογίων$, 5.12) and the other as unwillingness to penetrate further than the beginnings of the Christian message ($τὸν$ $τῆς$ $ἀρχῆς$ $τοῦ$ $Χριστοῦ$ $λόγον$, 6.1). While the two are distinguishable, they nevertheless represent symptomatically the same disease.[67]

The conception we are to have, then, of the Old Testament as Word of God in the Christian community involves at least three elements in a complex interrelationship. The first (not necessarily in a temporal or logical sequence) is that the Old Testament text must be made present as *logos* (λόγος) usually through the creative, interpretative, reflective activity of one member of the congregation for the others (though on occasion the λόγος παρακλήσεως can be spoken of as mediated directly through the text itself, 12.5). In our case this function is fulfilled by the writer of the epistle, but this does not affect the process in any material way. Because we may sit in, so to speak, on this particular interpretative attempt we may observe at first hand the way in which not only the *logion* Psalm 110.4, but indeed all the Old Testament *logia* (λόγια) used by our author are turned into *logoi*, or words which communicate something akin to the Word of God itself. The epistle has as its overriding concern the strengthening of this community in its Christian profession. The endeavour takes numerous forms - threats, pleadings, warnings, encouragements - but takes as its primary motivating conception that of Jesus' exaltation to be the Christians' highpriest; from this central motif are the implications for Christian understanding and conduct drawn out. In course of this a good many Old Testament *logia* are employed. But every one of these is turned toward this all-consuming end - that the priesthood of Christ and its implications for the Christian community should be expounded.

We have, in fact, already seen in our exegesis of the Melchizedek passage in chapter 7 (pp. 14ff above) how this happens with respect to Psalm 110.4. Using the standard exegetical techniques of the day, the writer builds around this text and others from Genesis 14 a midrashic construction. But that which controls the discussion throughout is the conception of Christ as eschatological highpriest. It is the finality of Jesus' priestly work which on one hand finds its point of contact with the Old Testament text ἱερεὺς εἰς τὸν αἰῶνα and which, on the other, is organised in such a way as to stimulate hope and consequently faithfulness in the Christian readers. Thus the *logion*, through the medium of the writer's theological and Christological reflection, becomes a λόγος παρακλήσεως, perhaps we may even say a λόγος τοῦ θεοῦ.[68]

The second element we have found to be requisite in this process is that of a Christian (i.e. a faith-) context. We see this not only from the way in which the *logion* becomes *logos* when it is brought into relationship with Christ[69] (e.g., in the case of Ps. 110.4 in Heb. 7), but from the fact that these Christians' sluggishness *as Christians* is the limiting factor in their hearing the 'Word' through the Old Testament text. As we noticed, this inertness before the scripture text is exactly to be paralleled to their lethargy regarding the Christian gospel, and indeed is a secondary feature of it.[70]

Thirdly, and as a partial corollary to both these, there is demanded an ongoing situation of growth, an openness to and receptivity for the Word of God in both its forms on the part of the hearers.[71] In one way, of course, the Word of God is a creative and recreative force in itself (καὶ τοῦτο ποιήσομεν, ἐάνπερ ἐπιτρέπη ὁ θεός, 6.3), but it is clear that from the author's point of view it is possible to become *so* 'dull of hearing' that the Word is no longer heard in spite of the seriousness of its warnings. Thus there is understood to be, where the Word of God is allowed to do its work in a Christian community, a constantly developing situation in which the amalgam of the various elements - text, interpretation, apprehension - is ever being made afresh, producing a new *logos* in an ever-deepening situation of obedience and apprehension by the hearers of that Word.[72]

Turning our attention to the 'corrective' part of the passage (6.9-20) we find laid out before us a precise demonstration of what is meant by the hearing of the λόγος παρακλήσεως through an Old Testament *logion*.

The *logion* in this case is the Promise-Word to Abraham, now located in Genesis 22.17. But the setting in which it is presented to the readers has already constituted it a λόγος παρακλήσεως for them. This comes about through the interpretative application of it to their situation by the writer. The point of his reference to the patriarchs in general and Abraham in particular is left quite unambiguous - they are intended to provide not only an example of, but (ἐπιθυμοῦμεν δέ . . .) also a stimulus to 'enthusiasm' (σπουδή), 'the assurance of hope' (πληροφορία τῆς ἐλπίδος), 'faith' (πίστις), 'perseverance' (μακροθυμία) - and all this in relation to the 'promises' (ἐπαγγελίαι) about which the readers have so far been indifferent (νωθροί). Here then we see the author actually engaged in the παράκλησις process.

We observed above that one prerequisite for the Word of God to be heard in the Old Testament *logion* was an openness toward the hearing of that Word. We have therefore now to notice that a rather dramatic shift in the interpretation of the readers' attitude to the Word has been introduced - whereas the earlier part had raised the question as to the possibility of persons who are 'dull of hearing' being able to hear the Word at all, and had sketched in the possibility of the fatal παραπίπτειν, the congregation is now clearly distinguished from such a radical situation (6.9). The possibility of a *logion* becoming a *logos* demands a situation of openness, and such openness is understood still to exist in the readers' present situation, as indicated by their ethical sensitivity.[73]

Finally, this Word comes about in a specifically Christian context. This is seen in the curiously abrupt way the discussion moves from the form in which the Word was present to Abraham (as the Promise-Oath) to the immediate situation, and to the form in which Christians now have that same Word. For them, the final and definitive form of the Word of God consists in the promise held out by the fact of Jesus' presence in the heavenly sanctuary (6.18-20). It is the function of this new form of the promise to encourage Christians to persevere also in their way toward that heavenly goal; that is to say, to encourage them in the 'enthusiastic realisation of the assurance of hope until the end' (6.11). But that, in turn, is to say that it functions as a λόγος παρακλήσεως. And that *is* what this Old Testament word becomes when read with reference to Jesus' exaltation, that is, in a Christian setting. For in its specification of God's Word to Abraham as 'Promise-Oath' it becomes for Christians a new παράκλησις with respect to the 'hope which is set before them' (6.18)!

It thus emerges that the openness of the hearers for the Word of God or otherwise is at most a limiting factor. It does not, in itself, make possible or constitute the event in which the Old Testament word becomes a *logos* for the Christian community. The possibility of this happening depends in the last analysis on the conformity, the inner congruity, between the old and the new forms of God's Word. It was for Abraham as it is for us: God's promise for the future.

In this fragment of concrete exegesis (i.e., the writer's exegesis of Genesis 22) we therefore gather up our more general observations in the preceding section and see the same conception of a historical expansion and development of God's Word here put to work. The form and character of the Word are the same, but the content is now much enlarged and developed. It cannot be that *what* was promised to Abraham and the patriarchs is also now promised to Christians, for the fathers are said to have attained that which was promised them (6.15, 11.33) but not the larger promises which are held out to Christians (11.39).[74] Nor can it be a case of promise-fulfilment patterns, since here 'Christ himself, as the final form of the Word of God, still has the character of promise.'[75] Rather, we have to say that Jesus' exaltation is a *final and definitive* form of the promise (cf. 1.1 and especially 7.18-24)[76] as the Word to Abraham was an *earlier and more limited* form of promise.[77] In each case it moves at an entirely different level and with a different point of reference, but because it is the Word it bears at each level the same character of Promise-Oath and makes the same demands for faith-response.

Ultimately, therefore, the Old Testament *logion* contains the possibility of becoming a *logos* for the New Testament community precisely because each belongs within the expanding history of God's Word in the world, and, indeed ultimately, because God remains consistent in his Word throughout its course of development.

(b) The function of the Old Testament in the writer's theology of the Word of God

Hebrews 5.11–6.20 is the author's own account of the hermeneutical principles involved in the hearing of God's Word through the Old Testament scriptures. The right methodological approach to his own citations from the Old Testament is therefore obviously through the principles which are stated or implied in this passage. Accordingly, in turning now to the writer's wider use of the Old Testament we shall attempt to understand these citations in the light of what we have there discovered. Three distinguishable, though interrelated, themes may be specified.

(i) The fundamental role of scripture is a paraenetic one. This assertion touches on one of the most important and, at the moment, one of the most debated questions posed by the epistle - that is its purpose. Our analysis above (pp. 25ff) has shown that the position assumed in this essay is a mediating one. On one side, it is argued, the 'Jewishness' of the epistle cannot be resolved into mere symbolism and, on the other, that there are good reasons to suppose that the problem to which the epistle addresses itself is, certainly for the moment, an 'internal' one, i.e., no *explicit* polemic against contemporary Judaism is intended.[78]

The question as to the 'life-setting' is directly relevant to the present discussion since one's attitude to the scripture citations is directly governed by one's understanding of the letter's overall objectives, and vice versa, how one regards the writer's intentions will, to some degree, be influenced by what one thinks about the function of the citations. That is to say, where the epistle is regarded as having an immediately polemical intention, there will be felt acute misgivings about the suitability of the citations;[79] on the other hand queries about the suitability of the citations for a directly polemical situation may help to confirm an opinion against this as the ultimate intention of the epistle.

Moving out, therefore, from the passage we have taken as definitive, we notice that, as there, every other major citation or group of citations has as its express objective a 'word of exhortation'.[80] So we see that the purpose of the 'angel catena' of chapter 1 emerges at the beginning of chapter 2: 'On this account we must pay more strict attention to what we have heard . . .' Psalm 8.4–6 and the citations of chapter 2 are partially included in this *logos*, as explaining *how* the Word of God has come to us in Jesus, but as we shall see (below, pp. 58f) has as its own 'word of encouragement' the phrase 'We see Jesus' (2.9). Psalm 95 and the associated citations of chapters 3 and 4 have as their exhortation: 'Let us be zealous to enter into that Rest . . .' (4.11). The highpriesthood–new

covenant citations (Pss. 2.7 and 110.4; Jer. 31.31ff; Ps. 40.6-8) together
with their supplementary citations through chapters 5 to 10 of the epistle
may be regarded as having for their 'word of exhortation': 'Since we may
therefore confidently enter the sanctuary by the blood of Jesus ... let us
draw near' (10.19ff). The discussion on faith (Is. 29.20; Hab. 2.2) and the
catalogue of the Old Testament heroes of faith (chapter 11) have as their
purpose the encouragement: 'So, let us too run with endurance ...' (12.1),
as indeed do the quotations from Proverbs 3.11f, Isaiah 35.3 and the other
citations of chapter 12. The collection from the Pentateuch contrasting
the first revelation with the last and the citation from Haggai 2.6 toward
the end of chapter 12 are intended that 'We should be thankful, through
which we may offer worship which is acceptable ...' (12.28). Finally, the
minor citations and allusions of chapter 13 either bear their own message
of encouragement (as, e.g., verse 15) or are directly linked to one of the
author's (e.g., verse 5).

Since this pattern is so regularly maintained we may query whether the
critical approach which occurs so naturally to us, and which asks concerning the success or otherwise of each 'scripture proof',[81] is the right
one. Does this question not already have as its postulate that Hebrews is
written to a situation in which the author is trying to 'prove' the divinity
of Christ or his superior priesthood or the lasting validity of his work?

The regularity of the *logion-logos* pattern, or the way in which the
Old Testament text is so regularly arranged in such a way as to promote a
Christian steadfastness, suggests that the discussion is not in the first
instance an interfaith (that is, Jewish-Christian) one but an 'intramural'
one in which the articles which require to be 'proven' are in fact already
the confessional items.

It must be immediately obvious that such a situation requires no less a
commitment to the theological enterprise than a setting of open confrontation - for certainly the questions are not less real ones. To this
extent the advocates of what we have called the 'relapse theory' are certainly correct. If the Christians to whom the letter is being addressed are
in fact Jewish Christians, as we have said is most likely, then the past must
certainly be accounted for, and the impossibility demonstrated even of
contemplating a return to that now outmoded form of faith. We have
argued that this had been a major preoccupation for the writer of the letter
long before he sat down to write. At the same time, the immediate and
gathering circumstances which seem to confront the readers also constitute
the most seriously imaginable reality and thus lend a certain support to
some of the alternatively conceived 'persuasion for spiritual advancement'
interpretations. Both questions and answers, therefore, are intended to be

taken in all seriousness. But the nature and range of the questions must be
evaluated accurately, or we shall find ourselves trying to match the wrong
answers to them. The burden of this present study has been to show that
these are both Jewish and Christian. Jewish because for the writer certainly,
and probably his readers too, the main theological problems can be seen to
have turned around the old covenant-new covenant relationship. And
Christian, because as far as we can see they, writer and readers, are still
talking between themselves, and not (yet) across the boundaries of faith to
Jewish opponents or would-be seducers.

This demand, then, that the writer should 'prove' to his friends why
they should not abandon their faith in Christ the eschatological priest but,
on the contrary, press on with their confession in spite of any discouraging
circumstances, is met by the author, working within the range of exegetical
devices available to him. None of those to be found in his letter are other
than from the common stock-in-trade of the exegete of his day. These
include the manipulation of the text form,[82] the isolation of a text from
its context,[83] the conjoining of two otherwise unrelated texts on the
basis of a catchword,[84] and, above all, the reinterpretation of a text or
word in light of the changed situation, that is to say, his conviction that
God has spoken again in Christ.[85] But whatever technique is used, the
guiding consideration is always that this *logion* be allowed to speak its 'word
of encouragement' in the present threatening situation. We have to say
quite simply that some of the devices used no longer meet the exegetical
standards required by the critical method. On the other hand, and this
needs to be said even more firmly in light of the all-but-universal disapproba-
tion accorded the writer's scripture usage,[86] the greatest part of his exegetical
work is built around the eminently sound principle of hearing what the
scriptures have to say about themselves.[87] It has certainly to be urged that
in comparison with other exegetical traditions of his time, the author of
the Epistle to the Hebrews has an appreciably high regard for the Old
Testament text and for historical principles of exegesis.

(ii) Christ is the final content of God's Word. We have seen from our study
of Hebrews 5.11-6.20 how, in the last analysis, the promise held out by
Jesus' presence, now, in the sanctuary is the ground and content for every
'word of encouragement'; it is this hope before him (ἡ προκειμένη ἐλπίς,
6.18) that provokes the Christian to hold fast, to run, to be faithful, to have
confidence. Jesus' sacrificial and priestly work therefore constitutes the
final stage in the historical development of God's promissory Word. We
have noted how the pattern developed in Hebrews 5.11-6.20 thus coincides
with that of the prologue statement.

It is also the pattern reflected in the citations themselves. Side by side with the 'arbitrary' methods of the writer's exegesis, modern scholars place as equally unpalatable his 'Christianising' of non-messianic texts.[88] Again this objection probably emerges out of a misconception of the way the citations are meant to function in the epistle, and indeed may represent a complete failure to understand the author's 'theology of the Word of God'. What we have to see is not an attempt to 'prove' that Jesus was Messiah, but the working out of this theology in which the inescapable conviction that Jesus is the final form of God's Word has to be reconciled with God's former modes of Speaking. The exact way this is seen to happen is that the previous form reaches its fullest meaning, and only reaches it, in the context of the new and final event of God's Address. And because the Word of God as a 'word of encouragement' arises out of *Jesus'* entry into the heavenly sanctuary, all previous forms now have their fullest significance within this *Christian* context. We are to understand, first, that the writer's conviction about the Christological form of the Word of God operates as the first and largest hermeneutical consideration in his handling of the Old Testament texts and, secondly, that this procedure emerges directly out of his overarching theology of revelation as it is laid out in the prologue statement and manifests itself again in 5.11ff.[89] Certainly it is an arbitrary approach. But it is not the cheap arbitrariness of 'proof' by subtle exegetical sleight-of-hand. The author's work with the Old Testament is relieved of this opprobrium by the inseparable association it has with the fundamental structures of his theology of the Word of God. Rather the process is reversed: what is to be 'proved' is already assumed:[90] the function of the scriptures is not to 'prove' but to communicate the 'encouraging word', which in the nature of things can only, for this author, be a Christian *logos*.

Some of the passages used, of course, have come to him already construed in a 'messianic' way (we can mention here, for example, Ps. 2.7[91] and 2 Sam. 7.14,[92] which had already been put together with Ps. 2 at Qumran;[93] Ps. 45;[94] and Ps. 110[95]). Others, as we have seen, are used in a more strictly rational or critical way, as bearing in themselves the message of their own futurity.

Yet others, however, neither come in a messianic setting nor bear in themselves any particularly obvious future meaning, but are taken as such by our author to the discomfort of his exegetes and interpreters. It is this group of citations which interests us here. They can, perhaps, be classified in three different classes – those used in a 'messianic' or eschatological way, though there was no such intention in the mind of the original poet; those which, in their original context, were addressed to Yahweh but are now taken as addressed to Jesus; and those which are placed on the lips of Jesus.

We may choose as an example of the first kind the use of Psalm 8 (Heb. 2.6ff), which 'is not, and never has been accounted by the Jews to be, directly messianic'.[96] It is, plainly and simply, a piece of reflective writing by a Hebrew poet on the created dignity of man. But in the hands of our writer its reference point becomes the eschatological 'world to come' (verse 5) and he who is 'crowned with glory and honour' is Jesus (verse 9). What are the interests and dynamics at work here?

According to the interpretation given above (pp. 8f) and which we will develop below (pp. 80ff) the context into which the citation is introduced (2.5–18) is concerned with the temptation to despair (i.e., in the terms of the letter, the antithesis of faith) created by the tension between the 'already' and the 'not yet' of Christian eschatological conviction. The author has spoken of the superlative Word that has come through Jesus (2.1–4), but he and his readers know only too acutely that 'we do not yet see every thing brought into submission' (verse 8). In a paradoxical way we have to say that the Word *already* given through Jesus (τὰ ἀκουσθέντα, verse 1) *still* has its reference point in the 'world to come' (verse 5). How then shall we exist in the interim? Why, we fix our gaze on Jesus already in his heavenly sanctuary (βλέπομεν 'Ιησοῦν ... δόξῃ καὶ τιμῇ ἐστεφανωμένον)[97] – he will help us through this time of waiting, for we know him to be a highpriest who is 'merciful and faithful' (verse 17).

The structure of 2.5–18 is therefore not essentially different to that of 5.11–6.20: the object of the author's concern is the possibility of despair, that is to say, faithlessness, which is in turn, apostasy; he counters this possibility by directing his readers' attention to the accomplished eschatological event of Jesus' exaltation (as he has had to teach himself to do?), and in this process an Old Testament text becomes the vehicle for the 'word of encouragement' which in this case takes the form: 'We see Jesus ... crowned' (βλέπομεν 'Ιησοῦν ... ἐστεφανωμένον).[98]

We are to say, therefore, that Psalm 8 functions in the same way here as Genesis 22 did at 6.13ff. That is to say, this prophetic Word of God (1.1) is now allowed to function in a new way in the light of the more recent event of God's Address through his exaltation of Jesus. We must say that it is no more the concern of the writer to force an identification of Jesus with the 'son of man'[99] than it was to identify the content of the Christians' promises with that given to Abraham. The whole interest lies in the apparent (to him)[100] contrast in status of one who for a short time (βραχύ τι) was humiliated but now is ἐστεφανωμένος. And *how* he is 'crowned'! For it says, 'You have put *every* thing under his feet' (πάντα ὑπέταξας ὑποκάτω τῶν ποδῶν αὐτοῦ). Here indeed is a timely word of promise: the *logion* has borne its *logos*.

Here, then, is seen that blending of elements in which the Word of God makes itself present in an ever new experience in each new situation: that creative process of which we spoke in our analysis of Hebrews 5.11ff. The first element is certainly the Old Testament *logion*. From it are drawn the absolutely crucial phrases: 'A little (or 'For a short time') lower than the angels' (βραχύ τι παρ' ἀγγέλους), 'You have crowned him with glory and honour' (δόξῃ καὶ τιμῇ ἐστεφάνωσας αὐτόν), 'You have set every thing under his feet' (παντα ὑπέταξας ὑποκάτω τῶν ποδῶν αὐτοῦ). These are to become the vehicles for the new *logos*, and without them it could not have come into existence.

But the way in which these phrases are woven into the author's own text in what we have learned to call the *pesher*-style (verses 8f) is an index of the contribution which the writer himself brings to the text in the creation of the new *logos*; Old Testament *logia* and New Testament reflection are blended to produce something really new. The psalmist contributes the former; the New Testament writer brings his own situation of need, his questions and uncertainties, and in this situation, or, we might say, into this situation, the *logos* is born. This contribution on the part of the latter can extend to the altering of the text to suit his situation more perfectly,[101] a technique common to all exegetes of his day.[102]

The most important element of all, however, if the Old Testament *logion* is to function as Word of God, is its new Christian setting, the bringing of it forward from its previous location and placing it in the light of the newest phase of God's Address. The setting in which these prophetic words are now to function as God's Word for this community is already established by the introductory remarks of verse 5; the context in which *all* our conversation now takes place is that of the 'world to come'.[103] In the Christian (i.e., eschatological) setting in which the writer and readers are to hear the Word of God the principal frame of reference for that Word will inevitably be God's newest form of promise, i.e., the exaltation of Jesus. In this setting the Old Testament *logion* takes a newer and deeper meaning than it could for the psalmist who penned it.[104]

The quotations of the second class mentioned, i.e., those in which a text addressed to God is now used with respect to Jesus, seem amenable to the same kind of approach. The two most important examples here are Deuteronomy 32.34 at Hebrews 1.6 and Psalm 102.25ff at Hebrews 1.10ff.

It is important that we analyse accurately and evaluate correctly the various interests present in these difficult citations. What is their function in the present location? What were the criteria controlling their choice? And what is the controlling factor under which their point of reference is changed from God to Jesus?

It is regularly assumed that they are cited to furnish scriptural proof for the divinity of Christ. Since most people in both the old and new worlds can be assumed to know that in their Old Testament location they had nothing to do with Jesus, not even with the Messiah, it is fairly clear that the 'proof' has short-circuited and fails to achieve its end. We may therefore either query the aptitude of the writer or re-examine the assumption that this is how he intended the citation to function.

He himself spells out the objective of the whole catena of quotations at 2.1-4; here there is no suggestion that they were to function as *Schrift-beweise* ('scriptural evidence') but as *Mahnwörter* ('exhortations'): 'On this account we must pay more strict attention to that which we have heard' (διὰ τοῦτο δεῖ περισσοτέρως προσέχειν ἡμᾶς τοῖς ἀκουσθεῖσιν).[105] The mention of 'that which we have heard' (τὰ ἀκουσθέντα) refers us back to the Word which has been spoken in the Son (1.1; cf. 2.3b, 4) and sets the whole intervening passage in this context. It is not the intention of the citations therefore to offer scripture proofs for the divinity of the Son, which is already assumed in the confessional statement of 1.3f,[106] but to indicate the heightened dignity of the Word which God has uttered in this form as compared with his previous forms of Address.

The first considerations regarding the choice of Deuteronomy 32.43 at Hebrews 1.6, therefore, were that this text speaks of a role of servitude for angels.[107] But what then is the function of the αὐτῷ ('worship *him*') which, we have seen, works so badly when we think of the verse as a 'scripture proof'? The way the text is introduced – 'And again, when he brings the firstborn into the world ...' – indicates that the same interpretative process has already taken place which we have observed in connection with Psalm 8 and Genesis 22; that is to say, this text is now understood to be functioning in the new context of God's eschatological form of Address. There is no more here the attempt to force an identification between the αὐτῷ and Jesus than there was there an identification between him and the psalmist's 'son of man' or between the 'promises' given to Abraham and to us. Rather, in the context of the Christian gospel this *logion* functions as a suitable vehicle for a Christian *logos* (2.1). For in speaking of the subserviency of angels (and, by implication, the inferiority of the revelation mediated by them) it brings to expression the superiority of the new form of the Word and therefore the need to pay good attention to that Word. These Old Testament citations are thus being brought into immediate relationship with the overall aim of the writer, the encouragement of his friends in the face of their lassitude.

If this is the right way to understand the citation, presumably this is also the way we are to take the κύριε ('Lord') of Hebrews 1.10. Here the interpretative cipher, shared with Psalm 45 (verses 8ff) is, 'Concerning the Son (it says) . . .' and, of course, the Christological introduction at verses 1–4 shared by all the citations. Again the question presents itself as to whether a 'proof' is intended here, and the same considerations militate against this interpretation. Quite apart from the immediate difficulty of the transference of the psalmist's reference from God to Jesus, which so patently fails to prove anything of Jesus' divinity,[108] we have now seen that the 'proof' conception runs counter to the tendency of the epistle as a whole. That κύριε here is referred to Jesus does not mean: this proves that Jesus is God, but: in light of our confession of Jesus as divine, and since we know that God has thus exalted him, here is a suitable text for saying that. The determinative considerations must be the confessional setting in which the citations are placed (1.1–4) and the objective to which they are all driving, that of the Christian 'word of encouragement' (2.1–4).

We can, accordingly, raise very sincere questions about the importance of the single word κύριε in the citation.[109] Would the citation have performed its intended function without this word, and is the word therefore the fundamental one governing the choice of the citation at this place? For it to function (however faultily) as a scripture 'proof', presumably the identification of this word with Jesus is so basic that apart from this the citation could not be used here. The contrast between the meniality of angels and the sovereignty of Jesus indicates, however, that the really important elements in the citation are its reference to lordship, creative power and eternity (qualities, incidentally, which have *already* been predicated of Jesus, 1.3f) just as the operative consideration in verses 6f was the association of angels with servitude. The overall framework of the contrast between an old, angelic dispensation of revelation and a new dispensation through Jesus as Son means that each set of quotations already has its reference point – servitude is to be predicated of angels, lordship of the Son. The appropriate expressions of meniality and lordliness therefore find their place over against each other because they *are* expressions of meniality and lordship, and not in the first instance because of αὐτῷ (Deut. 32) or κύριε (Ps. 102). Certainly in the new, Christian frame of reference these two words can be *suitably* referred to Jesus as Lord,[110] but the citation could equally well function without them.

The citations of the third class, those in which the words of an Old Testament citation are placed on the lips of Jesus (principally, Ps. 22.22 and Is. 8.17f at Heb. 2.12f and Ps. 40.6–8 at Heb. 10.5ff), are usually explained in terms of the writer's conception of the pre-incarnate existence of Jesus as Son.[111] Support is sometimes sought for this view in the writer's affirmation that Jesus is 'the same yesterday, today and forever' (13.8).[112]

That the pre-existence of the Son is an important element in the Christology of the Epistle to the Hebrews is beyond doubt. But is this the idea with which we have to do here? A moment's reflection indicates that if the pattern we have seen developing in our study of the writer's use of the Old Testament is a correct one, this particular usage would represent the clearest expression of that approach - the Old Testament *logia* would thus be 'updated' in the light of the new form of the Word so that they can actually be identified with the *logoi* of Jesus.

Immediately we put it this way we are confronted with the striking fact that the Synoptic and Fourth Gospels show that there were in the early church strong traditions of words and acts of Jesus which coincide with the attitudes here described in scripture words but attributed to him.[113] For instance, it is clearly remembered that Jesus *did* identify himself so closely with his followers as to call them his brothers (Matt. 12.46ff, par. Mark 3.31ff, Luke 8.19ff;[114] Matt. 25.40, 28.10; John 20.17; cf. also Rom. 8.14-17) and the Fourth Gospel, at least, speaks of Jesus declaring God's name to his followers (John 17.6, 26 etc.; cf. also 5.43, 12.28). Similarly, the characterisation of Jesus' life as wholly subordinate to the will of God (Heb. 10.5ff) has discernible links with the kerygmatic traditions (Matt. 6.10, 7.21, 12.50, par. Mark 3.35; Matt. 21.31 (?), 26.39-42, par. Luke 22.42; John 4.34, 5.30, 7.17) and especially with the passion narratives (compare Heb. 10.7: 'Behold I have come to do your will, O God ...' with Matt. 26.39-42 (par. Luke 22.42): 'My Father ... not as I will but as you wish ... Let your will be done').[115] These facts coincide with the patterns already discovered, i.e., that Hebrews' use of the Old Testament *logia* is always through the screen provided by the revelation in Jesus. That is to say, what is here in view is really the figure and character of Jesus as remembered in the traditions.[116] But the author sees such a close conformity between the Old Testament and New Testament forms of the Word of God that the former can now be appropriated to give expression to the latter.[117]

By way of summary, we conclude here that all three of these more problematic forms of scripture citation are amenable to the kind of interpretative principles we have analysed in the letter as a whole and in particular those laid out in the writer's own exposition of principles for reading the Old Testament (5.11-6.20). The most important of these, we decided (above, pp. 52f), was that, for the author, all understanding of God's declaration of his Word now has its meaning in terms of Christ as the fullest form of that Word. That is why no scripture text is left bare and uninterpreted, but is gathered up into the new Christian situation, in which synthesis both the old *logion* and the new situation are each indispensable elements.

(iii) The relationship between the old and new covenants is an 'historical' one. To claim that this writer's employment of the Old Testament, either in citations or more generally, embodies historical principles is to encounter diametrically the preponderant judgement of contemporary critical opinion. Most exegetes think that the way in which the citations are 'lifted' from their Old Testament contexts and brought into the New Testament indicates an understanding of the texts as timeless, the exact antithesis of an historical understanding.[118]

Moreover, the way in which we have ourselves spoken of the actively creative role of the author in bringing his own situation into the interpretation of the texts, and them into it, must certainly seem to involve an arbitrariness and subjectivity that run counter to the external, objective controls that any strictly historical understanding imposes.

What can be meant, therefore, in describing this as 'historical'?

To some extent, of course, we are up against conceptual and hermeneutical difficulties as soon as we use a term such as this which has been made to function in so highly technical a way for us and which can only therefore be used somewhat anachronistically with reference to an author who stands outside this modern, technical discussion. This recognition is acknowledged by the inverted commas used of the term in the heading above.

A further, and related, modification must be entered: this is that 'history' here must be understood in terms of the dialectical continuity, the progression, yet with constant reference backward, of the movement of God's promissory Word in history, as we have described it above. That this conception approximates only more or less to what we understand as 'history' is also reflected in the inverted commas.

And yet, with these recognitions, the term and the claim here made for the author are not by any means impossible. What is meant is that the organising of old and new into relationship with each other within the covenantal history is not a *purely* arbitrary or subjective exercise, the creative elements in the venture notwithstanding.[119] It is to claim that from either end of the hermeneutical work – that is to say, in terms of the texts and in terms of the interpretation of them – there are certain observable, outward factors which at least permit or even invite a relationship between the earlier forms and the later (Christian) interpretation made of them. Certainly the nature of this relationship must be stated carefully. There can be no question of an empirically necessary link or identification. As has frequently been observed,[120] the fact that the Old Testament could provide a basis for the whole course of rabbinic exegesis indicates as simply as is necessary that the texts cannot be said to point unambiguously toward the Christians' exegesis of them. On the other hand they may be said to *permit* their Christian interpretation; which of course is something different from demanding, or requiring, such.

Coming to the work of our writer, two factors may be said to be present which preserve it from pure subjectivity and thus allow (within the limits we have specified) the description of it as 'historical'.

The first is the indication of the Old Testament texts themselves of their own futurity; that is to say, the specific acknowledgement by the texts that their meaning is not exhausted in the objects of their immediate reference. It is salutary, indeed crucial, to recollect that the texts we have just discussed as problematical demanded our attention just because they *are* problems. In fact, the great bulk of the writer's citations, or at least the majority of those around which his argument turns, demand either explicitly or implicitly[121] an application future to themselves.[122] It is therefore important that we understand that those passages which seem to us to be problems are actually carried along by the much larger context created by the majority of texts which declare the limitations of their own environment and thereby themselves point toward the future. Accordingly we cannot here speak of a pure capriciousness. The futurity which the writer ascribes to the texts he draws from the Old Testament is indeed a possible, not unreasonable, interpretation drawn from the important majority of those texts themselves.

But there is an even more important way in which the exegetical work of the writer is subject to an external control, namely the memory of the life and character of Jesus as it is borne along in the church.[123] This is the screen through which the Old Testament is seen at every turning, and by which the meaning of any text is defined and therefore determined.

We use the word 'defined' advisedly; not that one can say in our (twentieth-century) sense that Jesus supplies the clear or compelling definition of the Old Testament texts, but in the sense that it is because Christian exegesis of the Old Testament is *delimited* (or defined) by a reference point at the near end (the observed and remembered events surrounding the life of Jesus) as well as the far end (the written texts) of the hermeneutical process, that there is achieved the possibility of an 'historical' relationship between these near and distant phenomena. It is therefore this aspect which separates the writer's exegesis from other (non-Christian) exegetes of his day, and allows us to speak of his approach as 'historical'.

What is meant here is probably best indicated by way of contrast with those other exegetical activities of the time. The most obvious contrast is presumably with Philo, whose reading of the biblical texts is the most advanced form of allegorical exegesis of the period. It is regularly observed of Philo that though he does not altogether abandon interest in the literal sense of the texts, his chief interest in them is not at all at this level, but in their provision of the 'bodily forms' for the philosophical truisms he is able to discover in them, allegorically.[124] This observation, which is true, does not really point up the distinctions between Philo and a writer like the author of Hebrews, however. It is not the historicity of the biblical events and persons which is in question but whether an historical *relationship* can be established between them, in their historical distance, and the present. It is because Philo has no such reference point at the near end of the hermeneutical process that his exegesis spills out into the broad plains of general, philosophical truth. By way of contrast, the author of Hebrews' exegesis is under the constant control of what he knows of the concrete *event* of Jesus as it is known in the kerygmatic traditions (see p. 169 n. 123). A ready example is to be found in the different approaches to Melchizedek by the two authors. For neither is there any apparent question concerning Melchizedek's actual historicity. But for Philo his significance is as a *symbol* for the *idea* of benevolent kingship (*Leg. All*. III. 79ff) whereas for the writer of Hebrews he stands in relationship to the *man* Jesus.[125]

Nor can it be said that the Rabbis were uninterested in the historical persons and events in the bible. But again, because the whole of the scriptural revelation had passed into history with no fixed reference point on the near side of the increasingly wide gulf between those events and the present, genuinely historical perspectives tended to dissolve into perpetually valid religious truths.[126]

The Qumranites, with their conception of the new interpretations given through the Teacher of Righteousness, come nearer to the historical and exegetical perspectives of the letter to the Hebrews than any other non-Christian group.[127] But even for Qumran, the identification by the sect of its ongoing scripture study as revelation[128] means that this history cannot attain the same 'event quality', and therefore does not offer the same historical perspectives, as the Christ-event achieves for Christian thought.

We may say, then, that because for the Christian exegetes, including our author, the definitive hermeneutical reference point is in the remembered life of Jesus, this exegesis does not flow over into the boundless categories of speculation but is anchored in, or defined within, a history of revelation. Certainly, it is a history of *revelation*, which means a history of the activities of God or a history theologically conceived. But that this history is not conceived *apart* from the external, empirical qualities of regular historical reconstruction is seen by the normative importance the memory of the figure of Jesus plays in this writer's thinking. For it is only insofar as the events of that life – both what was said and what was done – can be seen to be conformable to the anticipatory forms of the previous dispensation of the Word that a correlation is permitted between them and the one can be seen as the fulfilment toward which the other was driving.[129]

The importance of the empirical, noetic qualities of this relationship is reflected in the diligence and the multiplicity of ways in which the author works at making it clear. The bulk of our essay has been devoted to showing how these correspondences bind the covenants together so that the same patterns can be discerned stretching from one end of the history to the other, even breaking through the boundaries and disjunctions which serve to separate the covenants one from the other. We need here only refer in passing to the way in which the typological patterns (from the Hebraic side)[130] and the 'shadow–substance' formulae (notable, we would say, for the way in which these Alexandrian motifs have been incorporated into the historical framework of the earlier and later covenants) are each brought in their own way to serve the elucidation of the scheme as a whole.

Here the discussion has led us on from the immediate vicinity of the Old Testament citations to the whole question of the relationship between the covenants. We started our investigations into this writer's use of the Old Testament from the point of view of finding the theological considerations controlling the use of his quotations. That this investigation should have led us out into the same patterns of revelation and history that we have discovered in other parts of his work indicates, perhaps, the extent to which these motifs are fundamental in his thinking.

3 The Word of God in the present and its meaning for the future: history and eschatology

The problem of the writer's Old Testament citations, stated from a theological point of view, we said, is in knowing how the Old Testament forms were and are God's Word and yet can be spoken of as outdated (above, p. 35). So far we have attended to the first half of this question, that is, with the *continuity* between the old and the new forms. But how do the patterns we have described as 'an ongoing developmental process' relate to the elements of sharp *discontinuity* which are no less apparent in the epistle?

It is clear that the discontinuity between the testaments is occasioned exactly by the fact that the eschatological division between the ages is held to have come with the declaration of the Word in the Son (1.1f). So that in raising the question of Christian discontinuity with the Old Testament we are at the same time raising the question of what it means to live within the eschaton.

In beginning our inquiry into the relationship between the Word of God and historical existence, we took as our point of departure the apocalyptically conceived section at the end of the letter, 12.18-29, where the history of the world and the history of the salvation process are seen to draw together in the establishment of the 'unshakeable kingdom'. We drew from that the implication that the Word of God in all its forms, even those which are located in history and in some sense share the forms of historical existence, is most fundamentally to be regarded as an eschatological phenomenon – having its essential locus not in history but in the βασιλεία.

Turning again to that passage, now with the question in mind as to the structures of eschatological existence, it becomes important to notice that as at 1.1f Christians are definitely seen as already sharing in the eschatological life: 'You *have come* to Mt Zion' (προσεληλύθατε Σιων ὄρει, verse 22), precisely the heavenly πόλις toward which, in other places in the letter, they must make their way with great perseverance. It must seem here as if all those exhortations have suddenly been evacuated.

But that impression can only be a fleeting one, for almost immediately the Christians are warned again that they do *not* yet stand securely within the βασιλεία and indeed may yet fail to do so: 'See that you do not reject him who speaks' (verse 25). And the actual futurity of that to which the Christians 'have come' is specified in the word 'promise' (verse 26). For all its concrete imagery, therefore, this apocalyptic passage only states more graphically the eschatological tensions of Christian existence as such[131] and which are to be found running throughout our letter.[132]

If one inquires as to what permits – given the seemingly clear futurity of the 'kingdom' or the 'city' – the strangely daring 'you have come', there is only one item in the catalogue of eschatological entities which can be regarded as establishing the proximity of Christians: that is the reference to Jesus and his 'sprinkled blood'. The significance of this within the letter is not hard to see: the death of Jesus (and then his exaltation) is singularly the factor which brings Christians within the sphere of eschatological existence, that is to say, as members of his new covenant (verse 24). If one then asks, on the other hand, in what way the *futurity* of the covenant comes to expression, it is in the *warning* 'Do not refuse him ...' with its implication 'You have not yet arrived.'

A pattern thus begins to be apparent in which the variation in eschatological stances within the letter, the alternation between 'realised' and 'futurist' eschatologies, is completely synonymous with the theology-paraenesis disjunction. Insofar as the Christian is aware of his eschatological status – the knowledge that he has in some sense already 'come' into proximity with the heavenly realities – that awareness is totally dependent on his convictions regarding the finality of the 'Word in the Son', which is to say, his convictions about the definitive effectiveness of Jesus' death and exaltation. It is entirely consistent therefore that in the theological-Christological sections of the letter in which the meaning of the death of Jesus is explored, the eschatological viewpoint should be a 'realised' one.

On the other hand, the Christian's paradoxical awareness of his continuing *historicity*, that aspect of his existence which makes the 'city' or 'kingdom' appear yet a long way off in an anything-but-clear future, is what constitutes his membership within the eschaton as a still open question and which makes exhortation among the Christians, from one to the other, the order of the day (3.13, 10.25). It is therefore no more coincidental that the paraenetic passages of the letter should assume a 'futurist' aspect than that the theological sections should be cast in 'realised' terms.[133]

These patterns can be worked out exegetically.

It is simply to be observed that almost uniformly the theological-Christological parts of the epistle assume a finality of revelational and saving significance with respect to the life, and death and exaltation, of Jesus.[134] This is seen not only in the explicit ways in which those events are described ('in these last days', 1.2;[135] 'at the close of the age', 9.26 etc.), but in the way they represent the summation of the whole development of Old Testament religion. It is here certainly that the 'once-for-all' (ἐφάπαξ) quality of Christ's work belongs: everything that went before, by way of anticipation, in the Old Testament cultus was repetitive, unfinished (7.23; 9.6–10, 25; 10.1–3), but Jesus' priestly and sacrificial act was of final and definitive quality (7.27; 9.12, 26, 28; 10.10). It is interesting that the word ἅπαξ (lifted from the Hosea quotation, 12.26) in fact appears in the description of the eschatological tribulations of chapter 12 (12.27), so that the repeated designation of Jesus' work in these terms is possibly a further reference to the eschatology-in-history character which that event assumes. That this event (or rather, cluster of events) assumes a finally *revelatory* significance as well as saving significance was the thesis offered in the first chapter of this book.[136] It is not at all coincidental, therefore, that we should notice that terms such as 'eternal' (αἰώνιος, 5.9; 9.12, 14, 15; 13.20)[137] and 'for ever' (εἰς τὸν αἰῶνα, 6.20; 7.17, 21, 24, 28; εἰς τὸ διηνεκές, 7.3; 10.12, 14) should be frequently associated with this work and its effects. Finally, it is also wholly significant that this ministry is essentially a heavenly one in distinction to the levitical one performed on earth (4.14; 8.1f; 9.9ff, 23f) (see above pp. 45f). The event which thus

prematurely bears about it all the marks of an end-event is in fact already
an accomplished event; Jesus *has* been exalted, (2.9); he *has* brought in the
new eschatological covenant promised by Jeremiah (7.22, 8.6ff, 10.16ff); in
his death he *has* destroyed the power of death (2.14f) and has obtained an
eternal redemption (9.15).[138]
    This 'realised' eschatological understanding also applies to the 'ecclesiology'
of the letter, such as it is: the Christians *are* Christ's house (3.6); they can
say, 'We *have become* (γεγόναμεν) the companions of Christ' (3.14);
they can speak of themselves as having 'received the evangel' (4.2); and can
say, 'We are entering into the Rest' (4.3). They regard themselves as sanctified (ἡγιασμένοι ἐσμέν, 10.10; cf. 10.14, 29), and when they gather in
worship they do so as the eschatologically purified community (10.22).[139]
    It is also here that the writer's conception of sin, so problematic for
Christian exegetes, is to be located.[140] It is really questionable whether the
point of view expressed is that of some sections in the later church, that
individual sins can so seriously invalidate one's baptismal purity that there
is no possibility of repentance for post-baptismal sins.[141] In continuity
with the rest of the New Testament, Hebrews is not concerned with sins[142]
but with sin. The impossibility of further forgiveness after the deliberate and
resolute turning away from the place of grace (10.26) follows quite logically
(and psychologically?)[143] from the finality of the eschatological gift (6.4ff)
and of the eschatological worth of the death of Christ (6.6, 9.26, 10.26).[144]
    Over against these 'realised' eschatological perspectives which adhere
almost uniformly to the Christological sections, that the paraenetic parts
of the letter manifest a 'futurist' aspect hardly needs further detailed
documentation. It can be shown without trouble, for instance, how the
'enthronement scene' of chapter 1 (if that is the right way to take it), which
must on any account be reckoned as 'realised' eschatology, suddenly switches
to the exhortation to the readers to 'pay attention' lest they be 'swept away',
in the opening verses of chapter 2; with this goes the accompanying implication (which we must investigate more carefully in a moment) that Christians
stand exactly where hearers of the Old Testament Word were placed (2.2f)
except that Christians shall be deemed to be even more responsible and judged
accordingly. Similarly, the Moses comparison with Jesus (in which Christians
are Christ's 'companions', 3.1, 14, his 'house', 3.6) flows over into reflection
on the wilderness scene in which Christians are linked with the Exodus community as 'pilgrims' on their way toward the promised Rest (4.1, 11 etc.). On
an even larger scale it can be seen how the long discussion about Jesus' eschatological priesthood and sacrifice (chapters 5-10) gives way, or rather leads
into (10.19ff), the discussion on 'holding fast' (10.23) and the nature of faith
(chapter 11), the climax of which comes at 12.1: 'Let us run with patience . . .'

But now the hermeneutical significance of these patterns may by no means be overlooked.

For it turns out that not only can clear links be made between the theology-paraenesis division and the eschatological perspectives, but that the continuity-discontinuity dialectic with respect to the scriptures of the previous covenant is also fashioned within this scheme. So that in the theologically orientated passages ('realised' eschatology) the discontinuity with the old covenant is written large; in the exhortatory passages ('futurist' eschatology) the continuity between old and new covenants is such that one might almost think the Christian era had never dawned.[145]

Certainly, together with this general statement we must add a twofold refinement and correction: even in the theological parts of the letter the same *structures* of priesthood, cultus and sacrifice are seen to be operative in the new as in the old, though now on an eschatological scale. Further, it is also clear that the Old Testament *citations* when brought forward from their original settings to function as Christian λόγοι are seen not as outmoded but as present forms of the Word of God, whether in theology or paraenesis.[146]

But these modifications do not alter the substantial facts that in the *theology* of the letter the two covenants are set over against each other in the sharpest possible way and, contrariwise, that in the *paraenesis* a continuity between the communities emerges in a particularly clear way.

The reasons for this are not hard to see. We have now several times remarked upon the sense of existential identity which, in places in the letter, seems to bind the Christian to his Old Testament counterpart. But now, of course, we can see that that only happens from one aspect of the Christian eschatological bipolar experience. It is precisely the elements which remind him of his historicity – the distance and futurity of his eschatological goal, the promise-nature of the Word of God with its consequent requirement for him to persevere in faith and faithfulness, in short all those aspects of his existence which dictate that he should be encouraged, exhorted in the keeping of his confession – which identify the Christian most closely with the hearers of the Old Testament form of the Word of God. It is therefore perfectly understandable that it is in the exhortatory parts of the letter, with their futurist eschatological point of view, that the continuity between Israel and the Christians emerges either as warning (2.1–4, 3.7–4.13, 12.16 etc.) or as encouragement (6.11ff, 11.1–40).

But when the Christian community reflects on the meaning of the life, death and exaltation of Jesus, it cannot but become aware of its own significance as the community which has been brought into existence by those events and, accordingly, of its own standing as part of, or within, the community of the eschaton. Just as the Word which has been declared in the Son stands in its finality over against those previous, anticipatory forms which have led up to this definitive form (above, chapter 1), so the community brought into being by that Word stands over against its predecessor, Israel. From the point of view of the death of Christ, therefore (i.e., the perspectives of the theological–Christological passages in the letter), the Old Testament (covenant) and all that it represents must be regarded as simply preparatory and now quite outdated.

What this must mean is that the dialectic, or rather the bipolarity, of Christian eschatological existence has become a hermeneutical screen which has been placed across the Old Testament scriptures, not so much to allow some parts of them to come through into the Christian situation, unchanged, while other elements of them are blocked off as now outdated; but rather to let them speak to different elements within the Christian experience. It does not require that such a hermeneutical scheme should have been worked out deliberately or methodically for it nevertheless to be at work effectively.

It can be seen, then, that we have come quite some distance toward an answer to the question from which we set out at the head of this chapter: 'How in one context can the scriptures of the Old Testament function so immediately as a vehicle for the Word of God while in other contexts the covenant which those same scriptures enshrine is unceremoniously dismissed as outmoded?' (p. 35). The determinative word thus now appears to be 'context'. It depends on which context or from which perspective, eschatologically speaking, the scriptures of the Old Testament are being approached – if with reference to the difficulties, the conditionedness and responsibilities, within historical existence, then the Word of God in the Old Testament may be as meaningful to Christians as to its original recipients. But from the point of view of what is now considered to have taken place in the advent of Jesus Christ, those words can only be seen as preparatory, witnessing, some of them at least, to their own futurity and hence unfinality.[147] The processes involved, albeit unconsciously, we may accordingly term 'The hermeneutic of eschatological existence'.

Our investigation of the eschatological patterns within our letter has thus yielded valuable pointers in our hermeneutical inquiries. One or two other elements perhaps still deserve our attention. The fact is that so far our analysis has seemed to suggest an unbridgeable chasm between the theological and paraenetic or realised and futuristic eschatological sections of the epistle. Probably it is quite true that such a description reflects something of the tensions of Christian eschatological existence itself. But to leave them like this as impossible contradictions would not only be rather less than fair to the author (for whom they are not so much contradictions, but complements), but would also be to fail to carry through our investigation of his theology to its conclusion.

For it is here in fact that a synoptic view of the letter as a whole, and a careful appraisal of the relationship between theology and paraenesis, can preserve us from quite momentous misreadings of his text.[148] Because in spite of the tensions *we* may be able to locate in his eschatological perspectives, there is not the slightest indication that these were cause for embarrassment on the part of the author. On the contrary the two are set up side by side and made to work in one comprehensive scheme. That is not to say, of course, that the tensions are thereby eliminated; it is to suggest that our author has accepted them in his acceptance of the Christian faith,[149] so that they, these essentially contradictory points of view and the way in which they are related, in fact become themselves important hermeneutical pointers within the theology of the writer.

In the overall structure of the letter, theology has been made to serve the paraenesis. Careful examination shows that this pattern is preserved in detail as well as comprehensively.

It is in the words 'we have' (ἔχομεν), which have already engaged our attention (p. 27), that the relationship between present and future, theology and paraenesis, comes to its most concentrated expression. For here in one word (in Greek) is represented the strongest expression of a present, realised eschatology.[150] Invariably the content of the 'we have' indicates a summation of one of the central theological–Christological themes of our author: 'Since we have (ἔχοντες) a great highpriest...' (4.14); 'We have (ἔχομεν) such a highpriest...' (8.1); 'Since we have (ἔχοντες) confidence to enter the sanctuary...' (10.19); 'We have (ἔχομεν) an altar...a permanent city...' (13.10, 14).[151] But almost equally without exception (the one exception is 8.1) the 'we have' with its summary theological or Christological statement leads directly into, or supplies the ground for, an exhortation to faithfulness in day-to-day Christian confession. This applies throughout, but it is most clearly seen at 4.14–16 and 10.19ff. At both these places the 'we have' summarises the end-event quality[152] of the access which Christians *now* have (προσεληλύθατε, 12.22) to the heavenly realm in the midst of their temporal flux and perplexity; but so long as they *are* in history the access thus gained functions exactly as a stimulus to *continue* in their earthly, 'historical' confession of faith. That is to say, the 'realised' eschatological elements of the 'we have' statements are ordered in such a way as to promote a future-orientated, historical faithfulness: 'Let us hold fast...' (κρατῶμεν, 4.14; κατέχωμεν τὴν ὁμολογίαν, 10.23).

But, as we have noticed, the 'we have' and 'let us hold fast', though

standing in such close physical relationship, actually stand in tension if
not contradiction. For exhortation, we said, starts out from the real possibility of failure and consequently implies that the hoped-for eschatological
goal might yet be missed. It speaks of the futurity of the heavenly realities
and therefore stands in contradiction to the 'we have' which has immediately
preceded.

There can only be one way in which this tension is, if not resolved, at
least made to work in an effective theological, pastoral synthesis. That is in
the highpriest conception itself.[153] It is Jesus, the priest who now transcends
history in his exaltation but who is knowable among men by reason of his
humanity (p. 169 n. 123), who can help his people in their need (4.16) and
who appears for them before God himself (7.25, 9.24ff etc.). On closer
inspection we see that the 'we have' and 'let us hold fast' are in fact related
through an intermediate term, 'let us draw near' ($\pi\rho\sigma\epsilon\rho\chi\omega\mu\epsilon\vartheta\alpha$, 4.16,
10.22). In his intercessory function Jesus the priest clearly demonstrates
his eschatological status: 'Christ has entered ... into heaven itself, now to
appear in the presence of God on our behalf' (9.24). The end-quality of
this entry is specifically delineated: 'Now, once-for-all at the close of the
age, he has appeared, to put away sin through the offering of himself'
(9.26).[154] And yet these statements are closely followed by the clearest expression in the New Testament of the second coming: 'He will appear a second
time, quite apart from sin, for the salvation of those who await him' (9.28).
As the Christians' highpriest, therefore, Jesus has become a history-spanning
figure, the only means whereby Christians can sustain their paradoxical status
as the eschatological people in history.

The significance of this formulation for our present study lies in the way
that the author's theology has been shaped to his readers' needs. If the
argument of our first chapter is able to be sustained, a great deal of the
reflection about Jesus' priesthood has taken place prior to, and to some
extent independently of, the present shape those ideas assume in the
author's pastoral letter. The question for the author, we might have suggested, has been something like: how is the Word of God located in history?
which is simply a variation of the question: how does God's Word have
earlier and later forms? It was out of his reflection on this question, we
said, that his theology of the two covenants was created with their dialectical pattern of historical continuity and discontinuity, in which the forms
of priesthood, sacrifice and cultic approach have been preserved though
now enlarged into eschatological proportions.

But in the letter to his friends in trouble the conception of Jesus as
eschatological priest has taken an especially cogent and practical form of
pastoral encouragement.[155] The problem for these readers, as is widely

accepted, is some form of spiritual lethargy, a weariness before the seemingly interminable pilgrimage before them.[156] There are good reasons to suppose that this doubt and despondency are being especially quickened by gathering clouds on the political horizon (above, p. 38). In all this it is not too fanciful to sum up their attitudes in the question: why are *we* (still) in history? or perhaps a little more realistically: why should we persevere in our confession in history?[157]

If we are right in positing a formulation of the priesthood Christology earlier than in the immediate needs of this pastoral letter, then we have an especially provocative instance of the author's own hermeneutical activities at a second stage. The primary work has been his own deeply theological reflection on the relationship between old and new forms of God's Word. But now the products of that reflection have been brought to bear on what is an essentially different, though not dissimilar, question, and the hermeneutical reflection has accordingly been taken a stage further and in a different direction.

Can the letter itself support such a hypothesis? As we have it, it is undoubtedly a literary unit and no suggestion is being made here that we might detect 'seams' or other indications of a 'literary history' in its composition. The 'history' is rather that of the development of the author's own reflection. And for this, the important methodological question which we raised in chapter 1 (p. 28) as to whether this letter of the moment really requires such a large and detailed exploration of salvation-historical principles must also be the operative one here. If, as has been argued, the foundational conceptions have been worked out independently, then the letter itself inevitably represents a new and applied stage of the reflection which lies behind it. If that is not sufficiently clear, then we must content ourselves with the (still by no means inconsiderable) single achievement of the Christology of Jesus the priest who enables his people to make their way through history and towards the eschatological goal.

3

JESUS

It is immediately clear (whatever we say about the writer's practical application of his theology; above, pp. 73f) that the conception of Jesus as
eschatological highpriest involves not only a deeply serious interaction
with the scriptures and their presentation of the ways of atonement, but
with the traditions about Jesus himself. The writer's hermeneutics, therefore, involve more than an interpretational relationship with *texts* of the
past. We must speak also of an hermeneutic of, or with reference to, *Jesus*.

It can hardly be accidental that the modern preoccupation with the
meaning of interpretation should be discovered also to be deeply involved
in questions about Jesus and his accessibility. For each is a facet of the
same question: namely, how and to what extent can contingent events of
the historical past be for us the vehicles of divine self-disclosure? Alternatively expressed, the question of the historical Jesus simply raises, in
another and perhaps more urgent form, the questions of faith and history
with which, in his own way, we have said, the writer of our letter has been
most deeply engaged.

1 Hebrews and the quest for the historical Jesus

It is frequently observed that no other document in the New Testament,
apart from the gospels, displays more interest in the human Jesus than
the Epistle to the Hebrews.[1] It is therefore slightly surprising that this
writer has been allowed to contribute so little to the now lengthy debate
about Jesus[2] and the relationship of the New Testament church to him.[3]
The immediate short (and therefore suspect?) reply doubtless is that
Hebrews, or for that matter any of the New Testament letters, is so
manifestly a product of, and is directed to, the church of the post-
resurrection period, not even purporting to give an account of Jesus'
previous life, that its usefulness with regard to the 'quest' is limited from
the outset.[4]

From one point of view, the formal differences between a letter and a
gospel must seem to be so complete that this objection to the usefulness

of Hebrews is indeed all but valid. It is precisely because the evangelists present their story in the form of a narrative account of Jesus in his humanity that they thereby expose themselves to critical testing in a way which an epistle does not. That is to say, no matter how expressly theological is their intention, the evangelists do undertake to narrate events, or depict a figure, so that their *account* fairly naturally invites comparison with whatever can be recovered of the events or the figure they thus undertake to present.[5]

Yet even here, where the formal and material differences must seem to be quite overwhelming, it is possible to achieve a point of view from which certain comparisons may be made, and even some moderately important methodological observations. For even if the evangelists relate a great many more reminiscences of Jesus in terms of events and sayings of the earthly Jesus than Hebrews does, they, no less than our writer, are dependent on the kerygmatic traditions. The problem of the historical Jesus *as* an historical problem is to discern the extent to which the early Christian communities have imposed their own awareness on the traditions which they have passed on. In the case of the Epistle to the Hebrews we have before our very eyes one important theologian in the early church who both stood under the received traditions about Jesus and who was also a transmitter of them, along with his own highly distinctive interpretation of them. It may be possible, therefore, that Hebrews provides us with a kind of test case at a certain point in the transmission process.[6] If we may decide in this case in which direction the process is moving, that is to say, whether the life of Jesus is being deduced from the writer's theology or whether the church's memories of Jesus are the occasion for his theology, this may be a significant indicator for the processes under way in the wider church (see further below, pp. 90ff).

Even at this historical level, that is, with respect to our inquiry into the conformity of the traditions with the actual events, there is therefore a degree of similarity between Hebrews and the gospels and therefore the possibility of a contribution (admittedly a small one) from Hebrews to the quest for the historical Jesus.

On another front, however, the degree of similarity with the evangelists is very much greater. That is to say, whatever else they are, both groups of writers are theologians. Moreover, since both stand under a historically mediated tradition and yet at the same time are occupied with the theological interpretation of this tradition in and for their particular circumstances, the fundamental structure of this theological task is the same in spite of their so widely differing circumstances. This task is the exposition of the relation between faith and history. Certainly it is never formulated so explicitly. And yet in choosing to present their understanding of the exalted Christ in the form of a narrative of the life of Jesus the evangelists are indicating their conviction that the content of faith (the risen Christ) is informed and shaped by, and yet not exhausted in, events of history (the remembered life of Jesus).[7] This theological task is accomplished in its most sophisticated form by the Fourth Evangelist,[8] but insofar as they all attempted to relate the story of Jesus in such a way that faith would be born, it is the occupation of them all.

Here the differences from the Epistle to the Hebrews have been narrowed almost to elimination. Despite the differences in form and idiom this is also this writer's all-but-consuming task. The crisis to which he writes is one of faith – his friends stand in imminent danger of despair, that is to say, unbelief. The Christ whom he depicts is certainly the kerygmatic, faith-summoning Christ. And yet we shall see how completely this representation of Christ is informed by what the author knows of the man Jesus. In the exploration of the relationship between the human Jesus and the exalted highpriest of the writer's Christology, we shall therefore be engaged in the problem of the relationship between faith and history.

Since, at least on its theological side, this is precisely the question at the heart of the present debate about Jesus, the relevance of Hebrews to this part of the discussion is by no means negligible.

The so-called 'quest' has two aspects which we have chosen to call its 'historical' and its 'theological' sides.[9] The one has to do with whether *in fact* we have access to the historical Jesus; the other raises the question as to the theological importance such knowledge can have for faith in the risen Christ. The following discussion attempts to appreciate both the strengths and limitations of the letter's contribution to this debate. On the one side, we shall argue, a knowledge of the life of Jesus is *theologically* indispensable for the author. On the other side it is recognised from the outset that the letter to the Hebrews does not help us greatly with our *historical* questions; not only is the writer's information acknowledged to be mediated via the tradition (2.3, 13.7), so that the picture of Jesus pre-sented comes already at second or third hand, but the points of contact with other streams of tradition, e.g., the Synoptic ones, are so few that the possibility of setting up comparative tests between them is disallowed.[10] Nevertheless it is imperative, if the Jesus of Hebrews is to be more than the product of the writer's highpriestly Christology, to be able to show the *direction* of his thought, i.e., that it runs from what he knows of Jesus (via the traditions) *to* his theology, and not vice versa.[11] Here there are few enough checks, to be sure, and it should not be thought that the main burden of the present study will be on the 'historical' side; that is to say, we shall not be engaged in an attempt to 'vindicate' the picture of Jesus, historically speaking. The main interest will be where Hebrews helps us most, in the semi-theoretical discussion of the relationship between faith and history. But that this is not *wholly* theoretical and that there are *sufficient* hints and indications that the Jesus of Hebrews is not the product of the author's theology will also be shown.[12]

2 Jesus' life as a basis for faith

What does it mean to say: God has spoken to us in a Son? The concern of our previous explorations has been the meaning of the formal designation of Jesus as Son, as understood in its salvation-historical context by the writer of Hebrews. But *what* is said? So far the term Son has in itself communicated little more than *that* God has spoken and that this form of Speaking stands in a dialectical relationship of continuity and discontinuity with the previous forms of his Speaking. Is an awareness of this mere That (R. Bultmann's famous 'das blosse Dass') sufficient to sustain or engender faith?

As we have said so frequently, Hebrews is designed from beginning to end as a faith-engendering instrument. It is written to a crisis in confidence; its theology is expressly bent to the service of paraenesis. The Christ who is presented in course of this is unambiguously the exalted Christ; the declaration and exposition of Christ's highpriestly work is this writer's means of reviving his readers' hope, which is to say the confidence and determination to press on with maintaining their confession, which in turn - since this is with reference to their heavenward calling - means faith.

But this presentation or proclamation of the exalted highpriest is never abstracted from an accompanying portrayal of the earthly Jesus. On the contrary the picture of the highpriest is wholly informed and made possible by what is known of Jesus. Though the lines along which this is done intersect and occasionally overlap, still two more or less clearly defined ways can be discerned in which the humanity of Jesus provides a basis for faith according to the understanding of the writer. We might describe these in terms of 'Jesus the pioneer' (or 'the *model* of faith') and 'Jesus the priest' (or 'the *means* of faith'). The two groups of ideas may also be seen to cohere with the 'history-eschatology' demarcation in the writer's thought which we have already noted.

(a) Jesus the pioneer

The author of our letter is responsible for two of the four occasions in the New Testament upon which Jesus is described as 'leader' or 'pioneer' (ἀρχηγός): at 2.10 he is spoken of as 'pioneer of salvation' (ἀρχηγὸς τῆς σωτηρίας) and at 12.2 as 'pioneer and perfecter of faith' (ὁ τῆς πίστεως ἀρχηγὸς καὶ τελειωτής).[13] The range of possible connotations for the term[14] indicates that the meaning is best decided from the contexts themselves. Since our question has to do with Jesus and faith, the second of these passages, that which describes Jesus as 'pioneer of faith', offers itself suggestively for our inspection.

As has been frequently noticed[15] it can hardly be coincidental that this description should come so hard upon the great list of Old Testament faith-heroes, with its accompanying plea that the readers should, in their turn, 'run with patience the course set before' them (δι' ὑπομονῆς τρέχωμεν τὸν προκείμενον ἡμῖν ἀγῶνα, 12.1). The catalogue of heroes was itself introduced, we may recall, by way of depicting the kind of believing perseverance (ὑπομονή) which God requires (ἵνα τὸ θέλημα τοῦ θεοῦ ποιήσαντες) if the promises are to be attained (10.36).

It is true that this understanding of faith has been regarded particularly critically, as indicating the extent to which 'faith' in Hebrews has been devalued from the *fides salvifica* conception, normative for the New Testament, into a more ethically conceived 'faithfulness'.[16] But as we have already noticed in passing (p. 148 n. 38) such an interpretation quite seriously fails to reckon on *that with respect to which* this faith-perseverance is called for by the epistle. Because the believing-maintenance of their 'confession of hope' (10.23; cf. 3.6 and 4.14) is, in the last analysis, the measure of their estimation of *God's* dependability (11.11: 'By faith . . . since she reckoned him to be faithful who had promised' is especially clear and should be regarded as definitive rather than exceptional), words such as 'perseverance' (ὑπομονή) or 'steadfastness' (ὑπόστασις) should not too quickly be taken as clear indices 'of the transformation of faith into behaviour'.[17] Because such 'behaviour' stands itself as an index of a responsiveness to God and to his promise-quality Word (or alternatively, because its antithesis would be the outward sign of the apostasy-sin which hangs so ominously over the community; cf. how 10.26ff stands in such close proximity to 10.23), it would be much better described as a 'believing faithfulness', i.e., faith which *issues in* certain behavioural and character qualities.

Such is the 'faith' which is shown in the lives of the 'great cloud of witnesses' who are seen as surrounding the Christians as they in their turn 'run with patience . . .'

Such also is the faith of which Jesus is the 'pioneer and perfecter' (12.2). The problem here is in knowing whether Jesus, as the one to whom the Christians must look in their persevering 'faith-marathon', is to be thought

of as the *source* of such faith, or its greatest *exemplar*. The English versions
are almost unanimous, and many of the commentators agree, in taking the
former line. So that the phrase is rendered 'pioneer and perfecter of our
faith' (RSV), 'Jesus, on whom our faith depends from start to finish'
(NEB), 'on whom our faith depends from beginning to end' (TEV).[18] The
reason for this, as F. F. Bruce suggests, may lie in an attempt to represent
the article with 'faith',[19] but perhaps at least as influential is a partly
subconscious unwillingness to see that Jesus can be spoken of in the New
Testament, albeit infrequently, as a participant *in* faith as well as the object
of faith.[20] At this particular point, however, there really can be little doubt.
Even if linguistically the sentence allowed some uncertainty, which is
doubtful,[21] the way in which Jesus is brought into direct continuity with
the readers in their situation must make this clear: 'Let us run with perseverance (or 'endurance' to make the parallel more obvious) the course
which lies before us'; 'who for the joy which lay before him endured . . .'
(δι' ὑπομονῆς τρέχωμεν τὸν προκείμενον ἡμῖν ἀγῶνα / ὃς ἀντὶ τῆς προκειμένης
αὐτῷ χαρᾶς ὑπέμεινεν).[22] This can only mean that here Jesus is understood,
as in his humanity he stands before the dark uncertainty of his impending
death, to be repudiating the possibility of unbelief and on the contrary
allowing that threatening present to be illuminated by his confidence in
the future (ἀντὶ τῆς προκειμένης αὐτῷ χαρᾶς).[23] In this, of course, he
becomes a perfect model for the Christian readers,[24] whose own darkly
threatening future seems to be an important, if not the most important,
factor in their contemplation of the abandonment of their confession
(above p. 38). It is exactly *in* his endurance (ὑπέμεινεν) that he shows
for his followers the quality of endurance (ὑπομονή) which God requires
in the troublesome uncertainties of historical existence (10.32ff, esp.
verse 36); but the degree to which, or the manner in which, he carries this
through is what allows him to be called 'pioneer and perfecter'.[25]

The other occurrence of the term ἀρχηγός is at 2.10; that is, within the
passage 2.5-18, which in our initial exploration of the letter and its themes
we bracketed off as something of an interruption to the thrust of the arguments there being pursued. By way of investigating this term as applied
to Jesus now, we are therefore obliged to attend more carefully to the
passage as a whole, and to justify that exegetical judgement (above, pp. 8f).
    Our claim was that the passage fits only awkwardly into the expanding
pattern of three cycles of comparison of Jesus: with the angels, with Moses,
and with the Aaronic Priesthood. In fact that assessment, namely that
2.5-18 intrudes itself into this pattern, might quite well stand on its own -
it *does* intrude, with its early references to the priesthood of Jesus and so on,

into such a scheme. But since the idea of the three circles of comparison
was itself part of our hypothesis, additional support is required and can
be found.

The clearest indicator that some sort of dislocation is taking place is
exactly the statement with which the passage begins: that the reference
point in all that is being said is 'the world to come' (τὴν οἰκουμένην τὴν
μέλλουσαν). The strangeness in this is that so far the reference has *not* been
at all to a future aeon, but has been cast in terms of the present state of
things - the 'end of days' into which the Christians have entered in their
hearing of the Word in the Son (1.1f); the present exaltation of the Son
'already seated [aorist tense] at the right hand of the Majesty on High'
(1.3); now that he has achieved purification for sins (1.3) and has entered
into the Lordly dignity worthy of his name (1.4). Perhaps even more
striking is the reference to the Son's coming into the world (οἰκουμένη,
1.6) which is cast not as a humiliating descent into the phenomenal world,
or this world as over against a future world, but is a statement as to how
it is, now, concerning the entry of the regal Son into a present οἰκουμένη.[26]
This stance is continued, not just through the eloquent references to the
enthronement of the Son, but more importantly in the description of the
Word which has been made present to the community, originating in Jesus
and attested as it has been with signs of eschatological power and persuasiveness (2.4). All this is a statement of 'things as they are' - that is to say, a
description of how things now stand between God and the οἰκουμένη in
this new, eschatological age in which the Christians themselves are participants.

The statement, abruptly introduced at 2.5, indicating that the real
reference point is not a present οἰκουμένη, but one still to come, must
therefore be seen as a sudden shift in perspective.[27] In this respect the
concession - concession, that is, in view of the strong eschatological affirmations of the first chapter - that 'as yet we do not see ...' (νῦν δὲ οὔπω
ὁρῶμεν ..., 2.8) must further witness to this change. In terms of the letter
as a whole, of course, there is nothing here which does not accommodate
perfectly well within the eschatological bipolarity we have already explored
in some detail. What is to the point here, however, is that the reference in
2.5 to the futurity of the Christian eschaton is the first such reference and
comes with a somewhat surprising abruptness.

Another change of perspective must be with respect to the quite different picture of Christ which the passage introduces. The princely heir of
the angel-comparison in chapter 1 is suddenly seen as the humiliated
ἀρχηγός who must 'taste death on behalf of all' (2.9).[28] Of course it is
true again that no fundamental clash is to be found with the themes of

the letter as a whole - it is just that here elements are suddenly present which stand so strikingly in contrast to the picture so far given in the letter, and which indeed will not themselves be explored in any depth until considerably later on in the discussion. This is true, too, as part of the same phenomenon, of the unheralded first reference to the highpriest conception which rather suddenly makes its appearance at the end of the passage;[29] apart from the fleeting reference at 3.1, this centrally important theme is not taken up for elaboration until 4.14ff, giving to 2.17 the appearance of an isolated outcrop of subterranean material. The brief, and perhaps liturgically structured, reference to the 'achieving of cleansing from sins' at 1.3, or to the futurity of 'salvation' of 2.3,[30] should not be allowed to detract from the essential change of direction we have here described.

What can account for this sudden alteration of perspective? The point must lie in the change of eschatological viewpoint as signified by the references to the οἰκουμένη of 1.6 which is a *present* reality to Christians, and the οἰκουμένη μέλλουσα (still *future* world) of 2.5. We have seen that the fundamental eschatological orientation of the writer's theology - that is to say, his preoccupation with the Word in the Son and how this relates to the previous forms of the Word - is toward a *present*, 'realised' point of view. But when this theology is drawn upon for the immediate pastoral needs of the present letter, it must be addressed to a different, though not unrelated, question - one involving the problems of Christians in history, i.e., the presence of the eschatological community in the old orders of existence. This, we have said, is the readers' question: why are we (still) in history?[31] which, in all realism, can only be resolved in a *futuristically* conceived eschatology.

That is why the perspectives have to alter so abruptly at 2.5ff. The writer has been depicting his own great confidence in the fact of the turn of the ages in the advent of the Son. But the most bright-eyed idealism imaginable cannot alter the fact that, when all is said and done, that 'world' remains a 'world to come'. The most fundamental question to which the present passage is addressed is, therefore: what is the basis for faith in the *Zwischenzeit* (eschatological interval)?[32] And the answer which shapes itself under the writer's hand continues to flow from his preoccupation with Jesus the Son, but now with much greater attention to the humanity of Jesus, the Jesus who in his earthly life has both set the pattern of, and provides the reasons for, persevering hope among 'those who are tested' (2.18).

In fact so completely is the passage taken up in its contemplation of the figure of Jesus, and so tightly are the various elements compacted, that it is not easy to separate them out into clearly defined categories. Some sort of division, as follows, may be attempted.

(a) *Psalm 8 and the humiliation-exaltation pattern.* It is regularly observed that though the LXX translation *permits* the sequential ordering of the 'little lower than the angels' and 'crowned with glory and honour' statements of the psalm, it by no means *requires* it.[33] The obvious implication is that in so construing it, the writer is reading it quite unambiguously in the light of his understanding of the humiliation and exaltation of Jesus. Many attempts have been made to describe how this is done,[34] which attempts - collectively - presumably come as close as we are likely to get to an understanding of the processes involved.[35] Our interest, rather, is to see how, when the identification has been achieved, it is made to function as a basis for encouragement for the Christian readers. In the frank recognition that 'as yet we do not see all things brought into submission to him (mankind)' it is difficult not to hear an overt reference to the readers' own situation. Certainly this will become much more explicit in the next few verses, as the redemptive values of Jesus' suffering are explored.[36] It is true that the political clouds, which we have suggested are beginning to gather threateningly for the community (above, p. 38), can only be found here by implication, though in the references to the Devil and the power of death (2.14f) it is by no means unreasonable to hear veiled ideas about possible martyrdom,[37] and the concluding statement about 'those who are being tested' (οἱ πειραζόμενοι, 2.18) can hardly be for nothing.

At any rate it is clear that the importance of Jesus, in the first instance, lies precisely in the fact that he was 'for a short time made lower', for that is also where the Christians find themselves: 'In his physical being, Jesus is bound by space and time, by the laws of physical [i.e., 'historical'!] existence.'[38] 'For a short time' he was part not of that 'world to come', but was deeply enmeshed, at least as deeply as the readers themselves, if not more so, in 'this' world. But this 'short time' was succeeded by a moment of 'crowning'. Which, of course, is why the Christians look so intently toward him,[39] Jesus,[40] who in this alone, quite apart from everything else he stands for, thus becomes a reason for hope and encouragement among those who are still only on their way toward 'glory' (2.10).

But this leads us into a second discernible theme: (b) *The disclosure of the purpose of suffering.* In the statement 'It was appropriate that he (God) . . . should make perfect, through suffering, the pioneer of salvation' (ἔπρεπεν γὰρ αὐτῷ . . . τὸν ἀρχηγὸν τῆς σωτηρίας . . . διὰ παθημάτων τελειῶσαι, 2.10), it is impossible not to hear a striking similarity to the statement about 'the will of God' in 10.36, which, we saw, is most clearly exemplified in Jesus' attitudes toward the shame of the cross (12.2). In both cases the stance of Jesus becomes what might be called a 'disclosure situation',[41] God's election of 'suffering' as an appropriate way to glory is

shown nowhere more clearly than in the prototypal life of 'the pioneer'.
The clear link between the sufferings which the 'many sons' may therefore
quite well expect as they 'are led' and those of their 'leader'[42] hardly needs
further elaboration.

A third possibly identifiable strand is (c) *the unity of the sons with the
Son*, though certainly this does include elements already mentioned. The
specific point at issue here is that the identification of Jesus with the 'many
sons' provides a reassurance that as he *has been* lifted up to glory, so they
will be. This seems to be the intention in the link specified (2.11) between
'the Sanctifier' and 'the sanctified' in their common origin, whatever is
meant exactly by that.[43] Given their common situation, his fortune augurs
well for theirs. This is why such heavy emphasis is placed on Jesus' identification of himself with his 'brothers' through the scripture citations
placed upon his lips (2.12f). In view of our observations about the faith
of the earthly Jesus at 12.2, the statement – precisely in the context of
his self-identification with the human race – 'I shall trust in him' (2.13)
cannot fail to attract our interest here, even if the more significant term
$\pi \iota \sigma \tau \iota \varsigma$ is not present.[44] Trust, hope, confidence should be the definitive
marks of the believing community in history, and in his participation in
this community for a short time Jesus, the Christians' 'brother', both
exemplifies and also elicits such 'faith'.

A fourth category is more clearly separable, not insofar as it employs
different conceptions from those we have already examined, but because
it represents a rather different emphasis. (d) *Jesus the pioneer* includes
not just an identification of Jesus with the 'many sons', but also involves
a uniquely pioneering role *on their behalf*. He did for them what they
could not have done for themselves and so is distinct from them as well
as sharing a unity with them: 'the church . . . does not become his *alter ego*.
It has no status or life apart from his atoning deed.'[45] This becomes especially clear in the statements about his 'breaking the power' (NEB) of the
Devil in death (2.14) and his deliverance of those who 'for the whole of
life had been subjected to bondage through fear of death' (2.15). These are
the statements, of course, which have given most encouragement to
those exegetes who see behind the Christology of Hebrews the gnostic
conception of the 'redeemed–Redeemer', however questionable that
remains for others.[46] Rather more to our point, here, than saying whence
these ideas are drawn is to see how they are made to serve the purpose of
establishing or encouraging faith. That Jesus, the pioneer, in his total involvement in our 'flesh and blood' *has defeated* the lord of death, and has
therefore freed Christians to believe and hope, is the clear implication of
the passage.

It is true that these statements about the humanity of Jesus flow right
on into, and become the basis for, the conception of his priesthood (2.17f),
which, we have suggested, belongs to a rather different range of ideas within
the faith-conceptions of the letter. We may reserve these for more detailed
observation shortly.

For the moment, however, it is worth pausing to draw together some
intermediate conclusion about the role of the humanity of Jesus, at least
with respect to that function which describes him as pioneer and as this is
used in a faith-encouraging way within the letter.

First, it is impossible to overlook the high degree of 'content' which is
brought into this writer's portrayal of Jesus and the constitutive importance this content has in his call for faith among his readers. It is true that
we may not yet decide whether this content is present to the writer as
kerygmatic traditions created, or at least elaborated, within the early
church in response to its need to know 'what sort of person Jesus was'. It
is hard to see how the statements concerning Jesus' exaltation ('crowned
with glory and honour') or about his overcoming of the power of the
Devil may be subjected to historical scrutiny or verification. But on the
other hand the consciousness, not just that Jesus was a man totally immersed
in the only kind of existence we know, i.e., historical existence, but that
he responded to the conditions of that form of existence *in a particular
way* is that which provides the indispensable starting point for reflection
upon his role as the pioneer who establishes the pattern for others. Here,
of course, 'historical existence' means rather more than the simple limitations of space and time, though certainly it includes those, circumscribing
as they do our human ability to discern with assurance the future and
thus, for this reason alone, casting Christian existence into the form of
faith or hope (11.1; see above, pp. 40ff, 43). It means more specifically
the experience of a world 'not yet brought into submission', a world in
which Christians, in spite of their confession and paradoxically just because
of their confession,[47] are harassed by spirits and agencies still, apparently,
very much in ascendance.

When, in both the passages we have here examined, the writer makes
his urgent summons that his readers should 'look to Jesus'[48] it seems
inconceivable that he is not instinctively assuming that there is a 'conception' of Jesus to be had, known both to himself and his readers, and which
may be held out as a 'model' of faith-existence in face of the 'agonies'
(τὸν προκείμενον ἀγῶνα, 12.1) of flesh-and-blood-conditioned life. It
cannot be the case that all that matters is merely 'that' Jesus has shared
in this order: to 'look to Jesus' means to envisage to oneself a person of a
definite kind and who lived and died in a particular way.

Secondly, it was hinted at the outset of our discussion (p. 78) that the ordering of Jesus' importance for faith into the categories 'pioneer' and 'priest' corresponds in some sense to the history–eschatology division we have already explored as running through the letter. That observation may now be elaborated. It is by no means insignificant that both these passages (which are certainly not the only ones to attend to Jesus' humanity, but which have been taken as examples) fall into the paraenetic sections of the letter,[49] which, we have seen, regularly adopt a futurist eschatology with the effect that the situation of the Christians in history becomes altogether continuous with the covenant people throughout history. This could hardly be expressed more clearly than it is in 12.1f where the consideration of Jesus as pioneer comes as the climax of the lengthy review of the Old Testament exemplars of faith, and certainly – insofar as he stands at the head of this roll-call – he is seen in complete continuity with it.[50] Even at 2.5–18, where the historical continuity with members of the previous covenant is not in view, it may nevertheless be deduced from the total self-identification by Jesus with the human race, as the reference to 'the seed of Abraham' makes clear. All this is to say that just as we saw that when viewed from the point of view of its historical existence there is no real difference between the Christian community and Israel, when seen strictly in terms of his humanity there is no essential difference between *Jesus* and other members of the *faith-community*. To the extent that he has taken upon himself 'flesh and blood' as a form of existence, he belongs within the history of people who thus look to the future and must trust as a way of life.[51]

By all means, as pioneer, he stands at the head of this community, not in terms of temporal precedence, but as the most accomplished exponent of the way of life to which it is called. He is not, as we saw, *just* example;[52] he is the 'Bahnbrecher',[53] one who actually *creates* the new way in which others may follow. Nevertheless as 'model' he also belongs *to* this community and its history.[54]

This means, thirdly, that whatever misgivings Christians (including, quite possibly, other New Testament writers)[55] may have and have had about ascribing to Jesus – now known as Jesus Christ, the focal point for Christian faith – a faith of his own, the writer of Hebrews is not at all afraid to grasp this as among the clearest implications of incarnation and accordingly as neither an inappropriate nor unwelcome aspect of Jesus' meaning as 'pioneer' of, or model for, faith.[56]

(b) Jesus the priest

It would, however, be an inadmissible distortion to see the Jesus of Hebrews *only* as the model for faith, no matter how inspiring or encouraging such a model might be. Of much greater importance within the letter is his function as the one who, now as their interceding representative before the presence of God, makes faith possible; that is to say, he is also the *means* of faith.[57] We have seen (p. 73) how, regularly, interposed between the writer's theological, or rather Christological, reflections on the eschatological priesthood of Jesus and his summons to the community for more zealous commitment to their confession, is an intermediate exhortation that they 'draw near' so as to 'partake in mercy and find grace' (4.16) precisely in order to be able to continue steadfastly in their confession.

But the question now presents itself as to how the Christians know these things about the priest who 'lives forever to make intercession on their behalf' (7.25). And the clear answer is that this aspect of Jesus' significance is also drawn from what is known, or presumed by way of the traditions to be known, of the priest's human personality.

(*a*) This, in fact, is seen as clearly as anywhere in the passage we have just explored, 2.5-18; for it is precisely the reflection on Jesus' faithfulness in his identification with his 'brethren' - 'in every way' (κατὰ πάντα, 2.17) - which permits the judgement that he may therefore be seen as 'faithful and merciful' in his present highpriestly capacity. It is true that to some extent it is the mere fact 'that' he became so fully enmeshed in history which allows this insight; i.e., the presence of Jesus among men is in itself the sign of the compassion of the cosmic Christ. But that this gains immeasurably in colour and richness through the further information that 'he is able to help those who are being tested, insofar as he himself (αὐτός) suffered in testing' (2.18), is also indisputable.[58]

(*b*) The same interests are certainly present in the drawing out of the similarities between Jesus and his priestly counterparts of the old covenant, and consequently of his formal as well as his real authorisation as eternal highpriest (5.1-10). Of course it can only be of the utmost significance that this passage - often acknowledged as among the most frank portrayals of Jesus' humanity in the whole New Testament[59] - should follow so immediately upon the urgent plea that the readers should 'draw near' through their great highpriest, to find in the mercy and grace available in him a 'timely help' (4.14-16). This they should do, we are told, 'in confidence' (4.16). The subsequent passage is obviously, then, an exposition of the reasons for that confidence which Christians clearly may and should have, but which this group all too apparently does not.

One element of the reasoning certainly lies in God's divine election of Jesus to his priesthood, as worked out in the scripture citations from Psalms 2 and 110. But at least as important for the writer, in establishing the 'confidence' Christians may have in their highpriest, are exactly the insights drawn from knowledge of the priest's own deep engagement in humanity. In fact, though this passage is directed specifically toward clarification of Jesus' role as priest, many of the elements in it are those we have already noted in the passage 2.5-18, which is more interested, as we said, in his significance as the pioneer: suffering as part of the process of 'perfection', for example, is found here (5.8) as in 2.10; also present is a preoccupation with fear in association with death (5.7; cf. 2.14f); the involvement in 'flesh' (2.7; cf. 2.14) as the sphere of 'testing' or 'temptation' (4.15; cf. 2.18); and of course there is a mutual interest in Jesus' commitment to humanity generally.

The point at issue here, however, is not now to establish his identification with Christians as their 'prototype' (so to speak), but his credentials as the priest in whom they may take confidence amid the uncertainties of historical pilgrimage. Yet still it is his humanity, and again the particular qualities of *his* humanity, which allows the judgement about the priest. It is unfortunately true that difficult and consequential exegetical problems present themselves precisely in verses 7 and 8 of our passage where the involvement of Jesus in the toils of humankind is most deeply explored.[60] The difficulties in detail, however, are not sufficient to obscure the overall intention of the passage, which is to allow the humanity of Jesus to be the window upon his capacities and interests as eschatological priest: 'That Jesus or the Son is [the Christians'] highpriest has already been asserted in outline. Now the *kind* of priesthood he exercises is shown by means of the weakness, suffering and temptation which are bound up with his merciful, sympathetic saving assistance.'[61] Not only does the direction of the passage as a whole, namely the reference to Jesus' human experiences by way of response to the question about 'confidence' in him as eschatological priest, reflect an instinctive awareness of the significance of knowledge about Jesus for Christological judgements; it also raises the question whether there could in fact be knowledge of the priest if knowledge of the person was neither available nor important.[62]

(c) Finally we may observe the same awareness in a passage which stands very near the conclusion of the Christological part of the letter, and must in many ways be seen as the climax of the statements about Christ, namely 10.1-10, in which he is seen as making the offering of himself in place of the offerings of the priests under the old dispensation.

The author of Hebrews is very frequently represented as taking up and reaffirming, without reflection, the Old Testament conviction that sacrificial blood has a mysterious, expiatory power.[63] It is observed that he simply throws out the comment: 'Without shedding of blood there is no forgiveness' (9.22).

In fact it is more than questionable whether this does not do a grave injustice to the writer's penetration. For the phrase just cited is not at all his own unqualified judgement, but is a simple observation of what happened inside the old, legal dispensation: '*Under the Law* almost everything is purified with blood, and without shedding of blood there is no forgiveness of sins.' On the contrary the author *has* reflected at impressive depth upon this system and is very clear in his assessment of it: 'It is impossible that the blood of bulls and goats should remove sins' (10.4). In his massive reinterpretation of the Old Testament cultus (here anticipated by some Old Testament writers and, for that matter, by some of his own near-contemporaries)[64] he has actually replaced the sacrificial ritual with the infinitely more profound concept of the sacrifice of the will.[65] In his understanding, the sacrificial worth of Jesus' death therefore consists not so much in his physical death as in the sacrifice of his human will which that death presupposes:[66] 'In burnt offerings and sin offerings you take no pleasure. Then I said, "Behold I have come . . . to do your will, O God." '[67]

There can be no question but that this psalm statement has been thought through and applied to Jesus in such a way that the principle of radical obedience has replaced the outward, ineffective, constantly repeated sacrificial ritual of the old covenant: 'He abolishes the old ($\tau\grave{o}\ \pi\rho\tilde{\omega}\tau o\nu$) in order to establish the new ($\tau\grave{o}\ \delta\epsilon\acute{u}\tau\epsilon\rho o\nu$)' (10.10).

But again the interest does not lie quite as much in the offering as in the priest who makes it, though of course the two come so close that it is difficult to separate out one from the other. The point can best be seen by noting the comparison made with the old priests who stand 'daily' to make their offerings 'repeatedly', the offerings which 'can never take away sins' (10.11). In contrast Christ offered a single sacrifice for sins, effective for ever ($o\grave{u}\tau o\varsigma\ \delta\grave{\epsilon}\ \mu\acute{\iota}\alpha\nu\ \grave{u}\pi\grave{\epsilon}\rho\ \grave{\alpha}\mu\alpha\rho\tau\iota\tilde{\omega}\nu\ \pi\rho o\sigma\epsilon\nu\acute{\epsilon}\gamma\kappa\alpha\varsigma\ \vartheta\acute{u}\sigma\iota\alpha\nu\ \epsilon\grave{\iota}\varsigma\ \tau\grave{o}\ \delta\iota\eta\nu\epsilon\kappa\acute{\epsilon}\varsigma\ldots$ 10.12). That is to say, in the light of 10.5–10, Christ is a priest who *has offered himself*; and therein is precisely his excellence.[68]

But in this case the degree to which the whole construction depends upon the humanity of Jesus can hardly escape our attention. For here everything turns upon the actual volitional state of the man Jesus as he approached his death. Clearly the figure here spoken of is the Christ of Christian faith, of the church's kerygma. Moreover the interpretation of his death is a theological one from start to finish; even the historical bases on which it rests are notoriously difficult to test.[69] Yet the observation stands. This early Christian theologian is content to let his understanding of Jesus the Christ (or in this case, Jesus the priest) be developed out of what he knows, or believes he knows, of Jesus the man. To lapse into more contemporary idiom, if the historical conditions could not be fulfilled, that is to say, if under historical testing it could be shown that this was not, or is unlikely to have been, the way the man met his death, the whole theology of the eschatological priest would necessarily collapse in ruins.

These various samples, to which others might be added,[70] seem to indicate the consistency with which the remembered life of Jesus is taken as the point of departure not just for the conception of him as the pioneer, the one who reveals God's will for persevering pilgrimage on the part of the covenant people, but equally for an understanding of the priest who 'lives for ever to make intercession'. Since he is one and the same person,[71] the conception of the priest is nothing other than the projection upon the celestial screen of the knowledge one may have of the man upon earth.[72] Whatever 'time' is put upon the verse – i.e., whether 'yesterday' refers to the immediate past of Jesus' historical existence,[73] or alternatively to the distant past of the Son's pre-existence[74] – that must be the significance of the acclamation of him as 'the same yesterday, today and for ever' (13.8).[75] The one who has shown himself faithful in one moment of his existence, and in one capacity, may certainly be trusted in another.

Though knowledge of the person of Jesus is therefore taken as the basis for both aspects of his saving function in the letter,[76] so that it is not always easy to see just which element is being deduced from his engagement in humanity, the two are nevertheless reasonably distinctive. We said previously (p. 86) that the role of the pioneer is best understood in terms of the continuity of the pilgrim community throughout history. This continuity is the presupposition of the futurist eschatology of the letter. But, in contradistinction, the priesthood of Jesus is a clear index of his eschatological immediacy. He is the one through whom the Christians may have direct access to the heavenly realities which, from other perspectives, still seem to lie a great way off in the future.[77] Through his representation Christians *now* may enter the sanctuary (10.19ff etc.) to stand in the Presence (4.16, 12.22ff). The importance of this, not only for a balanced understanding of the eschatological perspectives of the writer and of the more 'devotional' or 'personal' aspects of his faith-understanding, but also by way of estimating his place in relationship to other New Testament writers,[78] is difficult to overestimate.[79] Our main interest in this chapter, however, has been to see how both ministries of Jesus represent interpretations by this creative Christian pastor and theologian of the basic memory in the church of the earthly Jesus.

3 Faith and history

Though we have been speaking continually of the human personality of Jesus it must nevertheless be obvious that the points at which this figure is actually exposed to normal historical processes are remarkably few. Precisely because the humanity of Jesus, in the letter, is so integrally related to the writer's theology of the priest, the figure to whom that humanity is ascribed is rendered elusive to the historian's grasp. Who shall say whether the humanity of Jesus is a construct demanded by the writer's theology or whether the theological construction is the product of his encounter with the church's memory of the man?[80]

In this way the question of the degree to which the interpretation of the writer (his conception of Christ) was subject to historical controls (his knowledge of Jesus) is raised particularly acutely.

But are we to assume that this is only a question for us? Is it not conceivable that the writer himself could also have discerned the danger of a circular movement between a Jesus-myth and a priest-Christology? Since this possibility may not be rejected out of hand, our investigation of the relationship between history and the faith (interpretation) of the writer needs to proceed at two different levels. It is necessary, first, that we conduct our own inquiry into the concrete relationship between the writer and the traditions. Here we are obviously obliged to stand apart from his account of the Jesus-priest relationship and inspect his work critically and objectively. But, secondly, if we satisfy ourselves that this early Christian theologian does have sufficient historical control over his materials, it will not be inappropriate to attend to whatever statements he may be making, directly or indirectly, about the relationships between faith and history.

The starting point must be his own affirmation at 2.3 that the salvation-bearing Word (λόγος) has, from its origins in Jesus, been transmitted through a definite history of tradition. Here, certainly, there are involved a number of factors not readily accessible to historical inquiry: 'Salvation', 'Word', 'Lord' all bear about them certain imponderable qualities, not to speak of the 'signs' (σημεῖα), and 'wonders' (τέρατα), the 'various manifestations of power' (ποικίλαι δυνάμεις) and 'gifts of the Holy Spirit' (Πνεύματος Ἁγίου μερισμοί) by which God has witnessed persuasively to the traditions (verse 4). But the 'beginning' (ἀρχή), 'those who heard' (οἱ ἀκούσαντες) and the 'we' among whom the writer includes himself (εἰς ἡμᾶς) are all sufficiently concrete in themselves to form definite reference points, and that which they form collectively, namely, an observable process of tradition, is well within the historian's orbit.[81] The chief interest here, however, is not so much what a modern historian might learn of this process in particular (which might not be very much) but that it was of such a public kind that he *could* begin to investigate it without disruption of his historical principles. That is to say, his only limitation here is his lack of information, not the impropriety of the subject matter.

But this, in turn, implies that for those who lived as contemporaries with the transmission process, there was a genuine possibility of testing the information given by the writer of Hebrews over against the traditions, the public property of the community within which the traditions have been received (εἰς ἡμᾶς); the writer is already opening himself to critical review in light of the traditions themselves.[82] But this implies, in turn, that his picture of Jesus is not at his beck and call but is subject to some degree of historical scrutiny.[83]

The same kinds of considerations may be brought to bear on the statement at 13.7 where the 'leaders' (ἡγούμενοι) are said to have declared the Word of God to the community. Here certainly the issues are not quite so clear, since the writer's use of the second person plural (ὑμῶν, ὑμῖν) does not identify him so immediately with the congregation. Also the loose relationship between verses 7 and 8 makes it problematic whether the 'leaders' (verse 7) can be linked with the 'yesterday' of verse 8, thus identifying 'yesterday' with the historical phase of Jesus' existence and the 'leaders' with 'those who heard' of 2.3, though neither is this improbable.[84] Nevertheless the fundamental point, that the Word is mediated by a public tradition, is maintained.

Of course we cannot lose sight of the limited nature of such historical controls as are here claimed. There is no possibility now of demonstrating the existence of a 'hot line' leading back from the community to the actual Jesus. The possibility, even, of conferring with 'those who heard' (2.3) is probably no longer present, especially if these are in fact the same people described as 'leaders' in 13.7, who certainly are by now dead or have gone away ('remember ...!' 13.7). So that even the traditions against which the writer is willing to be compared have *already* long since been the bearers of a post-Easter, kerygmatic interpretation of Jesus. And yet such observations as we have made are not without their importance. For they point up the public character of what we earlier called 'the memory of the life and character of Jesus ... in the church' (p. 64). This means that though the process of interpretation of the event and events of this life went on (and where more strikingly than in our document?), where this involved an *aberration* from the public memory, that interpretation might be itself discredited.[85] This signifies that though the system was not foolproof, the memory of Jesus *was* understood to be asserting an historical control upon the theology built on that memory by the early church.

We may be permitted to say, therefore, that what the author has to say about both the outward circumstances (as, for instance, his birth within the tribe of Judah, 7.14, or his death outside the city gates, 13.12) and the inner crises of spirit (e.g., 5.7, 10.5-7 or 12.2) of the life of Jesus has a greater possibility of having reached him in the traditions[86] than of having been thrown up by his theology of the eschatological priest, even though it is invariably the case that these details are utilised in the purposes of that theology.[87]

At 7.14, a particularly confident appeal is made to historical 'warrants':[88] 'For it is quite evident that Jesus was born of the tribe of Judah.'[89] Here, therefore, we have a useful starting point to see how faith and history (or history and interpretation) function together in the understanding of the author. Is faith here being 'legitimised' by an appeal to history in the way which was stigmatised in the theology of much of this century and associated especially with the name of R. Bultmann?[90]

Whatever else may be happening in this text, a direct line of argument from historical facts to justification for the conception of Jesus as eschatological highpriest is not in view. For the fact is, that in itself birth within the tribe of Judah really establishes nothing with respect to the messianic, or eschatological, status of a person. There were even countless descendants of David who were not thereby entitled to be called Messiah. Rather the appeal to Jesus' human parentage is designed to show that, *given* his status as eschatological priest (which for the author is established on quite different grounds), then the levitical institutions, and the Mosaic regulations on which they are dependent, have been relativised effectually and for ever. How? By the fact (indisputable) that Jesus was born outside them! So that the argument from history clearly carries conviction only when one is already a believer.

On the other hand, the construction is not pointless. For the historical circumstances certainly create or, perhaps more accurately, sustain the *possibility* of faith. For given belief in Jesus and his eschatological importance, the facts of his birth say something of great significance about him and his kind of priesthood: that is, here is a priest who did *not* depend for his authority upon the fragile institutions of levitical inheritance, but who contained within himself his own authorisation, specifically in the quality and dimensions of his life.[91] Therefore we are to say that though history does not 'prove' faith's claims, it nevertheless both provides the opportunity for faith and, certainly, informs the content of faith. That is why this particular fact is seized upon so triumphantly by the writer.

It is important, also, that we notice the degree of historical 'risk' involved in this appeal, and the reasons for taking it; for the extent to which faith may properly put itself at the mercy of historical findings has been an element of central importance in the discussions about faith and history. It must be quite to the point that the ancestry of Jesus has sometimes been thought to depend more upon the confessional needs of the church than upon historical fact.[92] Now it is clear that if some ancient investigator, who had more ready access to the facts than we can now have, had managed to show that the claim made by this writer, among others, rested not on historical grounds but on dogmatic formulation, not only is this particular argument of Hebrews wrecked, but faith itself is in some jeopardy. For in this case, faith would be seen to be appealing to itself. The appeal to history here therefore reflects both the writer's awareness that faith is obliged to indicate its relationship to concrete, objective 'facts' - details of information which are beyond the possibility of its own manipulation - and the confidence that this is both legitimate and possible.

From the way in which this particular fragment of historical knowledge is introduced to the argument it is perhaps permissible to draw more general inferences about the relationship of faith and history. It is not, as we have seen, that faith looks to history in an effort to 'prove' or vindicate itself. For faith *necessarily* assumes a point of view from beyond the boundaries of historical existence, and therefore beyond the limits of legitimate ('legitimate' is our word and is therefore anachronistic, but usefully makes more precise what is at stake) historical inquiry: confidence in Jesus' priesthood is not established merely by reference to his birth of the tribe of Judah. Yet faith is nevertheless committed to inquiry into its own historical origins precisely because the *elimination* of its historical content threatens, if not eliminates, its own possibility. That is, the relationship is strictly one-directional; all the historical evidence in the world would still not vindicate faith, but the erosion of its historical grounds spells the end of its own possibility. In brief, history is the necessary, but not sufficient, basis for Christian faith.[93]

This is seen even more clearly when we turn to the inner, rather than the outer, circumstances of Jesus' life as they are handled by the writer. According to our analysis above, the volitional state of Jesus as he faced his death is made the very kernel of the reason for confidence in Jesus the priest. It is just here that the writer locates Jesus' disclosure of God's will for his people in history as well as the disclosure of Jesus' eternal willingness to be a merciful and faithful intercessory priest on their behalf. Certainly it is true that these details are much harder to pin down than the kind relating to his birth in a particular family.[94] Accordingly the same kind of confident appeal to history as at 7.14 is not made in this case. But nor may these inner, spiritual facts be regarded as less historical *in principle*. Significantly, perhaps, Jesus' human decisions and crises of prayer are specifically designated by the writer as within the sphere of history: 'in the days of his flesh', 5.7; 'when he came into the world', 10.5.[95] It might, of course, be objected that such statements are no more than confessional ciphers. Nevertheless they signify that here are statements about a man who was genuinely historically observable and who, confronted with certain possibilities, made specific decisions, which decisions have left an overall impression upon those who knew him and who have preserved that memory of him.[96]

Given that this historical information about Jesus is of much greater importance to the writer than even the outward details of his birth (7.14) and death (13.12), he (the writer) has clearly exposed himself to a quite alarming degree of historical 'risk'. For if it can be shown, historically, that Jesus' actual behaviour was such as to render unlikely the account of his response to the threat of death[97] or, as is more nearly within the bounds of possibility, that the account shows signs of Christian manufacture,[98] then the structures of Christian theology must fall into ruin. The necessary basis for its statements about itself, about the world, the future, its hope, and about God, will have been undercut. That is what it means, in part, to have a theology of incarnation.[99]

One question which presents itself somewhat urgently in this respect has therefore to do with the extent to which the early Christians, and very possibly this writer in particular, have engaged in creative reconstructions of Jesus' inner life which show all the signs of having been moulded out of LXX texts, as many scholars believe has been the case at 5.7f of our letter.[100] Coupled with this, though not presenting such clear examples in Hebrews, is the possibility of the elaboration of, or additions to, the remembered traditions of Jesus through the activities of Christian prophets in the church,[101] which is of course simply a more specialised form of the tortuous question as to how seriously the traditions have been modified or overlaid by the needs of the early church.[102]

Clearly the simple fact that there are signs of creative activity on the part of the church of the New Testament does not *in itself* render the traditions historically unreliable, for it is entirely appropriate to ask: what were the reasons which prompted the gathering of scriptures, or the production of oracles, *of the kind* which were assembled or produced? To this, the answer, at least in part, must be: because they were found to be conformable with the *person* who was remembered to be of such a kind.[103] At the same time it must be seen that there is a point (and the judgement of this will vary from scholar to scholar) at which the creative reworking of the traditions is no longer sufficiently under control, and at which point faith becomes suspect on both its theological and historical sides: theologically because the reference to an external *datum* has become tenuous or at last non-existent, a *credo* which simply affirms itself (we must say more about this shortly); and historically, because then it is vunerable to historical discrediting.[104] Amid the many and vexatious questions in this respect,

and notwithstanding them, there are in fact not an inconsiderable number
of scholars who espouse a reasoned confidence that historical controls, of
some such order as we have noted above about the public nature of the
traditions, did ensure that a reliable picture of Jesus was preserved in the
church and functioned more nearly as the basis of its theology than as that
theology's product.[105] Precisely that fact, however, dictates that historical
questions are real questions for theology (faith), and must be brought
repeatedly to its attention.

Not only is there at stake here a question of historical credibility,
however, but also one of theological authenticity; that is to say, it is in its
attention to history, specifically the history of its own origins, that faith
is rescued from the danger of its own self-affirmation and self-propagation,
i.e., in meeting its need for objectivity out of its own confessional formulation. We have seen how, in our letter, the designation of Jesus as pioneer
(which embraces, though we did not examine them in detail, the conception of him as 'forerunner' as well as the 'sinlessness' and 'once-for-all'
language) includes as at least part of its intention the separation out of
the faith of Jesus from the faith of the church (above, pp. 84, 86f). But this,
in turn, witnesses to a theological awareness of the necessary distinction
between the church's origins and its existence, that is to say, an awareness
that insofar as the church confesses its dependence on an event outside
itself and beyond its own manipulation, it knows itself not to be a self-
sufficient, self-generating organism.[106] 'History' is the name we give to
the discipline which, in our times at any rate, enables us to monitor the
relationships between cause and effect, the extent to which the church was
the outcome of Jesus' presence in history and, vice versa, to be able to
say, too, at which points the picture of Jesus is the creation of the church.[107]
For its own sake, quite apart from any question of credibility in the world,
it is of the most serious importance for Christian theology to be able to
give an account of its origins.[108] It is never finished with the possibility
of its own 'reflection'.[109]

Since the reopening of the discussion, early in the 1950s,[110] about our
access to the Jesus of history, the most pressing question has been whether,
and to what extent, we may speak of continuity between Jesus as he was
known as a man of Nazareth, and Jesus who is the content of Christian
preaching.[111] It is almost singularly this point which permits the scholars
involved in what has been called the 'new quest' properly to be called
'post-Bultmannians'.[112] For Bultmann it was simply inadmissible that
Christian faith could approximate to anything that lay prior to the decisive
events of the crucifixion and resurrection of Jesus.[113] That is why, in his
judgement, one should not speak of Jesus' faith,[114] nor in fact even include

him within the sphere of 'Christianity';[115] it is also the root of his famous understanding of the Old Testament as depicting essentially the 'miscarriage' of the covenant concept prior to God's 'new beginning in Christ'.[116] For him, therefore, the irrelevance of an inquiry into the life of Jesus had at its heart not so much the legitimacy or otherwise of historical investigation, but rather this strict definition of faith as 'faith in (the risen) Christ'. The ensuing discussion has largely taken its shape from this assertion.[117]

It is at just this point that the writer of Hebrews seems to offer an important contribution to the discussion, as a New Testament witness to whom not a great deal of attention has been paid. For in his preoccupation with the relationship of the covenants, how the Word in the Son relates to the Word to the fathers, he has seen that faith requires to be defined on a larger scale simply than as 'faith in Christ'. That is to say, 'faith' for this early Christian theologian has a theocentric, rather than a Christocentric, orientation. Because God, rather than Christ, is in the last analysis the object of faith, it is altogether possible for him to include the patriarchs within its scope, almost exactly continuous with the Christians, as we have seen.

Interestingly enough it is this preoccupation with the history of the covenants which produces his double understanding of Jesus within the categories we have labelled pioneer and priest; for as pioneer, we saw, Jesus stood firmly within the history of this people who must look to the future believingly, while as priest he is now the means of their participating, already, in the eschatological realities.

But this means that in being a *member* of the covenant community as well as being (now) the *content* of its faith in him as great highpriest, he, too, is seen in something of the duality – continuity-in-discontinuity – which attaches to that entire history; for that continuity–discontinuity must also be true of the community's relationship with Jesus insofar as he represents in himself one who has passed from one aeon to another, the 'forerunner' who already stands beyond the curtain (6.19f). It is as a 'believer' himself that the community can find a continuity with him: the basis for, and the content of, its understanding of the role to which it is called, as well as a paradigmatic example set before it. But in his achievement in principle, in his exaltation, and consecration (perfection), he is certainly *not* an example but the one who has done these things 'on their behalf'.[118]

It may be true that the writer's conception of faith is not as brilliantly sharp as the 'faith-in' formula of Paul and John. But that is yet a long way from supposing it not at all specifically 'Christian' or merely the product of general reflection on the nature of religious behaviour.[119] Indeed it is a matter of theological judgement as to whether an undue concentration upon that particular formulation – the elevating of it into a functional 'canon within the canon'[120] – has not been responsible for the problems encountered in the 'Jesus of history or Christ of faith' alternative. For to allow *God* to be the reference point of faith rather than restricting this to 'faith in Christ' permits just that continuity between Jesus and the church which has been such a problem, theologically, in recent decades,[121] between the church and the Old Testament community, and indeed between the covenant community in both its forms and the world in which it must bear witness.[122] This is because it is 'history', the experience of the world as time-bound and for that reason and others experienced as limitation and uncertainty,[123] which constitutes the continuum within which these various persons or groups of persons, from their widely differentiated times and circumstances, may nevertheless recognise and understand themselves in the experiences of one another; 'history', that is, as seen from a faith-perspective.

4 Faith and interpretation

Yet when all has been said which is to be said about the writer and his relationship to history, including the historically mediated traditions about Jesus, the absolute fact remains that the Jesus we meet in his writing has not existed – at any rate certainly not in this particular form – before this Christian thinker brought together in such creative synthesis all the elements of his conception of 'Jesus as priest'.

What *are* these elements and how does the product which emerges from them relate to the matters we have been discussing?

Obviously there are strongly flavoured Old Testament ingredients which have been brought out of the cultic understanding and practice within the previous covenant. The most superficial reading shows how 'priest', 'sacrifice', 'sanctuary' and a good number of other words and concepts have been made to play a new role in the Christological reflection of the author. We can say quite simply that without these conceptual 'frames' this Christian thinker could not have begun to fashion his own, highly original conception of Christ and his work. Yet, as we saw in our previous chapter (pp. 63f), however indispensable these conceptions have been for him, one cannot point to an obvious, or *necessary*, connection between the levitical institutions and Jesus in the sense that the former point with unambiguous or demonstrable clarity toward Jesus as their culmination. There is no especially obvious link between the priests and highpriests going about their appointed tasks and the death of the man Jesus, however impressively dignified this is remembered as being. This is to say, of course, that the bringing of these two things, these two series of conceptual 'frames' (as we may describe them)[124] into relationship with one another is something which has taken place under the hand of our writer in a completely creative way.

And yet, as we also saw (pp. 64ff), this is by no means the same as saying that such creativity is without any base in 'things as they are', or completely devoid of historical appropriateness. Another way of saying this is that though the range of ideas which *could* be fashioned interpretatively around the priestly–sacrificial theme of the old covenant is virtually limitless, not all these – in fact, probably very few – may properly be regarded as appropriate or possible hermeneutical developments. So that to say that Jesus *may* (properly) be predicated of the Old Testament Priesthood as its culmination is to say that such an interpretative relationship is *not impermissible*; that the subject of the interpretation (the Old Testament cultus) *allows* both by its existence and also by its form and content such an interpretational relationship. That the relationship cannot be seen as an obvious or necessary one means that no claim can be made upon it for its evidential qualities, as 'proving' any divine or even historical causality between the elements of the relationship. The interpretation cannot be 'vindicated' (as we said with respect to the historical Jesus); it is simply – though by no means unimportantly – that it is not illegitimate. The double negative thus expresses not what *must* follow, but what must not be excluded and hence *may* follow.

Now we can see that the same kinds of considerations apply to the highpriesthood Christology which has been developed out of the kerygmatic traditions about Jesus. The traditions themselves certainly did not require to be turned in this particular direction. That may be seen in that no one else in the early church, so far as we can be aware, ever thought of working them into this particular scheme. But, as with the Old Testament ideas, though these memories of Jesus may not have necessitated this interpretation in particular, they certainly – we have tried to show – *permitted* such a development. Without this 'permission' (in the existence and shape of the traditions) the interpretation could not have come into being. As we said previously (p. 94), history is the necessary, but not sufficient, basis for Christian faith.

This must mean, its dependence on history and what is historically knowable notwithstanding, that the most fundamental ingredient in the interpretation has been the faith-insight of the interpreter. It is this which has brought the several elements together – the Old Testament conceptual 'frames', the traditions about Jesus, and not least the situation of the readers in their predicament of confidence – in order to fuse all these together into a quite new and imaginative conception: the figure of a history-spanning eschatological priest who may be 'known' to be faithful and merciful, and through whom his followers may therefore have courage, at any point in their historical pilgrimage, to approach the heavenly sanctuary.

To speak of faith as the most fundamental ingredient in the interpretation means that this is the element which alone can supply the synthesising, creative ordering of the other elements, a capacity for which they can only supply the possibilities or suggestions. As we have now seen in several different ways, faith does depend upon these to the limited extent that without them, or without the 'permission' they give it, faith could not be, let alone set about its creative, interpretative work. But this dependence, we have suggested, can only be of a limited kind. For, given this 'permission', faith always (by definition) transcends the boundaries to the historical information with which it is supplied. In the end, then, interpretation is an act, or product, of faith. Interpretation therefore cannot finally give an account of itself; it can only end in speaking of 'mystery', 'silence',[125] an 'alien logic'[126] or some such quantity.[127] This can hardly be surprising, at any rate in the case of a Christian interpreter. For he is essentially a 'believer': not just in the rather superficial sense of that word which categorises his religious affiliation, but in the sense that, standing as he knows he does in the midst of history, he nevertheless chooses or dares or feels obliged not to understand that history - even his own history - from within itself, but from a different, transcendent perspective. This at least may be said to be what is happening when the writer of Hebrews describes Jesus, a man who is known to have lived in the recent past, 'in every way like ourselves', as one who now 'lives for ever, to make intercession on our behalf'.

4

HERMENEUTICS

The question to which at last we are directed by our study of the interpretative procedures of this first-century Christian is whether what we have
found in his work has any point of helpfulness for contemporary hermeneutical reflection. Immediately quite natural doubts present themselves –
raised by our deep awareness of the gulf created by the centuries of terminological and conceptual refinement which separate his times from ours. That,
as is stated often enough, *is* the hermeneutical problem.[1]

And yet, to be daunted by those doubts, in the first instance at any rate,
would entail a certain irony. For what we have been investigating is the
work of a man who has apparently accomplished with some success precisely that from before which we were ourselves in resignation. For the
distances, temporally and culturally, between this author and the subject
matter of his interpretation (the Old Testament rituals) can hardly be
regarded as inconsiderable either; yet obviously he has not been dissuaded
by that fact. That is not to exclude the possibility, of course, that in the
end we might have to admit that the distances between us are too great for
there to be more than tangential similarities between his questions and
answers and ours. To pursue the question, nevertheless – to raise the
possibility that there appertain to the processes of interpretation itself at
least a minimum of perennially significant elements – represents an attempt
to extend the horizons along which we have worked (to use H.-G. Gadamer's
metaphor)[2] toward some sort of meeting point between this ancient author's
presuppositions and our own.

In this concluding essay on hermeneutics we shall therefore try to isolate,
largely by way of revision, some of the leading ideas which we have said are
implicit in this Christian's interpretative work. Then we shall attempt the
rather more hazardous task of bringing his ideas into relationship with
some considerations which rule in our (modern) discussions on the theme.

1 Review

Starting from the writer's prologue, which, we claimed, intentionally repre-

sents a careful summing up of his theological principles, we isolated as of
basic importance in those principles a dialectical relationship in which the
past stands to the present in both continuity and discontinuity. In that
opening statement, we saw, the Speaking of God is understood as manifesting about itself an historical elongation so that that which was received by
'the fathers, through the prophets' may be recognised as that which has
also now come 'to us, in a Son'. It has been this 'historicising' of the Word
of God, we said, which has provided the central question for this Christian's
theological reflection: how *can* the Word of him who 'is the same', whose
'years have no end' (1.12), have a past and a present, have forms which
can be rendered obsolete by newer and more perfect forms? Yet it is the
conviction that God's disclosure of himself in the person of Jesus belongs
to the Old Testament institutions as their fulfilment which is the driving
force behind this monumental piece of Christian reflection and interpretation.

We saw that there is reason to believe that this nucleus conception of
the past and present forms of the Word of God has been worked out in
at least three expanding circles of comparison and contrast embracing
both revelational and redemptive categories: that Jesus, as Son, is compared
and contrasted with the angels as the mediators of the Torah of the old
covenant, with Moses the human intermediary in the reception of that Law,
and with the Aaronic priestly practitioners, whose own institution was so
closely bound up with the intentions and shortcomings of the Law. These
circles of comparison and contrast, we urged, really carry forward the
basic considerations raised in such abbreviated form in the prologue, and
may be regarded from both literary and theological points of view as
continuations of the thesis there set down. We suggested, too, that this
careful theological construction may well have been accomplished independently of, and prior to, its eventual employment in our present letter.

The three circles of comparison and contrast of Jesus with his Old
Testament predecessors are not the only way in which this historical
continuity between the dispensations comes to expression, however. We
saw at several points that there is a direct and material continuity between
the recipients of the Word of God in both its Old Testament and New
Testament forms: so that on both communities are laid the same qualities
of believing obedience, hope and confidence, though the degrees to which
this is so vary in accordance with the clarity and finality of the forms of
the Word received. The reasons for this continuity between the communities, we saw, had to do with the interplay between the Word of God
itself in its fundamentally eschatological orientation, and the conditionedness of historical existence in which the people of both communities find

themselves. Further, continuity between the dispensations is to be seen in what we chose to call the conceptual 'frames' within which faith-understanding (in both covenants) takes place. What is meant here is that the clusters of ideas employed in each cohere in discernibly similar patterns of relationships. So that `priest', 'atonement', 'sacrifice', 'approach' and so on belong to one another in the one dispensation as in the other, though in the new the whole complex of ideas has been thought through and radicalised to a quite remarkable depth. As we saw, 'sacrifice' now means not the bloody offering on an altar, but the bending of a man's will to the divine will. This parallelism of structures (or in our terms, 'frames') is, of course, more traditionally called typology.

In these several different ways, then, the continuity between the covenants as set down *in nuce* in the prologue statement is drawn out.

But now a quite different consideration presents itself. Already in the prologue, the forms which the Speaking of God took to itself in the previous dispensation are described as 'partial and piecemeal',[3] which suggests that at best they point only suggestively to their true meaning and significance. Their partial and scattered quality[4] means that their capacity for, or function as, the Word of God cannot with assurance be read off their surface, but may only be inferred; in other words, to see them as such (as forms of God's Speaking) is an interpretation of them which is not wholly borne out by those forms themselves. As one important commentator has it: 'That which is communicated in parts, sections, fragments must of necessity be imperfect; and so also a representation which is made in many modes cannot be other than provisional.'[5] That which is here spoken of with respect to the forms of God's Speaking also applies, we have seen, at every other level of the covenant relationships. So the levitical institutions are, in every way, only hesitant and partial expressions of what they themselves point to *in* their partiality, namely a means of total and permanent expiation of sin. Or the mediators of the Law in the earlier dispensation show themselves as (in comparison with Jesus the Son) subordinate servants of the Word rather than its very manifestation.

This means that the continuity of which we have previously spoken must now be seen as, at best, only partially discernible in the outward forms in which the Word of God is present.[6] This is clearly so of the relationships of the Old Testament forms themselves in their partiality and scatteredness. To see them as coherent and continuous, moments in an ongoing process, is to make a judgement about them beyond what they themselves will support. But that must also be true, by implication, of the relation between those forms in their suggestiveness and their culmination in Jesus as eschatological form of the Speaking of God. To describe them as πολυμερῶς καὶ πολυτρόπως says that they could only anticipate; their meaning was not wholly disclosed in them, but is only seen retrospectively in light of the culmination of that process of which they were, suggestively, a part. So we may ask: what, in fact, permits the judgement that the previous forms in their temporality and provisional quality are parts of the same process as that which happened in the life, death and (believed) exaltation of Jesus? Where are the material and empirical lines of communication which bind them to him and him to them? We have said, at various points, that a sufficient suggestiveness may be claimed of the forward-looking expectations of the Old Testament texts and the institutions of which they speak, to *permit* an interpretative relationship between them and what happens in Jesus. But it is *not* a *necessary* relationship. To see them in relationship is an interpretation, in the end a perspective of faith rather than of demonstration.

This is not accidental. For to ask concerning the basis on which these judgements are made is to receive a clear answer already within the opening statement: the single factor which allows these ostensibly disparate elements to be ordered meaningfully is that God is, or has been, experienced as speaking in them.[7] Whatever consistency attaches to these 'sundry times and divers manners' therefore cannot be something which is immediately accessible to historical scrutiny. Their continuity rests not in their own manifest connectedness but in the faithfulness or consistency of him for whose Word they have been the vehicles. He *gives* a continuity to them: 'For God, who is ever like himself, and whose word is the same, and whose truth is unchangeable, has spoken as to both [the Law and the gospel] in common.'[8]

But this, in turn, can only mean that in such judgements the faith of the interpreter himself, who believes that God has so spoken and is so speaking, is by no means the least considerable element. Just to the extent to which the events and phenomena in their episodic quality fall short of demonstrable connection is the assertion that they do nevertheless belong together an assessment of faith.

We spoke earlier about the historical continuity of the conceptual 'frames'. But now we must see the extent to which these connections are part of the interpretative activity of the writer himself, made in the conviction that the Word which 'the fathers' received is identical with that which has come 'to us, in a Son'.

As with the central cluster of ideas – the sacrifice which has become the sacrifice of a man's will, and the priest who offers himself, and so on – the points of outward (shall we say, empirical) continuity between other aspects of the earlier and latter situations are in fact quite minimal. For example, the 'call' which these Hellenistic-Jewish readers have received is not now the summons to journey to an actual place, but is the 'heavenly' call toward 'the city which is to come' (3.1, 13.14). The 'country' in which they are presently 'exiles and strangers' (11.13) is, in fact, this world. The promise which is confirmed by oath is not now for a son in old age, but is the promise held out by Jesus' presence in the sanctuary. In these ways and others the imaginative skill of the interpreter is evident, yet in such a way that (nearly always, at any rate) one can see his point and the reasons for his conviction that God has been involved in both situations. There is certainly a continuity between the 'frames', but it is a continuity which only becomes *apparent* under the hand of the interpreter.

This then becomes the crux of the hermeneutical question in Hebrews: what is the relationship between the conceptual 'frames' - which certainly are there independently of the interpreter and between which, when it is drawn to our attention, there can be seen an intriguing connectedness - and the faith-convictions of the interpreter apart from which this connectedness is at best but latent, suggestive? In more contemporary idiom, it is once more the question of the relationship between historical forms which may and must be investigated in their historicity and the faith-insights of the Christian, which are not amenable to the same orders of investigation or demonstration.

The formula which has been shaping itself in the course of our study, and which may be now drawn together in some finality, depends largely on the word or conception 'permission'. Side by side with this, indeed as part of the same conception, is what we called the 'double negation': in other words, what is 'permitted' to the interpreter by the historical forms is thereby 'not excluded'.

If we go back to our discussion in chapter 2 of the writer's organisation of the relationship between the Old Testament scriptures and a Christian understanding of them, it may be recalled that there was seen there an interplay between the actual text forms (the *logia*) and the faith-setting (i.e., the Christian setting) in which these become more than *just* oracles (*logia*); given the presence of a 'teacher' and a receptivity on the part of the Christian congregation, the *logia* may and do become 'words' - a 'word of exhortation' or even a 'Word of God' (see pp. 50f). And yet, we suggested, it was not inappropriate to see the connection between the Old Testament texts and this creative, faith-determined reinterpretation of them as 'historical'. Certainly 'history' here must be set in inverted commas, we decided, to indicate that the processes involved are only somewhat approximate to the more strictly scientific methodology of which we now naturally think in our use of that term (above, p. 63). But nor, given these limitations, was the term forbidden, we claimed; for there are present in this Christian's interpretative work at least two factors, open to inspection and to that extent exercising a control on the subjectivity of the interpretations offered. These were, first, the observable expectations of the Old Testament texts for a future fulfilment over against themselves in their historically localised settings, and, secondly, the measurable conformity of the person of Jesus to those expectations. It was this latter factor, especially, we said, which distinguishes almost all Christian interpretation of the Old Testament from other exegetical traditions of the time, insofar as it enables an 'historical' relationship to be set up between the near and distant points of the interpretative relationship. In contradistinction, almost all the other traditions, lacking this 'definition', spill out into the unbounded plains of philosophical and other speculation (pp. 64ff).

Now in this we clearly have to do with the same interplay of 'historical form' and 'faith-interpretation' which we discerned in the opening statement and in other places. But it was in this context that we first began to use the 'permission' language to describe what is happening: 'from either end of the hermeneutical work – that is to say, in terms of the texts and in terms of the interpretation of them – there are certain observable, outward factors which at least permit or even invite a relationship between the earlier forms and the later (Christian) interpretation made of them'; '... to *permit* their Christian interpretation; which of course is something different from demanding, or requiring, such' (pp. 63f; cf. also pp. 65f). In that context, also, the 'double negation' makes its appearance: 'the term ['history'] and the claim here made for the author are not by any means impossible' (p. 63).

When we turned to the other strand of the writer's interpretative work, that is, his shaping of the remembered traditions about Jesus into his distinctive highpriestly Christology, the same structures and considerations seemed to present themselves. It can hardly be the case, we decided, that the memories of Jesus in the early church necessarily or unambiguously pointed toward the priestly interpretation of them, if for no other reason than that prior to our writer it never occurred to anyone else, so far as we know, to shape them in this particular way. In any case it is according to the nature of faith itself that its judgements always stand beyond (though, we have seen, not independently of) what can be known or deduced on historical grounds. Certainly, here, the conception of Jesus as eschatological highpriest transcends the historical data with which it is supplied.

But here, too, the concept 'permission' became the operative one. In recognising that in the last analysis it is the faith-insight of the interpreter which brings together the various elements of the eschatological priest conception - Old Testament prototypes, New Testament traditions of Jesus and, in its present formulation, at any rate, the crisis of confidence on the part of the readers - we saw that the conception is only a valid one to the extent that it is 'permitted' by its several ingredients, or certainly by its kerygmatic and Old Testament traditions. It is not that these can 'prove' or vindicate its authenticity, but that the absence of these, or a false or forced use of them, would eliminate its validity. As we said there, 'The double negative thus expresses not what *must* follow but what must not be excluded and hence *may* follow' (p. 99).

To come back now to the prologue formulation, under which all these others have taken place, we have said, this now appears to be a suitable description of what is happening there, too. The problem, we said (p. 105), lies in the relationship between the conceptual 'frames' and the meaning which is found in them by the Christian interpreter. The 'frames', we saw, do apparently have an existence quite independently of their interpreter; yet their meaning and connectedness is something only found *in* their interpretation. And this is not other than an interpretation of faith insofar as it is one which arises from the conviction that God has been involved in them and has given them a meaning and continuity not immediately obvious in the phenomena themselves.

In fact, as must now be apparent, the idea of forms of the Word of God which, in themselves, are at best only πολυμερῶς καὶ πολυτρόπως, but which are seen and ordered as pointing to their own fulfilment 'in a Son', belongs to the same range of ideas as that we have been discussing. The forms may indeed be 'partial and piecemeal'; it is not supposed that in and of themselves they shall vindicate the linking of them to the newer forms of the Word in the Son. For this connection is known and acknowledged to rest nowhere else than in the fact that God has spoken in them. Such a judgement cannot, in the nature of things, be other than a judgement of faith. On the other hand neither is such a view of them and their various relationships *im*permissible. While in their contingency and scatteredness they do not force such an understanding of themselves, they certainly do not rule it out; indeed they may even suggest it. It is on the basis of this suggestiveness that the continuity between the covenants has been worked out in its many different facets in the theology of this writer. Yet in the end this continuity (empirically speaking) is no more than a suggestion; it is permitted, not required. For in the end it is, as it must be, an insight brought in faith.[9]

This whole hermeneutical formulation, we suggested, may well belong to a different stage of the writer's reflection than the one we presently have in his practical, pastoral letter. This scheme, we said, has the appearance of being an answer to some such question as; how does the (eschatological) Word of God relate to history? which perhaps has been the central question for his own theological reflection. This reflection and its products, we judged, have very probably provided the 'reservoir' out of which his letter has been written. But in developing the outcome of that reflection (his conception of the priest who in his own death has made the finally effective expiation for sins) to meet the needs of his friends (i.e., into the picture of a priest who lives ever to make intercession for his hard-pressed followers), the question to which he must now address himself, we said, seems more likely to have been: why are *we* (as the eschatological community) still in history? (above, pp. 73f). While not by any means unrelated to the question with which he himself has been confronted, this new question will have altered slightly the perspectives of the hermeneutical problem, which is now not quite: how do the new (Christian) insights through Jesus belong to the older conceptual 'frames' (of sacrifice, etc.)? but; in what ways do the Old Testament scriptures still apply to a New Testament congregation?

It is in this setting, we suggested, that the writer seems to develop a secondary hermeneutical consideration, the one we designated 'the hermeneutic of eschatological existence'. The details of this have already been spelled out (pp. 66ff, 71), and we need do no more here than recall that it turns around the bipolarity of the Christian eschatological experience. From the point of view of the Christian conviction that the events which comprise the life and death and exaltation of Jesus represent God's finally effective self-disclosure, the Old Testament forms, which are then so clearly anticipatory, may all be regarded as having been outmoded. This in fact is regularly the attitude adopted in the theological–Christological sections of the letter, which, we saw, just as uniformly adopt a 'realised' eschatological stance. But when the Christian community is forced to reckon with its own unfinality, as being still very much enmeshed in the processes of history, it then discovers a real and existential continuity between itself and the community of the old covenant.

From our present point of view, the significant element about this secondary hermeneutical conception is that in it too, just as in the earlier one, the ultimately important constituent element becomes the faith-perspectives brought by the Christian to the task of interpretation. As we said, the hermeneutical 'screen' which has been placed across the scriptures, allowing them to speak with immediacy or blocking them off as outdated, is this, essentially Christian, experience of the End-as-duality, the characteristic 'already but not yet'. In a quite real sense, the way in which this screening effect is carried through depends upon whichever aspect of their eschatological awareness it is from which the Christians approach the scriptures: 'if with reference to the difficulties, the conditionedness and responsibilities within historical existence, then the Word of God in the Old Testament may be as meaningful to Christians as to its original recipients. But from the point of view of what is now considered to have taken place in the advent of Jesus Christ, those words can only be seen as preparatory, witnessing, some of them at least, to their own futurity and hence unfinality' (p. 71 above). Again, however, as with the 'frames', that is not to say that the Old Testament texts can be made to say whatever the interpreter wants them to; it is simply that the interpreter as interpreter brings his own hermeneutical considerations to bear in determining how and where they may most usefully say what they have to say. And for Christians, these considerations will be Christian ones.

In drawing together, from both these hermeneutical conceptions, some concluding observations, it may be in order to reflect that after all it should not be too surprising to us that the faith of the interpreter should prove to be of such determinative importance in the processes of interpretation. In the end, we might say, interpretation is itself exactly an act of faith.

If, for instance, we have any historical imagination at all, we must discern the considerable awesomeness of the task this Christian, whose work we have surveyed, has taken upon himself. For this represents nothing less than a complete reworking and, in places, a profound criticism, of what we must assume had previously been for him almost inviolate religious truth. And yet this has been carried through without any trace of personal doubt or misgiving. On the contrary, the whole letter is filled with a confidence which can hardly be written off as propaganda over against his irresolute readers. Whence, we may ask, comes this manifest freedom, the confidence which is not arrogance, this combination of *hilaritas* and humility?

There can scarcely be any doubt that for this author the security from which he can be so bold is to be located precisely in his personal confidence in the things of which he writes to his friends. That is to say, quite simply, it is because he is so overwhelmed by the truth, for him, of what he describes as 'God's Word to us in (his) Son', that he can be so free in the criticism of his own past, however important that may once have been for him. In this sense we may say that his interpretation is the product of, or perhaps even an extension of, his faith.

But is this true only for this Christian writer? Must we not go on from there to say that in some sense every act of interpretation is an act of faith? When we dare to interpret statements of the past, is there not an element of 'risk', of openness and unfinality, an absence of mathematical precision,

something more akin to imagination or aesthetic practice?[10] Who is able
to say he has hit upon *the* meaning of a text or event? And yet, as in the
case of our writer, do we not have to speak also of a more or less joyful
'commitment' on the part of the interpreter to the meaning he thinks he
has found, since he cannot see better where else to turn?

If this is the case, a great deal more is being said in speaking of the faith-
confidence of the writer of Hebrews than a mere psychological description
of his approach to his task. To suggest that every act of interpretation is
in some degree an act of faith implies, at any rate certainly in the case of
Christian interpretation, that any proffered hermeneutical theory should
represent neither more nor less than an extension and formalisation of
the innermost structures of faith-existence, as applied to the texts and
traditions on which that faith is itself dependent. This is to suggest that
an understanding of Christian hermeneutics should be achieved out of
an analysis of faith's understanding of itself and its objects of reference.

This point of view, which arises from our reflection on the interplay
between the data (the conceptual 'frames') and the interpretative insights
of our ancient author, is the one we shall pursue in a more systematic way
in the following section.

2 Response

Interestingly, the modern hermeneutical problem is also constituted by
the interaction of forms and their meaning. Nearly always the forms in
question are written forms, texts, which have taken their shape in a past
now considerably distant from the interpreter. So that the question concerning their meaning is whether that meaning must be seen in terms of
their localised historical contexts and the limitations of their authors, or
whether the modern interpreter may bring to them an understanding of
his own, and find in them a meaning for his times not conceivable for the
ancient authors of the texts in question.

Though (as our study of Hebrews shows) the question about forms
and meanings can be found in biblical and classical authors,[11] the question
as it now presents itself is an essentially modern (i.e., post-Renaissance)
one. It has been brought about by, among other things, the increased
awareness of historical distances and, most especially since the seventeenth
century, by the elevation of rational principles as the primary method of
establishing the truth and falsity of things. The advancement of Reason as
that which alone has a self-evident cogency also set in motion the beginnings
of biblical criticism, in which the meanings of texts are brought under strict
and rationally conceived controls, with the consequent elimination of all
meanings arbitrarily or dogmatically conceived. As it has been put in a

sentence now quite widely known: 'Self-evident universal validity is now possessed only by what man as such with his rational and empirical faculties can know, perceive, prove and control.'[12] As a product of the modern age, the so-called critical historical method has learned to attend with ever sharpened vigilance to the actual text forms in their historical settings, in the knowledge that the only meanings now acceptable are those which are discovered on the basis of a rational investigation of the texts.

But the advent of the historical method, while eliminating the arbitrariness of speculative interpretation, has only sharpened the hermeneutical problem with respect to biblical texts. For, as is clear in the sentence just quoted, the rationalistic base of this method makes it necessarily a secular, humanistically orientated method. The secularity of the new method was, of course, implicit in the intellectual movements of the early seventeenth century in which demonstration and reasoned argument began to clash with theological opinion;[13] but what is there implicit becomes fully apparent in R. Descartes, in whose work 'the thinking subject . . . takes the place of the thought object', and in whom, consequently, 'the reflecting I moves to the centre of the universe'.[14] That these tendencies, which quickly caught the spirit of the age and were intensified through the period of the Deist controversies in England and of the Enlightenment in Germany, have continued to advance so as to become the hallmark of 'man come of age'[15] or 'the fourth man'[16] hardly needs elaboration. But the problem for the interpreter of biblical texts in an age such as this is that in the last analysis these methods, and their philosophical presuppositions, are found to be in fundamental opposition to the most obvious meaning and message of those texts. For, in their various ways, the intention of all of them is to speak in some way or another of God and his relationship with men.[17] How, when the ruling considerations of the time are secular ones, can an understanding be achieved of texts whose subject matter contradicts the most elementary presuppositions of the methods used to establish their meaning?

In this way the interchange between forms and meaning lies at the centre of the modern hermeneutical question, just as in the biblical formulation we have inspected. The history of the rise of critical biblical scholarship, with its hermeneutical consequences, has been reviewed often enough and need not be repeated here.[18] As perhaps might be expected, this history (i.e., from the late seventeenth century onwards) has manifested an oscillation between the two elements, so that interpreters have either preoccupied themselves with an historical consideration of the texts – attempting to establish their meaning on the basis of their lexical, gram-

matical and historical features – or, on the other hand, arguing that since
their subject matter (God) is not determined by such considerations,
neither is an understanding of their meaning so achieved. For the most
part, of course, interpreters of the modern period have been so impressed
by what has been called 'the new morality of judgement',[19] the self-
authenticating persuasiveness of the historical method, that it has been
this aspect of interpretation which has dominated very large tracts of the
discussion, while the question of the subject matter – God, and man in
relationship with him – has been allowed to assume very much the secondary
role. Nevertheless, from time to time, this other element in any genuine
understanding of the texts has been brought to the fore. This was most
impressively accomplished, of course, in the '180-degree turn' of K. Barth
in the early 1920s with his new realisation that 'the theme of the Bible is
the deity of *God*, more exactly God's *deity*'.[20] It was recognised at the
time, and is so now even more clearly, that this only raised the hermeneutical question more sharply than ever;[21] bringing the two elements of
biblical understanding more nearly into equipoise has not resolved the
problem. Indeed, R. Bultmann's dominant influence through the middle
and latter decades of this century has served in many ways to keep the two
apart, with his resolute reaffirmation of the Lessing principle that 'the
accidental truths of history can never establish the necessary truths of
reason',[22] and a consequent refusal to acknowledge that faith in God can
stand or fall with the fruits of scholarly industry. The subsequent misgivings about this point of view have served only to keep the hermeneutical
questions at the focal point of theological reflection.[23]

Yet even where the two aspects of biblical interpretation – the historically conditioned forms and their absolute subject matter – have been
seen as equally indispensable in any proper understanding of the bible,
there has nevertheless been a clear predisposition on the part of interpreters to give an account of the 'forms' and let the subject matter somehow take care of itself. Obviously the all-pervasive secularity in which all
interpretation now takes place, so that the model for, and the measure of,
appropriate understanding is the so-called 'modern man', is chiefly responsible for this. Moreover, the empirical, historical, objective elements of the
texts are clearly more easily discussed; it is easier to say what they 'meant'
than what they 'mean'.[24] But as we shall see, even the more sophisticated
hermeneutical inquiries, those which have preoccupied themselves with the
underlying structures of language and meaning, and attempt to give an
account from a phenomenological view as to how understanding of the
texts takes place, cannot in the end be said to be doing more than this
either. Even these efforts invariably end in the observation that language

(in the bible or in preaching etc.) opens up before people the decision or question of faith. Language as part of the structures of human existence, or existence itself, cannot contain, or offer, an understanding of 'God'.

In view of the intense preoccupation with the 'forms' of biblical expression, one fact must become quite striking: that is, the exact reversal of the priorities as seen by the bible writers, the interpretation of whose texts is here being attempted. As we saw in our study of Hebrews the forms for biblical expression are never more than 'partial and piecemeal' when seen in comparison with the meaning they are believed to contain. Even in respect to the traditions about Jesus, the interpretation of them outruns the information those traditions contain. What does in the end make those historically limited forms properly 'meaning-full' is not the meaning they hold within themselves, but is a meaning given to them, which may be spoken of either as the faith-insights brought by their interpreter, or as a meaning they acquire through God's Speaking in them.

In the bible as a whole, though undoubtedly a good deal of care has been given to the 'how' of communication, this seldom if ever rises to the surface of the discussion, as it constantly does in modern hermeneutical probing.[25] On the contrary, the texts themselves are fully taken up in pressing, pleading or proclaiming the fact and the person of God, apparently taking for granted that what 'God' means is either self-evident to the readers or listeners, or is able to make itself so. In fact, however religiously inclined or otherwise that world is judged to have been in comparison with our own, the insight that *God* makes *himself* understandable is apparent in every stream of the New Testament writings – either through the Holy Spirit,[26] or a concept of election,[27] or in faith's interpretation of otherwise inert phenomena, and so on. Moreover, it should not be assumed that 'God' functions meaningfully in the texts because they are 'intramural', i.e., written 'from faith to faith'; in fact the letter we have examined is written from faith to incipient non-faith. One might certainly object that there is a residual modicum of faith which facilitates understanding. That would be true, but does not alter the judgement that it must be God who will do the speaking if understanding is to take place (1.1f; cf. 6.3).

Is it even conceivable that a satisfactory theory of biblical hermeneutics might be formulated in the latter twentieth century which attempts to take altogether seriously the priority attributed by the texts themselves to the activity of God in the interpretative and communicative processes? As radical as that proposal might seem in face of the current preponderance of the critical method, several factors from various directions are at least suggestive. Not least is the already mentioned discrepancy between the methodological approach of the interpreter who seeks to understand texts which themselves manifest a quite opposite, or at least different, way of understanding their subject matter; additionally it seems not inappropriate to ask as soberly as possible how solid have been the advances in our understanding of the texts (as distinct, shall we say, from our knowledge about them) which two and a half centuries of critical refinement have brought,[28] and what can be the significance of the apparently mounting *un*certainty which attends current, technical biblical scholarship;[29] thirdly, though unusual, such a proposal is by no means unheard of. From time to time there have been statements of misgiving about the now customary weight of importance given to the critical procedures, including, of course, the major upheaval caused by the publication in 1917 of the first edition of K. Barth's commentary on Romans, but including also a number of other less-well-noticed protests.[30]

In our own attempts to understand how interpretation takes place in the Epistle to the Hebrews, we saw that this is not other than an extension and particular application of the interpreter's faith. We suggested accordingly that an understanding of (Christian) interpretation is likely to be most properly achieved by coming to it from an analysis of (Christian) faith and its organisation of its own interior understanding of itself. Whereas, we have seen, the priority of importance attached to the historical critical method in our age has dictated that hermeneutical procedures have moved from criticism of the texts to an attempted faith-understanding of them, we shall suggest that the more natural and useful order is to move from an analysis of faith-understanding to criticism.[31] This will be on the basis of the directions we have already uncovered in our examination of a biblical text, but will also be reinforced by certain inner contradictions which seem to be present in the currently prevailing movements from criticism to faith.

(a) Faith's referent

Every hermeneutical theory depends upon the assumption of a universal order or structure underlying the particularity of cultural conditionedness. It is only on the assumption of this kind of continuity that there can be any possibility of recognition by people in one moment of history of the self-expression of those belonging to others widely distant in custom as well as space and time. Only on the prior assumption that there is some continuity which transcends and is universally true of the human situation, can 'understanding' be safely assumed. The names and descriptions of this universal structure have varied widely; they include the Hegelian 'spirit' (*Geist*) or Romantic 'experience' (*Erlebnis*), the nineteenth-century preoccupation with history, and the Heideggerian, Bultmannian interest in existence. More recently there has been an intense interest in showing the overarching significance of language (M. Heidegger, E. Fuchs, G. Ebeling, H.-G. Gadamer), and the most newly emergent candidate has been structuralism (F. de Saussure, C. Lévi-Strauss). These have all been employed in the first instance as a way of giving an account of the world, but then as offering possibilities for the achievement of understanding across widely disparate situations.

Most of these represent in their own ways some form of metaphysical Idealism,[32] conceptions achieved by way of elaborate phenomenological analysis of 'how things are', before they can be put to their hermeneutical uses. There is thus always involved the so-called 'hermeneutical circle', an explanation of the general from the particular, which generality then provides the possibility for understanding particular situations. Frequently the idea of 'dialectic' or 'conversation' therefore is found involving something like the Bultmannian 'preunderstanding' apart from which 'understanding' cannot find its place.

One element of high significance in all this for the biblical interpreter is the near apotheosis to which some of these structures used as hermeneutical models are lifted. Admittedly, certainly in their Christian deployment, they do not ostensibly take the place of 'God', so that in Bultmann, Fuchs and Ebeling, existence or language is never seen as other than the instrument or medium through which the issues of faith and decision make themselves apparent. Yet it cannot be without significance that at least some of Bultmann's students were convinced that this differentiation of 'God' as a separate entity represented in Bultmann an essential inconsistency, so that instead of 'demythologisation' he should have gone on to 'dekerygmatisation' or a more radically 'secular gospel'.[33] The problems implicit in the attempt to separate off an outdated world-view ('the three-decker universe ... which Enlightenment old and new will never tire of referring to')[34] from the authentic understandings of existence in the biblical writings, and the limitations of the concept of self-understanding as a means of access to the biblical message,[35] have been reviewed often enough.[36] What is rather more to our point here is to note the 'phenomenological' character of all the Existence hermeneutical theories as these have been developed from the philosophies of E. Husserl and M. Heidegger through their Christian adaptations by Bultmann and Fuchs.[37] Consequently, as we said, it remains ambiguous in these hermeneutical structures as to what, precisely, it is which effects the connection between the biblical text and a contemporary reader – whether it is really God who speaks, or whether it is the summons to (by?) 'authentic existence' or 'the language character of existence'.

By way of example, a short exposition of E. Fuchs' formulation may be in order. One important way of construing the problem, for Fuchs, is in terms of the notion of the Real and how language functions in respect to this ('Das Problem der Wirklichkeit und die Sprache').[38] Fuchs notes that there are many different kinds of reality. The possibility of my becoming a murderer may haunt me just as effectively (*wirklich*) as if I were in fact (*in Wirklichkeit*) a murderer.[39] So the Real is not reducible to simple empirical categories. So then how shall we test our experience of the Real for truthfulness,[40] and how shall we relate the Reality which is thus not bound in space and time to the present moment of our time-bound existence?[41] The answer is that this is the function of language: 'There belongs to Reality the possibility of an appropriate *statement* concerning the presence of the Real!'[42] 'An eternal silence would mean the elimination of the Real.'[43] So that it is in language that 'the Real is helped to its *truth*: in language the truth of the Real first makes its appearance'.[44] It is also to be noted that it is in this coming of Reality into language that a man discovers his own existence: 'Man exists linguistically between summons and response.'[45] Now side by side with these statements, which are clearly enough phenomenological observations on the linguistic structures of Reality, we may be permitted to set other statements of Fuchs in which Jesus is presented as the 'text' for Christian or faith-understanding: 'Jesus' proclamation shows us that he understood himself as the one "who brought to speech" the call of God in the final hour';[46] indeed, Jesus 'intends to "bring God into speech" '.[47]

Now it is clearly not Fuchs' intention to confuse God with Reality, or equate them. But it is also clear that the model for a person's hearing of the gospel in texts now distant from him has been discovered, not in the inner dynamics of the gospel itself, but in the investigation of language as a phenomenon, quite generally. Whereas the earlier (Liberal) confidence in the capacities of historical investigation has been called seriously in question by the Existentialists (most radically by Bultmann), this seems to have been replaced by a confidence in, and dependence upon, other forms of human communicability.[48] God is not seen as the medium of his own communication of himself (i.e., in the Holy Spirit etc.); language is the bridge across which communication, or understanding, passes.

But as we saw with the biblical statements, any 'forms' which we can find for the expression of God's Word are always too small – neither the biblical texts nor language itself can contain *God*. This becomes clear as Fuchs finds that he has to distinguish between different levels of language – between language as 'event' and 'the word as brute fact', or between an inner and an outer hearing.[49] In fact it transpires that only when 'the word "gets home" ' can it be said to have been 'heard, in the sense of the New Testament texts';[50] so 'language, in its outer form, can basically be repeated at will, but is nevertheless unique, if indeed the word leads to the kind of hearing which unites mood and conscience in the hearer, because the word has "struck home" '.[51] But it is precisely this difference between inner and outer hearing which is said, by the New Testament, to be the work of the Holy Spirit;[52] between those who have 'ears to hear' and those who do not.[53] In short, 'language', no more than the text forms themselves, can do more than offer *possibilities* for the communication of the Word of God; to ask it to do more than that, to ask it to function as *the* medium for an understanding of faith-formulations in the past, is to ask it to do more than it is capable of achieving.

That Christian hermeneutical theorists should attempt to employ such conceptual tools from philosophical sources is altogether understandable in its motivation, given the problems our secularised age has with 'God'. For such concepts are obviously open to exploration and interrogation in a way which God is not. But in their parallelism to the old theologies based on an *analogia entis*, such formulations suffer similar frustrations: as we have seen, the subject of the analogy outstrips the analogues. And, further, to the extent that the subject is contained within the analogy, it is rendered other and less than was intended. That is to say, to the extent that language or existence is allowed to function in the place of God has the point of the exercise been defeated.[54] For, in contradistinction to the radicals who have seen fit to push on to give a 'godless' account of 'God', Bultmann and his more conservative disciples have certainly wanted to allow 'God' to be *God*.

Herein is something of the irony of so much recent hermeneutical exploration. Curiously, but quite clearly, those who have felt so strongly the need to give an account to others (to the so-called 'modern man') of how the bible functions in the modern world do so precisely because they find themselves so conscripted. It is precisely *as Christians* that they have been launched upon their phenomenological investigations.[55] This is not at all to deny that they may have found for themselves in the process considerable clarification as to how their understanding has come about. It nevertheless remains true that virtually no one, in the times in which we live, has the least interest in knowing how the bible may speak to 'modern man' without a vested interest, which is to say, without having himself been spoken *to*.[56]

To fail to see this, to attempt to investigate the persuasiveness of the 'forms' without perceiving the limited and at best suggestive nature of these - which is another way of saying that their meaning or significance is greater than, and is given to, them – is to commit oneself to endless discussion and confusion. For whatever forms we may find to help us 'give an account', these cannot give us God; that is why at the end of the labyrinthine discussions we are invariably left with words like 'silence', 'parable', 'metaphor'.[57]

Lest this be misunderstood, it is important to say at once that to speak about the Speaking of God as that which establishes hermeneutical continuity between the texts and their meaning is not to say that 'God' here has somehow been abstracted as a precondition for that which is (humanly) knowable or that he is knowable apart from the human formulations which are our biblical texts. It was the correct insight of R. Bultmann that the God there spoken of is never other than God in relationship with man, which means that man cannot be spoken of other than as before God. What was not correct was his inference that theology must therefore become anthropology.[58] It is 'man before God' in both covenants, in Hebrews, which necessitates the systems for expiation and atonement, and which, in turn, becomes so significant, hermeneutically, in the understanding of Jesus and his accomplishments.[59] Or it is 'man as summoned to pilgrimage' which sets up the correspondences between the wilderness generation and the Christians, and so on. Yet, we have seen, 'anthropologically' the similarities between these moments are slight; what permits them to be brought into continuity with one another is the conviction that God has been present in both.

In summary, the hermeneutical task, we said, is to find some way of giving an account of the way in which the *meaning* of the biblical texts may be discovered. Herein lies, at an initial level, the problem encountered in attempting to understand any formulation from a distant cultural setting, but for biblical interpreters there is entailed the much more problematic issue of achieving an understanding of the subject matter of *these* texts – which, if it ever was moderately readily understood, is, in our age, rapidly becoming less so. In this impasse, we have said, it has been the understandable, but eventually misleading, response of Christian hermeneutical theorists to investigate ever more intensively first the lexical forms themselves, and then the phenomenological factors behind the understanding of such forms, in the hope of discovering a key to their understanding. But we have already seen that the texts themselves indicate a quite different way to their own interpretation. Their meaning, they assert, is not to be read off their surface at all, but is a meaning which is brought to them by their believing interpreter, or is given to them by the God who is their subject matter. To reaffirm: a Christian hermeneutic cannot be other than a hermeneutic of faith.[60]

(b) Faith's self-criticism

To make the Speaking of God the beginning and basis for a Christian hermeneutic must certainly sound to many reminiscent of the early statements of K. Barth, or even more alarmingly as if the whole development of critical biblical scholarship is being abandoned in favour of a pre-critical arbitrariness. Since that is not what is being proposed we must now turn to the function of the text forms and their historical-contextual settings, in the overall determination of their meaning. The hermeneutical question, it will be recalled, is that which is constituted by the interrelationship of texts and their meanings.

Any word, any text, any statement which is not nonsense has somewhere a 'boundary' to its meaning. It is only insofar as it does not mean anything and everything that it can mean *something*. An important part of any serious discussion is the determination of what shall be the boundaries of the meaning of the words to be used, which is to say, the establishment of their definitions. Certainly it is true that these boundaries are not fixed immoveably; they can be stretched and changed. Nor do they form a mathematical line, so to speak; they have a certain breadth and areas of grey margin. But they certainly exist. Diagrammatically the thing might be put so:

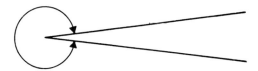

in which the area between the boundary lines represents the possible, or agreed, range of meanings of the words to be used, and the outer circle indicates the area of meanings which have been agreed to be 'out of bounds', or which would simply bring chaos into the discussion if such meanings were attached, without notice, to the words being used.

In terms of biblical interpretation, the rise of critical techniques from the seventeenth century onwards approximates in a real way to the establishment of such boundaries. It is true that the quest for proper meanings, or the elimination of the purely speculative, had been set in train as early as the reformers of the sixteenth century with their principles based on the grammatical sense of the words.[61] But it is also true that the motivations behind those principles were quite different to those which were coming into force in the middle seventeenth century which were rationally, rather than theologically, conceived.[62] The clashes between the Deists and their Orthodox opponents and the dawning of the Enlightenment in eighteenth-century Germany accelerated the need for, and the accomplishment of, clear and universally acceptable criteria for the establishment of meanings.[63] In sum these now amount to what we call the critical historical method: the definition, as accurately as can be achieved, of the actual lexical meanings of the words, the establishment of the historical context of the text and its author, and the establishment of the intention of the author. The more clearly the self-authenticating power of Reason asserted itself in this age of Reason the less possible it became for interpreters to attach meaning-at-will to the text forms. So, by and large, the situation remains.

But now the question must be: to which area, in terms of our diagram, do these critical principles belong? Inside the boundary lines, where the implication would be that meanings depend upon rational criteria? Or outside the lines, which would imply that their task is to eliminate all the false meanings, but not to do more than this? Or does it matter?

That it does matter, and matter seriously, needs no further demonstration than that till this very day the relationship between the critical investigation of the texts and the establishment of their meaning remains a vexatious question.[64]

Nor can there be a great deal of doubt that the origins of biblical criticism in the beginnings of the age of Reason gave strong impetus to an assumption that the critical method could and should be the means for establishing meanings (i.e., from within the boundary lines). Certainly it is true that there has always been an accompanying unease about this, felt more urgently in some Christian circles than others; but the tendency has been clear enough and is seen most obviously in the confidence with which the 'assured results' were greeted in late-nineteenth- and early-twentieth-century Liberalism. Even today, as many of those 'results' are known to have cracked or broken, and in an age which knows all too well that meticulous scholarship does not necessarily lead to a health-giving understanding of the texts, the anxiety persists that to abandon the reasonableness of the critical approach would be like casting off upon a trackless sea. The assumption prevails that it will be a critical interrogation of them which will yield up the meaning of the texts.[65] But we have already seen from the texts themselves that that is not their expectation. And now two more reasons can be found which challenge the assumption that criticism can establish meanings. The first challenge is directed toward the *rationalistic* bases of the critical method. This offensive has been mounted most magisterially in our times by H.-G. Gadamer, the ironic title of whose book *Truth and Method*, exactly states the dilemma. His point is that methods (scientifically conceived ones, at any rate) cannot establish truth, which is infinitely larger than to be confined within any methodology: '[This investigation] is concerned to seek that experience of truth that transcends the sphere of the control of scientific method wherever it is to be found ...'[66] It is for these reasons that he sets out from a consideration of aesthetic truth and is constantly preoccupied with the 'human sciences' as over against the 'physical sciences'.[67]

The problem of the rationalistic tendencies in critical methods may be exposed by asking about *the* meaning of any given text. Or, alternatively, one may ask: which of its innumerable interpreters may be said finally, definitively, exhaustively to have understood it? Has this been accomplished when at last the meaning or intention of its author has been established? Or can it not have an even more profoundly significant meaning for someone who comes upon it in an entirely different historical setting?[68] Is it not true that, often at any rate, an author may well not have understood the half of what he has written, so that in Schleiermacher's famous phrase the object of interpretation is 'to understand what has been said ... better than the originator'?[69] Rather clearly, the limit to which critical scholarship can go in this respect is to say what it was the author *meant*; but that is by no means the same as saying what his statement *means*.[70] For this, there is required not the elimination of imaginative skills as in the critical method, but precisely that creative flair which can make connections between two points – the text and the present situation – which do not lie upon the surface of either but, when made, result in an infinite and mutual enrichment of both.[71] That is why the 'application' of a text, regarded so suspiciously by critical scholarship, is necessarily part of any proper understanding of it.[72]

But a second problem, and from a Christian point of view an even more serious one, with the assumption that critical techniques may establish meanings lies in the profoundly *sceptical* qualities of the historical method. This is already perfectly apparent in R. Descartes, the founder of modern epistemology, one of whose first principles was 'Never to accept anything as true if I had not evident knowledge of its being so'.[73] We have already seen (above, p. 111) how the explicit secularism of modern (Cartesian) theories of knowledge has raised the hermeneutical problem to the sharpest possible pitch for biblical interpreters. For the subject matter, in one way or another, of practically every bible statement is God. But 'God' is precisely what is called in question by the anthropocentric modern methodology. To permit the critical method to operate inside the boundary lines of the determination of meanings of biblical texts is already to have silenced the texts in their intention. For, as is now recognised quite widely, the most basic posture of the critical practitioner is one of methodological doubt: 'A new ideal of judgement has gripped the intellect of Western man ... The old morality celebrated faith and belief as virtues and regarded doubt as sin. The new morality celebrates methodological scepticism and is distrustful of passion in matters of inquiry.'[74] So that the issue really may be put in its sharpest terms by asking wherein this systematised scepticism is supposed to prepare for faith, for that is the implicit assumption in supposing that critical methods can lead to an understanding of the biblical texts. Yet this is the programme to which modern hermeneutical theorists are committed in their elevation of the 'modern man' (which is in fact a euphemism for 'secular' or 'unbelieving' man) as the measure and model for how the texts may be understood.[75]

For all this, it is difficult to know how anyone can now seriously wish to abandon the critical method for the jungle of allegorical or speculative interpretation. And indeed the answer is not to call for its abandonment, as has occasionally happened, even quite recently, in more conservative Christian circles.[76] It is simply to demand that it functions where it properly belongs. In terms of our diagram, this means the setting of the boundary lines of meaning from the outside, or, more clearly, showing which meanings would be illegitimate, 'out of bounds'.

In point of fact, this is not at all inconsistent with the motives behind the erection of the critical method in its inception – the objects of its criticism were precisely the false and arbitrary meanings with which the texts were being festooned for dogmatic and personal reasons. Nor is it an unduly negative statement of the critical task to say that it functions from outside rather than inside the meanings of the texts; for as we saw in introducing our diagram, to state where are the boundary lines for meaning is of vital importance if a word or text is indeed to mean something. But now, just as its lack of suitability was exposed when seen in terms of its saying what a text means, precisely those same characteristics make it pre-eminently suitable for saying what the texts may not mean. So it is that its built-in scepticism allows it particularly well to uncover the false, the forced, the unjustified exegesis; and its rationalistic base permits it to show *reasons* why this or that interpretation is impermissible. We must reiterate: the establishing of boundaries for meaning is no secondary or negative task. Meaning could not exist without it.[77]

So far our discussion has proceeded in terms of the modern problems of texts and their meanings, especially as these problems have been brought about by the advent of the critical historical method. But now it is appropriate to gather up, from our reflections on the texts of Hebrews, our 'permission' and 'double negation' formulations (see above, pp. 105ff). At several different levels, most notably in connection with the Christians' use of the Old Testament texts, and in the author's interpretative reflection upon the traditions about Jesus, we established as a principle that while the interpretation could not be said to be based in the original data, nevertheless it was not thereby excluded and was accordingly 'permitted' by those data. In both cases, though especially in that of the 'Jesus as priest' interpretation, we saw that certain factors were easily imaginable which *would* render the interpretation illegitimate and hence untenable, namely, if what could be known, historically and empirically, contradicted the interpretation which was being attempted, or if the interpretation was seen to be 'manufacturing' too many of the 'facts' for its own viability. In these ways, we decided, the data could give or withhold 'permission'; interpretations were only possible ('permitted') which were *not* excluded. Yet, given this 'permission', we said, the interpretation always wants, indeed finds itself constrained, to pass beyond the data, to say more than can be shown. The same conceptions, we saw, could also be applied to the text forms which are acknowledged to be πολυμερῶς καὶ πολυτρόπως, yet certainly 'permit' an interpretation of themselves as linked to one another and to their own fulfilment in 'the Word in the Son'.

Now we are able to see that the same considerations apply to the modern problems of texts and meanings. While it cannot say, for the reasons we have seen, what the meaning of any given biblical text will be, the critical historical method can certainly say what that meaning shall not be.[78] So, in the lexicographical refinement of the definitions of words, the critical method forbids the false construing of those words; in determining the historical setting for a text, criticism eliminates a false, timeless view of them in which 'bible truths' can be linked together at random; and in clarifying the intentions of an author, any meanings which would contradict those intentions have already been ruled out of court.[79] But because the subject matter of the texts is bigger than the method (and indeed contradicts its presuppositions), and because the meaning of a text is not static but keeps finding new points of meaningfulness in various new contexts, in the end we have to say that the critical historical method cannot do more than draw the boundaries; all the meanings which are not excluded are possible or potential ones.

So far we have spoken mainly of the inappropriateness of the critical method within the faith-interpretation processes. It therefore remains to be said, more clearly, that faith itself *requires* the kind of critical controls which the historical method provides; just as words are meaningless if not defined, neither can faith be faith if it is not aware, deliberately, of what is believable and what is not (or not any longer). For example, we said in our discussion of Jesus that if certain things could be shown about the traditions, that they had been altered too seriously or even fabricated, the faith-interpretation of them was not free to disregard that knowledge.

To do so would already be to show the presence, not of faith, but of some form of ideology, self-contained, self-sufficient, self-propagating. The same things must now be said with respect to the biblical texts. For its own health and viability, faith *as faith* is committed to a knowledge of the fruits of scholarly industry. Not to be so committed is already to have passed from faith to ideology. This, then, is what is meant in the section heading above, 'Faith's self-criticism'. That, from the point of view here developed, is the correct designation of critical scholarship. To see it in this way is to move from faith to criticism. It is for faith continually to be asking itself: what is to be believed? what is believable? From this point of view critical and scholarly interrogation of the texts has a clear and necessary role. But that is quite otherwise when the directions are reversed, when the move is attempted from criticism to faith, when the goal and test case for authentic understanding of the texts is taken to be 'modern (unbelieving) man'. To try so to move, as the prevailing hermeneutical methods seem to do, can only result in endless confusion.

(c) Faith and its traditions

To be an interpreter means to be much more than a purveyor of information from the past. At the same time an interpreter is never done with that past with which he must continually be in touch if he is to be an interpreter of it. An interpreter who achieves an understanding of the biblical texts in terms of their subject matter is especially indebted to the traditions within which those texts have been interpreted before him. But because it is not just a matter of understanding the ways in which they have been understood, but of understanding them from within his own situation, he must exercise a freedom over against those traditions, even in his indebtedness to them.

We have seen this very clearly in our studies of the letter to the Hebrews. The author is a Christian who has inherited a very long and full tradition. Almost certainly we are right to assume that he has previously been a Jewish believer, but even if that has not been the case then at very least as a Christian he has made the Jewish traditions in scripture his own. But we have seen how, in his attention to those traditions, and in his concern to understand his new-found faith in light of them and vice versa, he has found a quite astonishing freedom with respect to the past from which he has come. It is now of importance for our understanding of the interpretative process itself that we pay attention to the precise balances in this relationship between the interpreter and his traditions.

In the first place we must certainly reaffirm this writer's complete dependence upon the traditions for all the conceptual 'frames' (as we have called them; pp. 99, 103f etc.) within which he sets about understanding Jesus as the Word of God.[80] We have set this out in the exegesis of chapters 1 and 2, and in more summary form at the head of this present chapter. It involves a multivalent application of Old Testament religious insights and expectations to the contents of Christian understanding – ranging from the central relationship between revelation and redemption categories to small illustrative details drawn from Old Testament personalities as warnings or examples for Christian behaviour. The sheer scale on which this has been accomplished may even occasionally prevent us from seeing it, so extensive has it been; to ask, for example, what this Christian's understanding of Christ and the Christian community would have been like without his Old Testament models is so hypothetical as to be pointless, *except* that it reminds us how dependent he has been, as is every thinker, upon the thought-forms of his past.

But we have already drawn attention to the freedom which permits this Christian to 'rework', in a most radical way, precisely these traditions on which he is so dependent, and from some points of view to reject them as outmoded. The previous 'frames' have now been made to function in quite new ways by the bringing of them into new contexts, so that the 'frames' are not destroyed, but take an entirely new meaning. It is clear that this kind of hermeneutical freedom and creativity is only possible where the 'meaning' of the original conception is not regarded as somehow intrinsically contained within it in its contextual setting; its meaning, or rather its meaning for the moment, is discovered for it, in some sense is given to it, by the interpreter's action in bringing it into the context of his own situation. When these two, conceptual 'frame' and present situation, are brought together in the freedom and creativity which belong to the interpreter's craft, then 'meaning' may be said to have been achieved. Yet this freedom is not by any means absolute. Just as we saw that the freedom to find the meaning of words is bounded by the lexical and historical limitations of the text, the interpreter of previous conceptions must maintain an identifiable correspondence with the 'frames' of the conceptions he is interpreting, if indeed he is to be their interpreter. To demonstrate this we might develop our previous diagrammatic model into three dimensions (see overleaf).

The earlier conceptual 'frame' manifests about itself a given sense content and also defines patterns of relationships. The example nearest to hand, of course, is the way in which the themes of sin, sacrifice, priesthood and atonement in Hebrews all stand together in a definite relationship, one to another, and which then belong to a larger relational pattern of revelation and redemption. It is this pattern of relationships, we have seen, which has

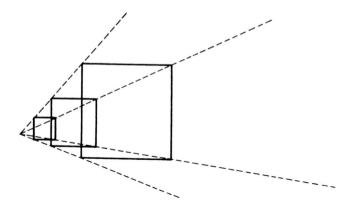

been preserved right across the divisions between the covenants in Hebrews and which allows us to speak of the new as an interpretation of the old. To interpret in any way adequately is to preserve, in all the divergence of the new situation, a recognisable continuity in terms of these inner and outer relationships. So that the previous 'frame' is seen to provide what again we might call boundaries, or (since we are now more conscious of the development inherent in proper interpretation) 'horizons' along which the interpreter may travel. To remain somewhere within these 'horizons', to show how earlier formulations may in new situations take quite new dimensions of meaning, yet in recognisable dependence upon and continuity with those earlier insights, is to be an interpreter of them. To move outside the horizons thus set for the interpreter (or at any rate, too seriously and too often) is to give not an interpretation, but a misinterpretation. It is to destroy the models in their givenness. Nevertheless, within the horizons the interpreter has freedom which indeed, to be an interpreter, he must use with all possible skill and creativity. Not to do so is again to fail to be an interpreter of the previous ideas; that is to be simply their custodian, a keeper of antiquities.[81]

The question of an interpreter and his traditions obviously touches upon at least two of the most pressing problems in biblical understanding today: these are the questions of the authority of the canonical scriptures in contemporary church life and theology, and the question of interpretations already within the canonical material, or of canon within the canon. These questions are too large to be opened up here in any depth, but one or two suggestions are perhaps provided from our reflections about one early Christian interpreter.

(a) The tradition, either in its elongated form as understood by Tridentine Roman Catholicism or in its authoritative beginnings as understood in the *sola scriptura* of Protestantism, has more regularly than otherwise been seen as exercising an authority over the church of any given age. As is well enough known, this is a characteristic of Christian self-organisation as far back as the New Testament and further. From the earliest times there seems to have been some sort of 'apostolic' *paradosis*, and the preservation of words and actions of Jesus signifies that these were held, from the beginning, to have more than usual importance and authority.[82] Side by side with these were set the scriptures of Judaism: 'Christianity is unique among the great religions in being born with a Bible in its cradle.'[83]

This authority, resident in the traditions, has caused endless discussion for the obvious reason that there is no clear demarcation between the tradition itself and that over which it is supposed to rule. The questions are summed up as crisply as one could wish in the classic conundrum: did the tradition produce the bible or did the bible produce the tradition? Nevertheless the authority with which the tradition has been supposed to be invested is seen as a safeguarding mechanism, a means of controlling the life and theology of Christians in the present on the basis of what has been understood in the past.

Today, for various reasons, the concept of authority - even with respect to authoritative traditions - has come under serious review.[84] Some of these reasons are rather clearly reflexive responses to the crisis in authoritarian relationships in the modern world at large, and some arise through genuine difficulty among Christians in seeing where the exact authority lies and how it is meant to bear upon the ongoing situation.

From our reflections on the attitudes of the author of Hebrews two insights may appear to have some relevance. One must be the sense of freedom, already remarked on, with which this early Christian has quite cheerfully taken upon himself his responsibilities as interpreter. We can only say that without this freedom over against his own traditions, his provocatively original conceptions of Christ as priest could never have come into being. We need also to be reminded, in this context, that one element of utmost importance in this creative interplay with the traditions has been the determinative influence of his own reading of his own situation; this in two respects. The first must be his personal convictions, which have sparked the whole great reinterpretative exercise of the Old Testament ordinances. We may say quite categorically that the most basic consideration of all in an estimation of the writer of Hebrews as interpreter is that *he is a Christian*. A moment's reflection will suffice to show that beneath every crucial interpretative insight or attitude which he brings to the Old Testament texts and institutions, it is his Christian convictions which are decisive. Other hermeneutical considerations - not without their importance, admittedly – such as his Alexandrian predispositions, are of much less importance relatively. To this extent, this early Christian interpreter has, necessarily, preserved an independence in face of his own traditions.

In a second, not unimportant, respect we can see this happening, too. That is in the way the so-called 'hermeneutic of eschatological existence' has been allowed to be the hermeneutical screen which governs the extent to which elements in the Old Testament are still relevant to Christians, and which irrelevant. Here, again, the interpretation is controlled by the needs of the present situation rather than by any authority from the past.

And yet, when all this has been said, we dare not lose sight of the indispensable importance that this past has for the writer, in providing for him what we have called the 'frames' within which to order his Christian reflection.[85] We have also seen that the task of interpretation is such that for all his freedom within them the interpreter, if he is to *be* their interpreter, is bounded by certain definable 'horizons'. It is possible to say what would be a *mis*translation of the old, or where the new point of view had ceased to be an interpretation at all.

To this consideration we may bring another similar to it but arising from our own situation now twenty centuries past the crucial foundational events for Christian faith. It emerged to some extent in our earlier reflections on the nature of the relationship between Christian interpretations of Jesus and the primitive memories of him, but may now be seen to have a rather different point of application. It will be recalled that we said that for faith to be faith and not a self-generating ideology there is required to be a clear distinction between the events which are being interpreted and the interpretations themselves.[86] It is this distinction which continues to remind believers that their faith has no independent existence of its own but depends upon a truth or a body of knowledge given to it (*extra nos*); only to the extent that it is able to state with clarity the direction of the relationship, from objective fact to creative interpretation, is it delivered from dangerous temptations of a faithless self-affirmation.

To bring these two considerations together is to see that no matter how courageously Christian interpreters take their stance in their present situations,[87] as long as they are *Christian* interpreters they are never done with the past, and especially the particular cluster of events in the past in which the Christian faith sees itself as grounded. To loose oneself from these, and from as accurate information as one can have of them, is to cease to be Christian, as well as to cease to be an interpreter. For, as we have just said, to lose sight of the 'givenness' of the originating events is to fall back into the self-authenticating, self-generating syndrome of ideology. However confused the motives may have been and however complicated the

specific historical details surrounding it may now seem, that is unambiguously the guiding consideration in the establishing of a Christian scriptural
canon,[88] namely, the recognition that ongoing interpretation, however
free within its horizons, must as long as it calls itself Christian have recourse
to the events which stand at its head.[89]

But again, this is now a recognition made by faith-interpretation itself
out of its own knowledge of itself and the conditions for its continuing
authenticity. As the attempt to extract the meaning of the words by critical techniques was seen to be quite the wrong way to come at the genuinely
important function of scholarly control, so here the attempt to set up the
tradition as an externally legislative directive for Christian life and theology
is quite to misunderstand the relationship. It is not that the tradition
asserts itself authoritatively over the church, or faith, but that faith out of
its knowledge of itself and its own criteria for authenticity, *recognises* and
submits itself to the normative importance of the traditions it has inherited, most especially (for Catholic and Protestant) the traditions which are
encapsulated in the documents now bound together as the New Testament.[90]

(*b*) We said that what we have seen from the letter to the Hebrews also
touches upon the question of a canon within the canon. Part of the scripture-tradition problem is that already within the New Testament scriptures
the process of interpretation has made some way. Especially in the case of
the parables, this is clear. Exacting research has shown that a very large
number of the parables had, in their telling, quite different settings, and
therefore rather different meanings, than the ones they now have.[91] But
in many other gospel narratives, too, the activity of early Christian interpreters seems quite evident, and our own letter, the Epistle to the Hebrews,
is an especially fine document in early Christian interpretation.[92] The
question then becomes: given the authoritative importance of the early
Christian traditions, which of these is to be taken as the more authoritative – the form they now exist in, or the form which may, more or less,
accurately, be recovered by patient scholarly research? Is one version
(shall we say, a Johannine version) more or less authoritative than a
Synoptic version of what is apparently the same incident? Is the Pauline
'justification by faith' formula to be regarded as *the* measure by which
everything else is to be assessed? (see above, pp. 97f).

Here the freedom of a Christian such as the writer of Hebrews, in allowing his own situation and that of his readers to be a factor in deciding the
applicability of the traditions under which they stand, seems to be instruc-
tive. This is not, as we have seen, to give the bible a nose of wax, for the
traditions themselves prescribe certain boundaries or horizons within
which they must speak if they are to be taken in any way seriously. In the

case in point (the question of interpretations already within the authoritative traditions), this must mean that a present-day interpreter is presented with a whole range of hermeneutical suggestions – some of which more clearly stand nearer to the origins of the traditions and some of which have already travelled some distance in terms of their interpretative development. The freedom of the modern interpreter then lies in his liberty to choose which of these several hermeneutical attempts applies most fittingly to his present situation, always in critical assessment of their own legitimacy *as* interpretations,[93] and endeavouring to understand as well as he can the factors which have given them their present shape.[94]

In this description of the hermeneutical task and its relationship to previous traditions has lain an implicit explanation of the questions which were stated at the outset of our own investigation of Hebrews to be the ones which would rule, as far as possible, in the inquiry. These, it may be recalled, were: 'If [the author] were here, would he recognise and give assent to the inferences we have drawn from his work? And in drawing up the formulations we have, could we have arrived at these quite independently of the text, or did it provide the indispensable starting point for our own reflections?' (p. 4 above). Now these may be clarified. To keep before one, as far as is humanly possible, the first of these questions is to recognise that while, however hard we may try, we cannot stand exactly where he stood by reason of the obvious differences between his times and ours, yet his work does provide certain definitions of meaning within which we must proceed if we are not to misinterpret, mistranslate, his theological achievements. And the second question recognises that no matter how far along these horizons we may find ourselves to have travelled in the centuries which divide his work from ours, ours simply could not even have begun without the conceptual 'frames' with which he has provided us, and which he in turn has inherited from his own past.

Such is the relation of each new interpreter to the tradition of which he is the inheritor and to which, in his own time, he makes his contribution.

(d) Faith and its questioners

One consequence of the directions set by the origins of the modern critical movement, we have seen, is its acceptance of unbelief as the criterion for Christian meaningfulness. This has generally been true throughout the development of critical techniques, with only a few exceptions, as in the hermeneutics of K. Barth. So, today, 'modern man' (which means 'secular man') is taken to be the norm towards which Christian interpretation should work: 'The decision not to contemplate this disjunction [between a modern man's understanding of himself and the understanding for which faith calls] is tantamount to the decision to withdraw into a linguistic ghetto.'[95] The question therefore occurs: in attempting to take faith as the starting point for a Christian hermeneutic, rather than its conclusion, has this or some such similar decision been made for a Christian ghetto existence?

It is true, certainly, that the people for whom the letter to the Hebrews is written are Christians, and that there is therefore a nucleus of common understanding between writer and readers. But it would be quite misleading to lose sight of the serious erosion of this Christian faith, and that the tendency on the part of the readers is in fact not toward a faith-commitment, but in the opposite direction. It is more accurate to say that the letter is written from faith to incipient unbelief than from faith to faith.

This suggests that the believing interpreter of the traditions is not necessarily to be daunted by the unbelief of his readers or hearers, but, from within those traditions themselves and the faith-understanding they exhibit, already finds reasons for attempting to address himself to interpreting for unbelief. This, we have suggested, is not a confidence in his own capacities as interpreter, or in the forms he is trying to interpret, but in the fact (experienced before and expected again) that the God to whom the traditions point has the capacity to make himself understandable. We have seen that that is true also, not just of the biblical writers, but of the modern-day hermeneutical theorists who, virtually without exception, are themselves committed *to* the hermeneutical task by way of their prior commitment to the believability of 'God'.

What in fact is required is not that the interpreter succeed in making the traditions believable for the unbeliever, but simply that he should find them believable himself.[96] For even the most superficial reflection can see the inherent paradox in accepting unbelief as the norm for believability. The end can only be a 'godless' interpretation of 'God'.

This ought not, however, to be taken as signifying that the faith-interpreter can contentedly proceed, talking only to himself and his fellows. The critical procedures, we said, cannot be allowed to decide what the texts mean, but do provide the indispensable indicators as to wherein that meaning must lie. Similarly, neither can 'modern man' be allowed to decide what is believable, but he does provide *horizons* for Christian meaningfulness; in its own reflection about what is believable, faith takes careful note of such horizons to preserve itself from speaking and thinking that which is nonsense.

The best example here does not come from Hebrews but from Paul. In speaking to the already chaotic situation in the Corinthian congregation created by the excessive attention to *glossalalia*, Paul asks his readers to consider the impression an 'outsider' or 'unbeliever' would take from the unrelieved use of tongues in an assembly (1 Cor. 14.20-5). It may safely be assumed that Paul is here much more preoccupied with the domestic situation, the edification (14.3, 5, 12 etc.) of the congregation, than with its mission to the world. But here in this 'internal' situation, the unbelieving man serves to indicate where the boundaries are between what is meaningful and that which is meaningless, for faith's own self-criticism and self-correction.[97]

As a matter of fact, for all the attention given to it by Christian hermeneutical theorists, it is not at all clear that 'God' is really the most accurate test sample for what is believable in the modern world, or that the parables, which have been investigated so thoroughly as examples of the 'language-event', are not relatively easily understood in comparison with other elements of biblical thought.[98] Actually, the 'Devil' is probably very much more difficult for modern Christians to conceptualise and thus to believe in, or understand, than 'God'. Even the 'Holy Spirit' seems likely to press against the limits of what is understandable. And 'miracle' must be much more difficult for the modern man (Christian or secular) than 'parable'. In these cases, rather more directly than in the case of 'God', we gain an insight into the boundaries, or horizons, provided for contemporary Christian interpretation by what is 'believable' in the world. Here, to the extent that Christian interpretation takes seriously the horizons of what it can meaningfully believe, it finds itself pressed back from the edges of the biblical traditions. It learns, as a matter of its own self-criticism, that it cannot put its hand to the interpretation of that which is no longer, or not for the moment,[99] 'believable' with any hope of successful interpretation. If, or when, it comes to the point where 'God' is similarly no longer believable (not for the critic but for the interpreter) then the only honest thing is for the interpreter to cease from his attempts at its interpretation. The boundaries have in this case closed too tightly. But to take what is believable for the interpreter as the measure of what is believable is one thing; to take the non-belief of the critic as the norm is quite another, and fraught with paradox.[100]

(e) Faith and the world

Even if he cannot allow unbelief to become the norm for his interpretation, yet the biblical interpreter knows he cannot, either, disregard the horizons set by 'modern man', for he himself *is* such a man in that he continues to live in the world and is very largely shaped by it.[101] It is this recognition on the part of our ancient writer which provides for a final hermeneutical consideration. What we are gathering up here for our own reflection is the insight already labelled the 'hermeneutic of eschatological existence'. This description is admittedly not as apt as it might be insofar as it is the continuing existence of the eschatological community *in history* which sets the exact prescription for a Christian hermeneutic, acutely conscious of the 'not yet' element of Christian faith. In allowing the bipolarity of the Christian's awareness of himself in history to become a hermeneutical device (even if this is only implicit) for the selection and ordering of scripture, the writer offers us some valuable suggestions with respect to our approaches to the Old Testament, and also with respect to a Christian freedom to make relationships between the bible and the world in which we live.

Very early in this book the opinions of several theologians were gathered who have seen that the relationship between the Old Testament and the New Testament is an important matrix for the whole hermeneutical question (ch. 1, n. 16). In essence, the questions run: what is the significance of the fact that Christians felt obliged to add a second canon to the canon of Jewish scripture? Is the New Testament regarded as fulfilment of, supplement to, or outmoding the Old Testament? And if more than one of these, in which relationships and at which points?[102]

Almost invariably the New Testament has been regarded as *the* hermeneutical key to the Old Testament; the Old Testament only finds its proper meaning in the New, so that the Christian interpreter has made it his business to come to the Old Testament only through the New Testament.[103] Many observations of our own about the writer of Hebrews conform to this pattern.

But we have also seen that there are points, specifically those at which the Christian community is aware of itself as not yet redeemed, as journeying with only a promise to guide it, where the writer of Hebrews is content to let the Old Testament ethos and directive come immediately into the Christian experience, almost, we said, as if the Christian era had never dawned.

Since the conditions of the bipolar experience still apply for Christians nineteen centuries later, might one not say that this hermeneutical screen also applies for us too? That is, are there not points in contemporary Christian experience which permit interpreters to make their way quite directly to the Old Testament, and allow it say what it has to say, without feeling the compulsion to approach it from New Testament perspectives?[104]

What, as we have seen them in Hebrews, are the differences between the two? Rather obviously, the Old Testament writings manifest, and address themselves to, a situation which is predominantly one of expectation. It is certainly true that this rough generalisation (which is frequently found in nearly such a bald way as a basis for hermeneutical structures)[105] is countered by a significantly high proportion of memory, and an even more important element of 'immediacy', that is, a direct involvement in their present moment by the politically minded prophets. Still, it remains generally true that an air of 'not yet' pervades – there is very much more to come. As our writer characterises it, 'They did not receive what God had promised' (11.39). In the same generalised way one may speak of the New Testament manifesting a sense of fulfilment. Again the element of expectation may not be discounted, but even in this, there is an unmistakable 'foreshortening' of history. The end is still to come, but the decisive acts have already happened. It cannot be too far off.

But now since the Christian, as long as he is in the world, experiences *both* those elements side by side, indeed intertwined, there seems to be no good reason why he should not let *each* covenant speak to him from its own point of view and as fitting whichever aspect of Christian existence seems appropriate.[106] This in fact, is exactly what has happened in the letter to the Hebrews.

Two points of application offer themselves in this respect. Christians find themselves in a highly complicated political world. With only intermittent and fortunate exceptions can it be said that they discover the conceptual wherewithal to become in any way deeply enmeshed in such political structures, or, even if they do happen to be Christians and politicians, to find Christian ways of being politicians. The church, generally, can hardly be described as a major political force in the world. Various reasons can be found for this, no doubt, but one of importance is likely to be that the New Testament is almost totally politically disengaged from the world round about it. The reasons for this are clear, too. Except for the later writers, the leaders in the New Testament church felt themselves quite overshadowed by the proximity of the End. So far as we can see, they saw no requirement laid upon them to engage in political reconstruction, with the Kingdom about to break in at any moment. But it is quite otherwise with the Old Testament. Here there is an abundance of models for the interaction of faith and politics. This is because the world is still felt to be very intact, or at least that is so wherever we find faith-inspired politicians. Of course it would be foolish for Christians to take over such models, *simpliciter*; that would run contrary to all we have discovered about interpretation. But it may be said with confidence that here are paradigms – 'frames', to fall back on the term we have used – which offer themselves immediately from the Old Testament for Christian interpreters.[107] Following the pattern of Hebrews, there is no clear reason why

these should first be 'Christianised' by approaching them through the New
Testament. For at this point the experience of the first covenant is nearer
to that of Christians in history than that of the new.[108]

Another possible point of departure from the Old Testament for Christians is in Christian-Jewish relationships. It must certainly seem paradoxical
that our document, which has so long been regarded as an anti-Jewish
polemic, should provide such a suggestion. Yet, as modern Judaism
attempts to say, after the 'holocaust', what it means to believe in God,
many statements emerge of quite astonishing similarity to the 'perseverance' statements in the letter to the Hebrews, including the dialectic between what is known and what is yet totally unknown: 'Neither Exodus
(nor Easter) wins out or is totally blotted out by Buchenwald, but we
encounter both polar experiences; the life of faith is lived between them.'[109]
Certainly the 'not yet' elements in Hebrews, precisely those places in which
the writer falls back upon the Old Testament, ought to warn Christians
away from any messianic triumphalism, and to this extent inject an apparently perennially necessary antidote against anti-Semitism in the
church.[110]

Yet to close our work in concentrating on the pilgrim theme in our
letter, with its implications of resigned determination, its call for the lift-
ing again of hanging arms and tired knees, would be a pity; for it would be
a failure to preserve that wholeness of the message which we have said is
the hallmark of authentic interpretation. Hebrews is certainly addressed to
a group of people in some despondency. But it is itself the outpouring of a
Christian who, while he understands that disenchantment and its reasons,
does not share it. As we have already had occasion to say, it is (often unwit-
tingly) the joyfully confident testimony of a Christian in that troubled late
first century, whose security palpably rests in the things of which he writes
to his friends.

To ask in what ways the closing decades of the twentieth century are
similar to those of the first is certainly to short-circuit, and thus to fuse by
overload, all the hermeneutical issues we have here tried to handle. And
yet it is difficult to resist the instinct that this message of buoyant hope
to Christians who are confused and dispirited is also a message for our times
as well as those in which it was written.

It is a message for tired *Christians*. Whether we like it or not, Hebrews
has no programme for 'mission' or 'evangelism'. And yet as we think about
the world in which Christians presently find themselves, and as we think
about this testimony which clearly knows about the hope to which it
summons its hearers, is it inconceivable that others apart from those already
committed to the Christian faith might also recognise a beacon for hope

and expectation, and join with the pilgrim people who have set their hearts on the city 'which is to come'?

We have said that it does not lie in the interpreter's hands to accomplish the miracle which leads to a faith-understanding of God and his universe. But we have said it is his task, if he is to be an interpreter of his traditions, to find for them new points of reference, new 'frames' which allow the previous 'frames' at least the possibility of disclosing their meaning. To learn from this thoughtful Christian in our past, whom we cannot greet other than as 'the writer', how we might frame for our times an expression of hope, as he has out of the legacy of his past, would be to have accomplished no insignificant interpretative task.

HEBREWS AS INTERPRETATION FOR A LATE-APOSTOLIC CHURCH SITUATION?

Methodological notes on the work of E. Grässer

Our study has been devoted to an investigation of the writer of Hebrews as an interpreter: an interpreter of his own past in the light of his newfound Christian convictions, and an interpreter of those convictions in the light of his past. But is that the only interpretation which is going on? Is the writer of Hebrews also interpreting the gospel in its more primitive, apostolic form for a late, or rather 'early catholic', church situation?

This is the thesis of E. Grässer in his book *Der Glaube im Hebräerbrief*, which, in its impressive size and detail, will undoubtedly continue to exercise a major influence in the understanding of our letter. Indeed Grässer's interests go well beyond the letter itself and are rather more concerned with the recovery of a picture of the developing church in the later first century. The faith-conception in Hebrews has really been selected as a means to this end; by it, Grässer hopes to see what is happening in the church to its 'central Christ-proclamation', its understanding of 'justification of sinners', of 'revelation', and the extent to which it sees 'the event of salvation as the "centre point" of its testimony'.[1] Formally, this inquiry is set out as one into the nature and limits of the New Testament canon, though in fact this is only mentioned in opening[2] and closing[3] remarks. Factually it is an inquiry into the development of the Christian church, employing the faith-conception in Hebrews as a kind of test case at a given point in that history.

The conclusions Grässer comes to are not generally encouraging; the pattern is not so much one of development as of devolution. Faith is discovered to be less than the personal, saving relationship with Jesus which it had been in Paul[4] and even in the Synoptic writers;[5] it has assumed a much more academic, noetic quality.[6] It is no longer Paul's existential decision - 'faith in Christ'[7] - but has turned into a Christian ethic, 'faithfulness'.[8] It can be imitated, an index, Grässer thinks, of the radical depersonalising of what had been Paul's understanding.[9]

With respect to eschatology, we find that the primitive Christian hope for the imminent breaking in of the Kingdom has been replaced by a 'spatially-conceived' (*räumlich*) eschatology.[10] There is now no particular sense of eschatologically qualified time, the sense of the 'already-but-not-yet' as in primitive Christian expectation. This has been transformed into 'the time of the not yet', a time of weary waiting.[11] Salvation is pushed forward into an indefinite future, and the events of Jesus' life and death are consequently devalued from being the definitive events of salvation (contrast Paul's faith 'in Jesus') to be merely the *promise* of (future) salvation.[12] The faith-conception in Hebrews represents in fact a reversion from specifically Christian faith to an Old Testament conception in some of its aspects,[13] or to a generalised religious quality in others.[14]

Behind this considerable transformation Grässer detects a single historical cause – the despair in the church at the delay of the parousia. It is this which indicates the church-historical situation of the writer and the community to which he writes. The distance in time from the cross has brought a depreciation of its saving significance, a tendency to despair by the community, and the need to rearrange the priorities among the various elements in the primitive church's theology. In his now quite well-known sentence Grässer reaches his judgement: 'The writer of Hebrews is therein the theologian on the doorstep from primitive Christianity to the post-apostolic period.'[15]

The methodological questions raised by Grässer's study fall into two separate groups.

(*a*) The first concerns the suitability of the πίστις group of words as an index for such important and far-reaching aspects of the theology of Hebrews as those into which Grässer is concerned to inquire. He himself draws attention early in his book to the relative paucity and very unequal distribution of these words in Hebrews – πίστις occurs thirty-two times but only six of these are outside chapter 11; πιστεύειν occurs only twice; πιστός five times; and ἀπιστία twice.[16] Moreover, we learn that of these forty-one occurrences, not one falls outside the paraenetic sections of the letter.[17] It must immediately appear hazardous for a balanced analysis of themes such as 'the centrality of the Christ-proclamation', or 'justification' or 'revelation' when we have at a stroke delimited ourselves to one word root and, at that, one so unrepresentative as the mere lexical statistics show it to be.

With this must be linked the semantic fallacy of supposing that a single word must be exactly coextensive in its meaning wherever, and by whomsoever, it is used.[18] Grässer's work certainly makes demonstrably clear what has long been guessed, namely that the πίστις words are put to a different work by the writer of Hebrews than by Paul or by John or perhaps even by the Synoptic writers.[19] But this does not in itself indicate that he has not preserved the substance of what they have tried to express in the πίστις words, even if he does it in different ways and with different vocabulary.[20]

Grässer comes, then, as we have mentioned, through an exhaustive interrogation of the πίστις words to the conclusion that 'faith' in Hebrews bears a much more academic and ethical quality than it could have done for Paul or the primitive church. It is no longer 'trust in Jesus', i.e., a present experience of salvation grounded in events already concluded.

But was not that conclusion already assured by the fact that the πίστις words happen to be used *exclusively* in paraenetic contexts, and consequently bear an exhortatory sense? We have seen from our own study that on the whole these sections of the letter consistently view salvation as a future entity, something which the congregation does not yet have within its grasp and which, in their complacency, its members may yet perfectly well lose. Naturally, then, the emphasis here is on faithfulness and steady determination as the antidotes to such dangerous lassitude.

But we also saw that this point of view, in the letter, stands in tension with, if not downright contradiction to, the stance adopted in the theological and Christological sections. Here the events which are together made up by the life, death and exaltation of Jesus are clearly seen as *the* eschatological events, and the covenant which has been brought into being by those events (of which covenant the Christians are members) is clearly identified with the eschatological covenant of forgiveness foreseen by Jeremiah. Within this covenant relationship are to be discovered all the more specifically 'religious' elements of faith which Grässer has not been able to find in his explorations of the πίστις words, such as the Christians' relationship with the compassionate, merciful highpriest, their access through him to the very courts of heaven, and so on.[21] And this because *already* they stand within the eschatological covenant. This quality of immediate, personal relationship reaches its most concentrated expression, we saw, in the 'we have' statements of the letter which not only represent a distillation of the now-quality of Christian experience but also, invariably, provide the ground and motive for exhortation to prayer and worship in times of weariness and uncertainty (see above, pp. 72f). Indeed we found reason to believe that the writer's presentation (adaptation?) of his highpriestly Christology, his most distinctive contribution to the New Testament corpus, represents precisely the attempt to hold together the divergent tendencies of New Testament eschatological awareness – the 'already' of the definitive revelation of the Word of God in the Son as over against an all-too-real awareness of the ongoing history of this world (above, pp. 73f, 82).

Grässer is certainly correct, therefore, to see a futuristic tendency in the πίστις words, and with this an interest in Christian conduct and a continuity with the Old Testament community. But to detach these elements from the 'already' quality of Christian life and understanding, inherent in the theological sections of the letter, is to create the most serious imbalances in any assessment of the letter, not to speak of a wider church situation into which an understanding is being sought. Though the πίστις words are not used to express relationship with the past saving events, as in Paul, and though there is nothing approximating to Paul's 'justification' scheme, the writer of Hebrews certainly *does* know about a personal relationship with Jesus, a relationship on which Christian salvation is wholly dependent. That can hardly be reckoned to be an altogether inadequate expression of what Paul was trying to say in his 'justification' formula.[22] That Grässer should have failed to find this has been, presumably, because he began with, and never moved beyond, the essentially simple lexical study of the πίστις words, even though the uneven distribution of these placed the inquiry in so much jeopardy from the start.[23]

(*b*) A second major criticism is to be located in the hermeneutical interplay Grässer sets up between the text of Hebrews and the church historical situation he envisages for the letter. It is quite clear that there is bound to be a certain circularity in the historical assessment of any ancient document – we have to know the situation into which the document fits in order to be able properly to interpret it, but in a measure the document itself is part of the evidence *for* the situation envisaged. This does not mean that investigation is crippled from the beginning, but it does mean that the greatest measure of control should be exercised to ensure that the direction of the argument flows as much as possible in one way and that circularity is kept to its minimum. It is not clear that this has been achieved by Grässer in his study.

Grässer places Hebrews late in the first century.[24] This judgement, however, rests almost wholly on Grässer's own evaluation of the internal evidence.[25] This is not an invalid procedure in itself, but attention is certainly to be drawn to the high degree of circularity involved when he then goes on to assess Hebrews' theology on the basis of this lateness: as a document of the late first century, Hebrews shows most clearly the change from the apostolic age to the time of the early church – but the *evidence* for this late date is contained precisely in its marks of *Frühkatholizismus!*[26]

Nevertheless, as we have said, we are inevitably shut up to some degree of circularity in an assessment of any ancient document. Is this circularity sufficiently under control in Grässer's work? Two features emerge which suggest that this is not so.

The first is the disconcertingly flexible way in which the evidence can be made to fit the theory of the parousia-delay *whichever way it runs*. The flexibility emerges especially clearly when the question is put: does the author of Hebrews write *to* or *within* a situation of despair at the delay of the parousia? That is to say, is he writing to *correct* the disappointment arising from this delay among his readers, or is he himself writing *under the influence* of this disappointment? Grässer has no hesitation in saying: Both! But this not only raises the suspicion that the canons for the inquiry have been constructed too loosely, so that *all* the evidence, whether for or against, fits the theory, but involves Grässer in some contradiction. For on one hand his book proceeds on the assumption that the writer discloses *himself* as a man who now despairs of the immediacy of the parousia-expectation and therefore of the 'already' of primitive-Christian eschatological awareness. On the other hand, confronted by some aspects of Hebrews which do *not* suggest this despair, Grässer must say that these statements represent old, formulaic expressions (see the subsequent criticism) or (and this is our point here) that the author is writing to *correct* this despair in his readers. But this assumes that he does *not* himself share in such despair, and where he sees it in others regards it as mistaken.[27]

The second mark of undue flexibility has to do with the important hermeneutical principle (for understanding Hebrews) of the ultimate significance of the paraenesis in the letter. This is a principle which Grässer vigorously underwrites.[28] But he is free to countermand it when his thesis so requires! This emerges particularly clearly in his discussion of eschatology in the letter. For the biggest part of his book, Grässer has been urging that, under the influence of the parousia-delay, the writer has pushed the definitive saving event into the future and has thus devalued the salvific worth of the events comprising the life and death of Jesus. But C. K. Barrett had already pressed these very qualities to indicate the continuity of Hebrews with the apocalyptically conceived primitive kerygma.[29] This is hardly compatible with Grässer's own view of a radical *change* in the primitive church's theology, as it has been effected by the parousia-delay. Reversing the canon of the hermeneutical priority of the paraenetic element in Hebrews, he therefore appeals to the *theology* of the epistle, which, as we know, assumes a present, 'realised' eschatological stance. This, he now says, is where we find the real originality of Hebrews – the paraenesis simply reproduces traditional language![30] Here he has not only contradicted the generally accepted hermeneutical principle of the ultimate importance of the exhortation – as supplying the *point* for the elaborate theological argumentation – but the greater part of his own work hitherto.[31]

From these two specific examples we are therefore bound to conclude

that the degree of control which Grässer has over the interaction between
the text and the historical situation envisaged for it is disconcertingly low.
When this is compounded with the partiality and selectivity to which we
have drawn attention in our first criticism, our unease is increased propor-
tionately.[32]

These criticisms should not be taken as a denial of the element of
despair on the part of the *readers*, which may certainly be inferred from
the Epistle to the Hebrews. One of the underlying themes of our own essay
has been to show that the document represents the attempt to meet this,
the problem of the readers, from the perspectives and insights gained from
the *author's* reflection around the problem of the historical setting of the
revealing Word of God. In fact, we suggested, he finds a certain analogy
and parallelism between the two sets of problems, i.e., between the problem of the eschatological *Word* of God in history and that of the eschatological *people* of God in history (above, pp. 73f, 82). But precisely
the fact that he has been able to find a way, through his own reflection on
the Word of God, to a solution, or at least the possibility of one, for his
readers, means that he himself does *not* despair of the future, but is joyful
and confident for it. And this in turn, must raise the question again as to
whether he does not really *mean* it when he writes: 'Yet just a little longer
and he who comes will come, he will not tarry' (10.37).[33] But this would
be to raise a question against Grässer's whole thesis, which is, as we saw,
'The writer of Hebrews is . . . the theologian on the doorstep from primitive Christianity to the post-apostolic period.'[34]

NOTES

Introduction

1   See, by way of random example, E. F. Scott, *The Epistle to the Hebrews* (Edinburgh, 1922), 1; William Neil, *Torch Commentary on Hebrews* (London, 1955), 13; F. F. Bruce, *The Epistle to the Hebrews* (The New London Commentary) (London, 1964), xi; or J. Héring, *Commentary on the Epistle to the Hebrews* (London, 1970), xi. In more detail, and more recently, is the essay by H.-M. Schenke, 'Erwägungen zum Rätsel des Hebräerbriefes' in *Neues Testament und christliche Existenz* (H. Braun Festschrift), ed. H. D. Betz and L. Schottroff (Tübingen, 1973), 421–37.

2   See, e.g., E. F. Scott, *Hebrews*, 52, 79ff, 116; J. Moffatt, *The Epistle to the Hebrews* (International Critical Commentary) (Edinburgh, 1924), xliv f; and W. Manson, *The Epistle to the Hebrews* (London, 1951), 68.

3   See Rowan A. Greer's recent important monograph on the uses made of the letter in Christological controversies up to the fourth century, *The Captain of Our Salvation* (Tübingen, 1973).

4   The only scholarly monographs to appear in English on the epistle in the last decade have been those of F. V. Filson, *Yesterday* (London, 1967), and of R. Williamson, *Philo and the Epistle to the Hebrews* (Leiden, 1970). In German there have appeared in this time, to my knowledge, F. Schröger's *Der Verfasser des Hebräerbriefes als Schriftausleger* (Regensburg, 1968); B. Klappert's *Die Eschatologie des Hebräerbriefes* (Munich, 1969); G. Theissen's *Untersuchungen zum Hebräerbrief* (Gütersloh, 1969); O. Hofius' two books, *Katapausis* (Tübingen, 1970) and *Der Vorhang vor dem Thron Gottes* (Tübingen, 1972); F. Renner's *'An die Hebräer' – ein pseudepigraphischer Brief* (Münsterschwarzach, 1970); and J. Thurén's *Das Lobopfer der Hebräer* (Abo, 1973). This list, in comparison with publications on most other New Testament documents, must seem to indicate only a fractional interest in scholarly research on Hebrews. Certainly some commentaries have been produced in this period, but even of these several have been contributions to wider series of commentaries, so that their significance as expressions of independent interest in the letter is uncertain. That of G. W. Buchanan, *'To the Hebrews'* (Anchor Bible Commentary) (New York, 1972), perhaps should be excepted from this generalisation in that it does attempt to offer an original thesis with respect to the epistle (see n. 11 below).

5   Cf. E. F. Scott, *Hebrews*, 124: 'We cannot but feel, as the writer elaborates his analogy [between Christ's work and the Old Testament Priesthood] that he is engaged in pouring new wine into old bottles which are burst under

the strain.' This is also one of the main theses of E. Grässer's book *Der Glaube in Hebräerbrief* (Marburg, 1965), though his references are confined more narrowly to the faith-conception in the letter: 'The fundamental structural elements of the conception of faith in the Epistle to the Hebrews – indeed more than any other New Testament writing – are rooted in the Old Testament' (p. 85, see also pp. 44, 105f, 144, 147, and cf. pp. 93f).

6   J. Moltmann, in his *Theology of Hope* (London, 1967), drew quite extensively on the letter for his exegetical base.

7   See C. F. D. Moule, *The Birth of the New Testament* (London, 1962), 77f, and also the questions taken up in more detail in ch. 2 (see pp. 54ff).

8   I use the term here in its traditional sense and not with reference to the newer discipline of 'structuralism'; for the latter, see the introductory essays by R. A. Spivey, R. Jacobson, R. C. Culley, R. Polzin and D. O. Via in the issue of *Interpretation* for April 1974 (vol. 28, no. 2). See also the extensive bibliography compiled by A. M. Johnson in *Structural Analysis and Biblical Exegesis* by R. Barthes *et al.* (Pittsburgh, 1974).

9   E. Grässer has catalogued the opinions on this as on every other aspect of research on the epistle, in his exhaustive survey article 'Der Hebräerbrief, 1938-63'. *ThR* n.s. 30 (1964-5), 138-236. For this topic in particular see pp. 160-7. I am not aware of any significant additions which have been published since and which should be made to this list.

10   Cf. Grässer, *ThR* n.s. 30 (1964-5), 161 'On these questions depend theological judgements of considerable weight'; also W. Nauck, 'Zum Aufbau des Hebräerbriefes' in *Judentum, Urchristentum, Kirche* (J. Jeremias Festschrift), ed. W. Eltester (Berlin, 1964), 201. 'The Epistle to the Hebrews remains closed, one cannot find his way in it, as long as one is not clear about the structure.' I regret especially that the work of A. Vanhoye, most notably his *Structure littéraire de l'épître aux Hébreux* (Paris and Brussels, 1963), was not available to me. See the discussion of this and similar essays in Grässer's article, pp. 164ff.

11   One exception must be the commentary of G. W. Buchanan (see n. 4 above) where the thesis is advanced that our document 'To the Hebrews' (Buchanan disputes that it was a letter) represents a Christian midrash on Ps. 110 addressed to a Jewish Christian community in Jerusalem. The thesis is assumed rather than argued, however; nowhere is any explanation offered of the fact that no elements of Ps. 110 other than verse 1 and verse 4 (and this only of the priesthood of Jesus in chs. 5 and 7) are ever alluded to by the writer.

12   Any number of writers could be cited. As E. F. Scott, *Hebrews*, 14, puts it, 'From an early time it has borne the title "To the Hebrews", and this conjecture of some ancient scholar embodies a view which has been endorsed by all subsequent criticism, down to our time.' The scholar best known to me holding firmly to this view was in fact the supervisor of this work, Professor C. F. D. Moule, with whom, as will become obvious, I enjoyed many vigorous exchanges. See, for example, his *Birth of the New Testament*, 76, and 'Sanctuary and Sacrifice in the Church of the New Testament', *JTS* n.s. 1 (1950), 37ff.

13   This shift in exegetical opinion is generally considered to date from the

publication of E. Käsemann's influential work *Das wandernde Gottesvolk* (Göttingen, 1939), though Käsemann had certainly been anticipated by J. Moffatt in his distinguished ICC commentary (1924) and in America by E. F. Scott, whose *Epistle to the Hebrews* was published in Edinburgh and in New York in 1922.

14 See the significant aside thrown out by M. D. Hooker, 'In His Own Image?' in *What about the New Testament?* (C. Evans Festschrift), ed. M. D. Hooker and C. Hickling (London, 1975), 41.

15 See especially G. Ebeling, *Word and Faith* (London, 1963), 32ff.

16 So ibid. 96 and more especially in 'Hermeneutik', *RGG³* III, col. 246; also J. Barr, *Old and New in Interpretation* (London, 1966), 11; K. Schwarzwäller, 'Das Verhältnis Altes Testament-Neues Testament im Lichte der gegenwärtigen Bestimmungen', *EvTh* 29 (1969), 281ff; and P. Ricoeur, 'Die Hermeneutik Rudolf Bultmanns', *EvTh* 33 (1973), 458ff.

17 J. Barr, *The Bible in the Modern World* (London, 1973), 46f.

18 So H.-G. Gadamer, *Truth and Method* (London, 1975), 274: 'Interpretation is not an occasional additional act subsequent to understanding, but rather understanding is always an interpretation, and hence interpretation is the explicit form of understanding.' H. W. Frei, *The Eclipse of Biblical Narrative* (New Haven, 1974), 288, says that since Schleiermacher 'the aim of hermeneutical procedure must be to answer the question: What does it mean to understand?'

19 These methodological questions are taken up and explained in more detail on p. 130.

20 G. Tyrrell, *Christianity at the Crossroads* (London, 1909), 44. For a more recent statement of the same fallacy see Hooker, 'In His Own Image?', *passim*.

Chapter 1. The Son

1 So E. Grässer, 'Hebräer 1.1-4: ein exegetischer Versuch' in *Evangelisch-Katholischer Kommentar zum Neuen Testament* (preliminary fascicle 3) (Zurich and Neukirchen, 1971), 55f.

2 Moule, *Birth*, 167; see also Williamson, *Philo*, 410.

3 See Theissen, *Untersuchungen*, 43, and Williamson, *Philo*, 430f, together with the references collected by H. Clavier in 'ὁ λόγος τοῦ θεοῦ dans l'épître aux Hébreux' in *New Testament Essays - Studies in Memory of T. W. Manson*, ed. A. J. B. Higgins (Manchester, 1959), 81 n. 1. Clavier's attempt to demonstrate a relationship between the 'Word' theme and the Christology of the letter must be regarded as something of a *tour de force*.

4 Certainly, most interpreters see a connection between the prologue and the closely following comparison of Jesus with the angels as continuing the 'Word' theme (1.5-2.4). And some, we shall see, take this as far as the comparison of Jesus and Moses in ch. 3. None, to my knowledge, have taken the prologue as the definitive key to the letter as a whole and few see any connection between it and the highpriestly Christology. Indeed some see a sharp *disjunction* between the 'Word' and the 'priest' themes. See Nauck, 'Zum Aufbau des Hebräerbriefes', 205; F. J. Schierse, *Verheissung und Heilsvollendung* (Munich, 1955), 197 n. 6, and D. C. St V. Welander, 'Hebrews 1.1-3', *ExT* 65 (1953-4), 315.

5 E. Grässer, 'Hebräer 1.1-4', 61, 70f, draws attention to the interconnection of literary form and theological content. The statement in the text above should not be taken as setting out, programmatically, the course of the ensuing inquiry; it merely indicates the multi-level nature of that inquiry.

6 O. Michel, *Der Brief an die Hebräer* (Meyers Kommentar über das Neue Testament) (Göttingen, 1966[12]), 93; Héring, commentary, 1.

7 F. F. Bruce, quoted without reference by H. W. Montefiore, *A Commentary on the Epistle to the Hebrews* (Black's New Testament Commentaries) (London, 1964), 33.

8 Grässer, 'Hebräer 1.1-4', 74; see also J. Calvin, quoted above, p. 104.

9 Thus, within the first sentence of the letter we are brought into one of the storm-centres of its interpretation, namely whether the theology of the writer is conceived pre-eminently in 'horizontal', historical terms, or in 'vertical' dimensions; whether apocalyptic, Hebraistic ideas have been overtaken by Hellenistic, Platonic ones.

10 R. Deichgräber, *Gotteshymnus und Christushymnus in der Frühen Christenheit* (Göttingen, 1967), 174-8, has examined the claims of G. Schille and G. Friederich to have located hymn fragments in chs. 5 and 7 of Hebrews, and finds them mistaken. The attempts of G. Theissen are similarly unconvincing. See n. 46 below.

11 Deichgräber, *Gotteshymnus*, 137-40; Grässer, 'Hebräer 1.1-4', 62-7; Manson, *The Epistle to the Hebrews*, 91f; G. Bornkamm, 'Das Bekenntnis im Hebräerbrief' in *Studien zu Antike und Urchristentum* (collected essays, vol. II) (Munich, 1959), 198f; Michel, commentary, 94, 96f.

12 'Hebräer, 1.1-4', 62-7.

13 *Gotteshymnus*, 138.

14 As E. Grässer attempts to do; see 'Hebräer 1.1-4', esp. p. 88. See also Manson, *The Epistle to the Hebrews*, 91f.

15 So A. Baaker, 'Christ an Angel?', *ZNW* 32 (1933), 255ff; R. V. G. Tasker, *The Old Testament in the New Testament* (London, 1946[1]), 101; Y. Yadin, 'The Dead Sea Scrolls and the Epistle to the Hebrews' in *Scripta Hierosolymitana* IV, ed. C. Rabin and Y. Yadin (Jerusalem, 1965), 39f, 45; and the much more significant essay by M. de Jonge and A. S. van der Woude, '11Q Melchizedek and the New Testament', *NTS* 12 (1965-6), 301-26, esp. pp. 314ff. E. Grässer, however, rightly points out that such a possibility is completely absent from any of the paraenetic warnings of the letter ('Hebräer 1.1-4', 90).

16 *Gottesvolk*, 58-60, 66-71.

17 So, more precisely stated by C. Büchel than in most commentators: 'At 2.2 ὁ δι' ἀγγέλων λαληθεὶς λόγος is contrasted with the σωτηρία ἥτις ἀρχὴν λαβοῦσα λαλεῖσθαι διὰ τοῦ κυρίου' ('Der Hebräerbrief und das Alte Testament', *TSK* 79 (1906), 508; see also p. 554).

18 Montefiore, commentary, 52, and similarly in many other commentators.

19 So J. Jeremias, *TDNT* IV, 866 n. 210. H. L. Strack and P. Billerbeck, *Kommentar zum Neuen Testament aus Talmud and Midrasch* III (Munich, 1926), 554, similarly restrict themselves: 'The presence of angels at the giving of the Law is old Jewish tradition.'

20 Acts 7.53 and Gal. 3.19. If there really is a link between Hebrews and the circle of Stephen (Manson, *The Epistle to the Hebrews*, 25-46, but see

M. Simon, *St Stephen and the Hellenists in the Primitive Church* (New York, 1958), 100ff), then other New Testament witnesses would, of course, be reduced to Paul. It is at least interesting that whatever decision is reached about Stephen and Hebrews, in this particular case they stand antithetically to one another. For Stephen the mediation of the angels enhances the status of the Law; for Hebrews (and Paul!) it is a sign of inferiority.

21   W. D. Davies notwithstanding ('A Note on Josephus, Antiquities 15.136', *HTR* 47 (1954), 135–40), I think Josephus may well have been acquainted with it: ἡμῶν δὲ τὰ κάλλιστα τῶν δογμάτων καὶ τὰ ὁσιώτατα τῶν ἐν τοῖς νόμοις δι᾽ ἀγγέλων παρὰ τοῦ θεοῦ μαθόντων. I think the idea might also not unreasonably be found at b.Shabbath 89a, a passage not usually cited so far as I can discover (see the Soncino edition, pp. 422f). Finally, see Jubilees I.27 and R. H. Charles' note in his edition, *The Book of Jubilees* (London, 1902), 8.

22   See S. G. Sowers, *The Hermeneutics of Philo and Hebrews* (Zurich and Richmond, Va., 1965), 77 n. 9; also E. Grässer, 'Das Heil als Wort, Hebr. 2.1–4', in *Neues Testament und Geschichte* (O. Cullmann Festschrift), ed. H. Baltensweiler and B. Reicke (Tübingen, 1972), 271f.

23   See above, pp. 80ff, on the significance of Jesus' highpriesthood for the community yet involved in the tension between its apprehension of the eschatological Word and its present experience as οἱ πειραζόμενοι.

24   Many commentators are in concurrence. Cf., for example, B. F. Westcott, *The Epistle to the Hebrews* (London, 1889; repr. Grand Rapids, n.d.), 72: 'He has already shown that Christ (the Son) is superior to the angels, the spiritual agents in the giving of the Law; he now goes on to show that He is superior to the Human Lawgiver.' O. Michel and several others treat up to 4.13 of the letter under some such heading as that of J. Schneider, 'The Uniqueness of the Divine Bearer of Revelation', *The Letter to the Hebrews* (Grand Rapids, 1957).

25   See Grässer, *Glaube*, 19 n. 42.

26   E. L. Allen, 'Jesus and Moses in the New Testament', *ExT* 67 (1955-6), 105.

27   F. F. Bruce, ' "To the Hebrews" or "To the Essenes"?', *NTS* 9 (1962-3), 222.

28   Grässer, *Glaube*, 19 n. 42, in contending against the polemical interpretation, goes too far in the opposite direction when he writes: 'The argument [for the exaltation of Jesus over Moses] fails on the decisive point: in their quality as πιστός there is absolutely no distinction.' Grässer has been misled by assumptions of his own, for faithfulness is only one of the elements of the comparison. There are others (no less decisive!) in which Moses is clearly subordinated.

29   Some of the unresolved questions with respect to verses 3 and 4 are: who is envisaged as ὁ κατασκευάσας αὐτόν in verse 3? What is the significance of the seemingly obvious assertations that 'every house is built by someone' and 'God is the creator of all' (verse 4)? How does the glory of Christ depend on his being the architect of the house if God is the architect (verse 4b)? What is Moses' relation to Christ in terms of the building metaphor, i.e., does verse 3 imply that Christ, as builder of the house, is also Moses' fashioner? F. J. Schierse, *Heilsvollendung*, 108–12, attributes this 'obscure middle,

verses 2b-5' to the determination of exegetes to see the Moses-Jesus comparison in terms of the relationship between the two economies. But his own explanation of the house as a 'heavenly dwelling' ('Himmelswohnung'), p. 111, does not appear to cast much light on the puzzles mentioned.

30 W. Bauer, *A Greek-English Lexicon of the New Testament*, tr. and ed. W. F. Arndt and F. W. Gingrich (Chicago, 1957): οἶκος, 2.

31 The most recent studies have been those of Klappert, *Eschatologie*, 33ff, and of Theissen, *Untersuchungen*, 43ff, but the most influential essay of recent times has been that of Bornkamm, 'Das Bekenntnis'.

32 K. Bornhäuser, 'Die Versuchungen Jesu nach dem Hebräerbrief' in *Theologische Studien Martin Kähler dargebracht* (Leipzig, 1905), 77.

33 Jeremias, *TDNT* IV, 861f.

34 E. Riggenbach, *Der Brief an die Hebräer* (Leipzig, 1913), 65; C. Chavasse, 'Jesus: Christ and Moses', *Theology* 54 (1951), 291; and Yadin, 'The Dead Sea Scrolls and the Epistle to the Hebrews', 41, 53f, who thinks the readers were in danger not only of confusing the mediators of the covenants but of associating Moses with the καινή διαθήκη!

35 In spite of Moses' importance as a mediator in Palestinian Judaism (Jeremias, *TDNT* IV, 852, and cf. N. Wieder, 'The "Law-Interpreter" of the Sect of the Dead Sea Scrolls: The Second Moses', *JJS* 4 (1953), 158-75, who is criticised, however, by P. Winter in *JQR* 45 (1954), 39-47), the term ἀπόστολος, שָׁלִיחַ, seems not to have been widely or especially used of him. W. A. Meeks, *The Prophet-King* (Leiden, 1967), 302 n. 4, adduces a few examples. Extant Samaritan documents in which great interest in Moses is shown (ibid. pp. 226f) are probably too late to be of certain use to us. R. J. Banks has submitted the whole question of New Moses and New Torah formulations prior to the New Testament to careful scrutiny and has concluded that evidence for these ideas is not forthcoming. See his *Jesus and the Law in the Synoptic Tradition* (Cambridge, 1975), 72f, 77-81, also 'The Eschatological Role of Law in Pre- and Post-Christian Jewish Thought' in *Reconcilation and Hope* (L. Morris Festschrift), ed. R. J. Banks (London, 1974), 173-85.

36 Michel, commentary, 197, but see Hofius, *Katapausis*, 139.

37 See Grässer, 'Hebräer 1.1-4', 72.

38 Grässer's attempt (*Glaube*, 14f) to distinguish the faith-conception in Hebrews from regulative New Testament understanding on the basis of the verb συνκεράννυμι (4.2), suggesting that the author thinks 'not of the faith-awakening proclamation, but of that capacity by means of which what is heard is secured for the hearer by means of faith; that is to say, faith must be already present when the Word reaches the hearer', seems to me forced and unconvincing. Faith, here as in other places in the letter, is not simply an ethical matter, faithfulness, though certainly it includes that. It stands as the index of one's preparedness or otherwise to trust God amid the inauspicious circumstances of historical existence, and is therefore the measure of one's estimate of the character and person of God. See Michel, commentary, 376; O. Kuss, 'Der Verfasser des Hebräerbriefes als Seelsorger', *Auslegung und Verkündigung* (collected essays, vol. I) (Regensburg, 1963), 344ff; Theissen, *Untersuchungen*, 100; and G. Dautzenberg, 'Der Glaube in Hebräerbrief', *BZ* n.s. 15 (1973), 165;

more generally, see Moltmann, *Hope*, 44, and Ebeling, *Word and Faith*, 211.
In fact, Grässer has since modified his views on the ethical qualities of the
faith-conception in Hebrews (as a devolution from central New Testament
understanding). See his 'Zur Christologie des Hebräerbriefes' in *Neues
Testament und christliche Existenz* (H. Braun Festschrift), ed. H. D. Betz
and L. Schottroff (Tübingen, 1973), 202ff, esp. p. 205 n. 38.

39 See Hofius, *Katapausis*, 138f.

40 See E. K. Simpson on κριτικός and τραχηλίζεω in *EQ* 18 (1946), 37f.

41 See Hofius, *Katapausis*, 127, and esp. the references he gives in n. 785.

42 G. Theissen, for example, has analysed the function of the Word of God
in Hebrews in particularly close conjunction with the 'inescapable wrath of
God' (*Untersuchungen*, 107f).

43 So, explicitly, A. B. Bruce, *The Epistle to the Hebrews* (Edinburgh, 1899),
17f, and E. F. Scott, *Hebrews*, 70.

44 That the three comparisons are meant to function as a series is proposed by
some scholars, notably: H. A. A. Kennedy, *The Theology of the Epistles*
(London, 1919), 192, 201ff; W. Leonard, *The Authorship of the Epistle to
the Hebrews* (London, 1939), 52; Yadin, 'The Dead Sea Scrolls and the
Epistle to the Hebrews', 38. With the exception of Kennedy, however, it
has not generally been perceived by these writers that the organising idea
around which the structure is built is that of God's revelation in its old and
new forms.

45 Cf., however, Williamson, *Philo*, 127-9.

46 It is true there is scholarly debate as to whether these words are the
author's own. O. Michel, commentary, 259, with reference to G. Wuttke,
thinks that the whole of verse 3 is 'a rhythmical structure of four lines . . .
a small, independent poem praising Melchizedek as the "Image of the
Son of God" ', which the writer has taken over preformed. Building on
this, and making great play with the changes between 'priest' and 'highpriest' throughout the chapter (noted at least as early as F. Delitzsch, who
is not cited, and B. Weiss, who is) G. Schille, 'Erwägungen zur Hohepriesterlehre des Hebräerbriefes', *ZNW* 46 (1955), 81-109, produces an
elaborate theory in which he discerns a primitive Christian hymn to Christ
to which our author has actually *added* the line in question (pp. 84-7). The
several logical lapses in this involved thesis tell sufficiently against it. See
Deichgräber, *Gotteshymnus*, 176ff. G. Theissen's attempt, *Untersuchungen*,
20-5, to reconstruct a Melchizedek hymn underlying the whole of Hebrews 7,
and of which verse 3 is only the first stanza, is admittedly (p. 24) speculative.
G. W. Buchanan, commentary, 117, 122, assumes a 'little poem that is
non-canonical' at 7.3 and another at 7.26, for which he produces no argument, however.

47 As some older commentators thought; see F. F. Bruce, commentary, 137
n. 20, and for a modern presentation, A. T. Hanson, *Jesus Christ in the
Old Testament* (London, 1965), 65-72.

48 The very limited role Melchizedek plays here seems to me to warn against
taking the reference to him too seriously as a pointer to the background of
the letter. Cf. Schenke, 'Erwägungen zum Rätsel', among others. It does
not seem apparent to me that the writer needed any knowledge of a 'Melchizedek
tradition' other than that which he found in the psalm, and to which he

has been attracted by the concept of a 'priest for ever'. See further n. 50 below.

49 And cf. Jubilees XIII.

50 Whatever we are to say about the original relationship of Ps. 110 to Gen. 14, there can be little doubt that the order in which the writer of Hebrews has thought through the relation of Jesus to Melchizedek has been, first, Jesus' definitive quality of priesthood, second, the psalm reference to describe this, and third, the Genesis reference to fill this out.

This order is actively contested by J. A. Fitzmyer, ' "Now This Melchizedek ...", Hebrews 7.1' in *Essays on the Semitic Background of the New Testament* (London, 1971), 221–43, who regards Hebrews 7 primarily as 'an excellent example of a midrash on Gen. 14.18–20' (p. 222), into which have been introduced phrases from Ps. 110.

But even if, as many exegetes agree (references by Fitzmyer, pp. 221f), there are midrashic elements in the way the Genesis passage has been used, it is incontestable that Ps. 110.4 has become an integral part of the discussion as early as Heb. 5.6 (which question Fitzmyer begs, p. 223) and, as we shall see, is the controlling idea throughout ch. 7. See Michel, commentary, 256, and A. G. Hebert, *The Authority of the Old Testament* (London, 1947), 214.

51 It is true that some exegetes take this as a reference to the distinction occasionally made in the Old Testament between the Aaronite priests and the Levites; that is to say, οἱ μέν . . . τὴν ἱερατείαν λαμβάνοντες are distinguished from the remainder of those who are ἐκ τῶν υἱῶν Λευει (see, e.g., Montefiore, commentary, 121, and cf. Westcott, commentary, 175). In this case the genitive is taken as partitive and the meaning given as: 'those of the sons of Levi who have received the priestly office'. The tithe mentioned is then 'the tithe of the tithes' (Num. 18.26), that taken by the Aaronite priests out of the tithes collected by the Levites from the people.

Three factors decide against this interpretation: (a) The tithe envisaged is not a secondary one, but that received by the Levites *from the people* as established by Deut. 10.8f (conceded by Montefiore in his very next paragraph). (b) According to Westcott, ἱερατεία 'in relation to ἱερωσύνη expresses the actual service of the priest and not the office of priesthood' (commentary, 176), in which case what is in view here is not the priestly *office* in distinction from other levitical rights and duties, but the actual *function* of being a priest, the necessary condition for which is that a man be ἐκ τῶν υἱῶν Λευει (though against this, see Moffatt, commentary, 95). (c) The μὲν–δέ construction makes it clear that this phrase is to be read in the light of μὴ γενεαλογούμενος in verse 6 (see esp. Riggenbach, commentary, 187).

52 See Josephus, *Life*, 1–6; also M. D. Johnson, *The Purpose of the Biblical Genealogies* (Cambidge, 1969), 96ff.

53 The importance of this for the writer is hard to overestimate; it is reflected in the reduplication and intensification in ἐντολὴν ἔχουσιν and κατὰ τὸν νόμον (verse 5). It is not simply an individual commandment which is in question here but the fundamental relationship within which the Priesthood is established by the Law. See especially W. Gutbrod, *TDNT* IV, 1078; also Schröger, *Ausleger*, 144f, and H. Strathmann, *Der Brief an die Hebräer* (Das Neue Testament Deutsch) (Göttingen, 1963[8]), 97.

54 "Ο πατριάρχης is thrown to the end of the sentence for emphasis' (Moffatt, commentary, 94); other commentators are in agreement.

55 See the collection of contemporary opinions regarding the permanency of the Priesthood assembled by Michel, commentary, 269f, and see the work of Banks, cited in n. 35 above, who has collected copious references for the idea of the eternity of the Law.

56 So nearly all the commentators. See esp. Montefiore, pp. 123f.

57 As witnessed by the textual confusion; see Moffatt, commentary, 95.

58 Bauer (Arndt and Gingrich) gives (s.v. ἐπί 1,1,b, β) 'on the basis of', and he is followed by almost all the commentators.

59 Moffatt, commentary, 96: '. . . "in connection with", since ἐπί and περί have a similar force with the genitive . . .'; 'in betreff . . .': Michel, commentary, 270, and similarly Riggenbach, commentary, 194.

60 See Moffatt, commentary, 96, and Gutbrod, TDNT IV, 1078.

61 εἰ μὲν οὖν τελειωσις διὰ τῆς Λευιτικῆς ἱερωσύνης ἦν . . . τίς ἔτι χρεία . . . ἐτερον ἀνίστασθαι ἱερέα καὶ οὐ κατὰ τὴν τάξω Ααρων λέγεσθαι; It is not clear that commentators have always grasped the importance of this statement for the author's *argument*. Montefiore, for instance, thinks that the important factor is that the psalm word comes later than the establishment of the levitical institutions. This argument has already been used at 4.7, of course, and will come again at verse 28 of the present chapter. But even if it lies in the background here, the explicit form of the argument is much simpler: there has, in history, been conceived a better order of priesthood than the levitical one, which means *ipso facto* that that is not a perfect form. Westcott, commentary, 181, says that the need for a change 'was found by experience . . . and was described long before it came to pass by one who lived under the Law and enjoyed its privileges'. The experiential sense of the Law's inadequacy is probably the material starting point of the gospel, but formally the argument here simply depends on the fact that a better institution can and has been conceived of. The principle is stated concisely by the author himself at 8.7: εἰ γὰρ ἡ πρώτη ἐκείνη ἦν ἄμεμπτος, οὐκ ἂν δευτέρας ἐζητεῖτο τόπος.

62 The distinction between σάρκινος and σαρκικός is fairly well established by modern lexicographers, even if some confusion existed in ancient writers and especially in copyists. Σάρκινος by consensus of modern opinion means 'of fleshly constitution, made of flesh', and should be distinguished from σαρκικός, 'belonging to the realm of flesh, the opposite of πνευματικός' (Westcott, commentary, 184; similarly Bauer (Arndt and Gingrich), s.v.v.; see also F. Blass and A. Debrunner, *A Greek Grammar of the New Testament* (Cambridge and Chicago, 1961), 62. In fact the distinction is not rigidly observed by ancient authors and the juxtaposition here of σαρκίνης with ζωῆς ἀκαταλύτου seems to demand rather the sense of σαρκικός - belonging to the *realm* of flesh. The fact that the author apparently uses the wrong word presents us with the alternative: either he was clumsy and unaware of the precise nuances of the two words; or he is deliberately setting up a harsh discontinuity to emphasise all the more strongly the opposition between the two kinds of priesthood (so Westcott).

63 The regular antithesis between fleshly, earthly and levitical entities and spiritual, heavenly and eschatological ones is, not unnaturally, of the great-

est importance to those exegetes who see the letter as dominated by the 'Alexandrian' type of dualism (see, e.g., Schierse on 'Fleisch und Gewissen', *Heilsvollendung*, 38–40). Here, as everywhere in Hebrews, it is a question of evaluating the *role* these dualistic terms are playing and whether they have or have not been subordinated to traditional eschatological patterns. See above, pp. 42f, 45.

64 See the excursus on ' "Perfection" in the epistle' at the conclusion of this chapter.

65 See esp. Klappert, *Eschatologie*, 31ff, and also H. Köster, 'Die Auslegung der Abraham-Verheissung in Hebräer 6' in *Studien zur Theologie der alttestamentlichen Überlieferungen* (G. von Rad Festschrift), ed. R. Rendtorf and K. Koch (Neukirchen, 1961), 107. Cf. also Käsemann, *Gottesvolk*, 14 nn. 1, 2; Moule, *Birth*, 76 n. 2; Schröger, *Ausleger*, 154 n. 2; and Hofius, *Vorhang*, 86.

66 See a slightly different list in Klappert, *Eschatologie*, 32.

67 For a more detailed discussion of the dialectical role of the scriptures in the letter, see above, pp. 70ff.

68 Cf. C. Westermann, 'The Interpretation of the Old Testament' in *Essays in Old Testament Interpretation*, ed. C. Westermann (London, 1965), 48: 'Those who experienced the deliverance at the Red Sea ... could ... confess, praise and pass on this event as an act of God ... for the sole reason that this salvation had word-character ... a *factum* is recognised as a *dictum*.' And see C. F. D. Moule, *The Phenomenon of the New Testament* (London, 1967), 98: 'I feel myself driven to the conclusion that it was rather through what Christ *did* than anything he *said* that the lesson [of the redemptive significance of his death] was learnt' (his italics).

69 E. Grässer, in his detailed examination of the prologue, has made a connection between the 'Word' theme of the prologue and the letter's own description of itself as a 'word of encouragement' (λόγος παρακλήσεως, 13.22) ('Hebräer 1.1–4', 70f). See also his 'Das Heil als Wort', esp. p. 269.

70 Concisely stated with reference to Hebrews by A. Nairne in the Introduction to his Cambridge Greek Testament commentary, *The Epistle to the Hebrews* (Cambridge, 1922), lxxxi f, and by E. F. Scott, *The Literature of the New Testament* (New York, 1932), 199: 'To whom then does [the author] address himself? This is the most important of all the questions, since it affects our whole understanding of the purpose of the epistle.'

71 So R. Bultmann, 'The Problem of Hermeneutics', *Essays Philosophical and Theological* (London, n.d.), 236, 247f; also F. G. Downing, *The Church and Jesus* (London, 1968), 51ff.

72 Cf. G. N. Stanton, *Jesus of Nazareth in New Testament Preaching* (Cambridge, 1974), 11, 173, and see the criticisms directed toward the work of E. Grässer, above, pp. 140ff.

73 Eusebius, *Ecclesiastical History*, VI, 25, 11ff.

74 In particular, attempts to name the author of our document remain not only hypothetical, but fundamentally self-defeating, precisely because the *criteria* for the selection of this name or that *already* contain all the information we can garner about that person. So Nairne, commentary, lvii. See esp. Schenke, 'Erwägungen zum Rätsel', 425.

75 Grässer, 'Hebräer 1.1–4', 77, or 'analogy', in *Glaube*, 15. Cf. also H. Braun,

'Die Gewinnung der Gewissheit in dem Hebräerbrief', *ThLz* 96 (1971), col. 325.

76 Käsemann, *Gottesvolk*, 34.
77 Ibid. 34. See also Moffatt, commentary, xxvi.
78 E. F. Scott, *Hebrews*, 28, and see, further, E. Grässer, *ThR* n.s. 30 (1964-5), 149: 'The comparison of the old and new covenants is not an indication of the polemical, anti-Jewish character of the letter, since it represents for the author simply part of an hermeneutical method . . .'
79 This point is explored in greater detail on p. 43.
80 As a matter of fact, O. Hofius has gone a very long way toward showing that these conceptions could perfectly well have had a rabbinic or Merkabah provenance (*Vorhang*, section A). See also Schenke, 'Erwägungen zum Rätsel', esp. pp. 433ff.
81 See, for example, Grässer, *Glaube*, 19 and esp. n. 42 on that page; also his 'Hebräer 1.1-4', 75. Similarly, see E. F. Scott, *Hebrews*, 16.
82 Moffatt, commentary, xxiv f; E. F. Scott, *Hebrews*, 22 and frequently; Grässer, *Glaube*, 199, 212 *et al.*
83 See Moule, *Birth*, 76.
84 Moffatt, commentary, xvi; E. F. Scott, *Hebrews*, 16.
85 *JTS* n.s. 1 (1950), 37f.
86 Ibid. 37.
87 See Filson, *Yesterday*, 48ff.
88 See H. Köster, 'Outside the Camp: Hebrews 13.9-14', *HTR* 55 (1962), 312 n. 45.
89 Moule, *Birth*, 78.
90 Moffatt, commentary, xxiv.
91 One of the most frequently expressed dissatisfactions with the letter is with its 'scripture proofs'. This criticism, however, often proceeds on the assumption that it is written in a hard, polemical situation and *expects* to be persuasive in this way. Since the two questions, that of the 'life-situation' of Hebrews and that of the author's scripture citations, thus cohere very closely together, the present discussion is taken up and extended on pp. 54ff.
92 It is not intended here to raise the question of the actual literary form of Hebrews. It is sufficiently clear, I think, that it is directed to a definite community; the thesis of M. Dibelius, 'Der himmlische Kultus nach dem Hebräerbrief', *Botschaft und Geschichte* (collected essays, vol. II) (Tübingen, 1956), 161f, that it is a catholic document without a specific group in mind, does not seem to me to warrant serious attention. The more recent suggestion of G. W. Buchanan, commentary, 246, 255f, that it was not a letter, but a 'homiletical midrash' addressed to a monastic, Christian 'brotherhood' in Jerusalem, however convincing or otherwise that thesis is found to be (see the review by E. Grässer in *ThLz* 100 (1975), cols. 752-5), would not significantly affect the thesis here advanced, namely that it is primarily addressed 'to friends in trouble'.
93 Cf. O. Kuss, 'Der Verfasser des Hebräerbriefes als Seelsorger', 331: 'Pastoral care is applied, lived, 'concretised' theology . . .'
94 Williamson, *Philo*, 30, 78 *et al.*
95 See Williamson's comments, *Philo*, 14, on the literary and theological creativity of the writer.

96 E. F. Scott, *Hebrews*, 123f.
97 E. Grässer takes the strongly Old Testament character of the letter as a
     mark of the diminution of more characteristically New Testament attitudes
     (*Glaube*, 44 etc.) See above, Introduction, n. 5.
98 See, e.g., A. J. B. Higgins, 'The Priestly Messiah', *NTS* 13 (1966-7), 211-39,
     and M. Black, 'The Qumran Messiah and Related Beliefs', *The Scrolls and
     Christian Origins* (London, 1961), 145-63.
99 For Qumran see esp. K. G. Kuhn, 'The Two Messiahs of Aaron and Israel' in
     The Scrolls and the New Testament, ed. K. Stendahl (New York, 1957),
     54-64; A. S. van der Woude, *Die messianische Vorstellungen der Gemeinde
     von Qumran* (Assen, 1957); Johnson, *Biblical Genealogies*, 120-31; and
     many others. For the *Test. XII Patr.* see G. R. Beasley-Murray, 'The Two
     Messiahs in the Testaments of the Twelve Patriarchs', *JTS* 48 (1947), 1-12.
     M. de Jonge, at first convinced of the late (Christian) composition of the
     testaments (*The Testaments of the Twelve Patriarchs* (Assen, 1953)), and
     though still anxious to maintain that there has been an extensive Christian
     redaction process, has been willing, in light of the Qumran discoveries, to
     concede the probability of earlier Jewish sources embodying these ideas.
     See his 'Christian Influences in the Testaments of the Twelve Patriarchs',
     NovT 4 (1960), 182-235. (I regret that his most recent volume, *Studies on
     The Testaments of the Twelve Patriarchs* (Leiden, 1975), was not available
     to me.)
100 See Yadin, 'The Dead Sea Scrolls and the Epistle to the Hebrews', and
     H. Kosmala, *Hebräer-Essener-Christen* (Leiden, 1959), 76-96.
101 Yadin, 'Scrolls', 44.
102 See Filson, *Yesterday*, 35f, and F. Büchsel, *Die Christologie des.
     Hebräerbriefes* (Gütersloh, 1923), 10ff, who, though he detects many
     allusions to Jesus' eschatological rule, nevertheless affirms that 'the
     messianic idea is not of basic importance for the Christology of Hebrews'
     (p. 10); similarly, A. Oepke, *Das neue Gottesvolk* (Gütersloh, 1950), 18,
     and Moffatt, commentary, xxvii.
103 As claimed by Kosmala, *Essener*, 13, 87.
104 Filson, *Yesterday*, 36, 38.
105 Yadin, 'Scrolls', 42.
106 Even of the ἱερεὺς καινός of *T. Levi* 18.1, van der Woude remarks correctly:
     'That he is not of levitical origins is nowhere mentioned and cannot be
     deduced from the present text' (*Vorstellungen*, 210).
107 See Higgins, 'The Priestly Messiah', 233.
108 As Kosmala claims, *Essener*, 90; to the contrary, see F. Hahn, *The Titles of
     Jesus in Christology* (London, 1969), 230.
109 Yadin, 'Scrolls', 50.
110 As Yadin is himself aware; 'Scrolls', 50.
111 And for a rabbinic interpretation see b.Nedarim 32b; Strack and Billerbeck,
     Kommentar IV, 453.
112 See Williamson, *Philo*, 409-34.
113 So M. E. Clarkson, 'The Antecedents of the High-Priest Theme in Hebrews',
     AngTheolRev 29 (1947), 89-95; O. Cullmann, *The Christology of the New
     Testament* (London, 1963²), 87ff; G. Friedrich, 'Beobachtungen zur
     messianischen Hohepriestererwartung in den Synoptikern', *ZThK* 53 (1956),

265-311; A. J. B. Higgins, 'The Old Testament and Some Aspects of New
Testament Christology' in *Promise and Fulfilment*, ed. F. F. Bruce
(Edinburgh, 1963), 136ff; O. Moe, 'Das Priestertum Christi im Neuen
Testament ausserhalb des Hebräerbriefes', *ThLz* 72 (1947), cols. 335ff;
and S. Nomoto, 'Herkunft und Struktur der Hohenpriestervorstellung im
Hebräerbrief', *NovT* 10 (1968), 10-25.

114   See Hahn, *Titles*, 229-39, and H. Schlier, 'Grundelemente des priesterlichen
Amtes im Neuen Testament', *Theologie und Philosophie* 44 (1969), 162.

115   When all is said and done, it is in fact difficult to judge just how important
is the question of other sources, since even if it could be shown that the
writer had been aware of the eschatological highpriest idea in other writings, his own development of it is so highly personalised and clearly original.

116   It is a matter of surprise to me that O. Cullmann, *Salvation in History*
(London, 1967), scarcely seems to have recognised the contribution made
by our writer to his thesis. Cf. the few references on pp. 131f.

117   Dr G. C. O'Collins has suggested to me that we might describe his (the
writer of Hebrews') work as a 'hermeneutic of images' as distinct from
the 'language' category of ideas which has usually taken the attention of
modern theologians interested in hermeneutics.

118   It seems to me remarkable that the essays of E. Riggenbach, 'Der Begriff
der ΔΙΑΘΗΚΗ im Hebräerbrief' in *Theologische Studien Theodor Zahn
dargebracht* (Leipzig, 1908), 289-316, and of J. Behm, *Der Begriff
ΔΙΑΘΗΚΗ im Neuen Testament* (Leipzig, 1912), should scarcely touch the
question of the writer's interest in the *inter*relationship between the
covenants. E. Lohmeyer, *Diatheke* (Leipzig, 1913), sees only a negative
relationship. It is much more clearly understood by O. Schmitz, 'Das Alte
Testament im Neuen Testament' in *Wort und Geist* (Karl Heim Festschrift),
ed. A. Koberle and O. Schmitz (Berlin, 1934), 57: '...a peculiar double-
relationship of *heilsgeschichtlich* dialectic'.

119   So G. B. Caird, 'The Exegetical Method of the Epistle to the Hebrews',
CanJTheol 5 (1959), 45.

120   The change, at 9.20, from ἰδοὺ τὸ αἷμα (Ex. 24.8) to τοῦτο τὸ αἷμα has
frequently been noticed. Cf. Kennedy, *The Theology of the Epistles*, 198f,
and J. Jeremias, *The Eucharistic Words of Jesus* (London, 1966), 170, to
name just two such scholars. On the other hand of course, there are also
those who doubt whether the words καινὴ διαθήκη were in fact originally
part of the cupword. See W. G. Morrice, 'Covenant', *ExT* 86 (1974-5), 134f.

121   'Thus, this letter - often referred to as the "Epistle of Priesthood" - is also
"the Letter of the New Covenant" ' (Morrice, 'Covenant', 134).

Excursus 1. 'Perfection' in the epistle

1   See J. Kögel, 'Der Begriff τελειοῦν im Hebräerbrief', *Theologische Studien
Martin Kähler dargebracht* (Leipzig, 1905), 35-68.

2   *Gottesvolk*, 90.

3   See P. Vielhauer's review of his commentary, *VuF* (1951-2), 213-19.

4   Commentary, 146; O. Hofius has, of course, examined the theses of
Käsemann with great thoroughness and complains, with respect to the
'pilgrimage' motif at least, that even those scholars who do not share
Käsemann's assumptions regarding the background of the letter still concede

too many essential points to him. See *Katapausis*, esp. p. 116, and, more generally, pp. 6-12 (Michel is charged on p. 11 with 'an indecisive vacillation').

5 See among others, W. D. Davies, *The Setting of the Sermon on the Mount* (Cambridge, 1964), 211ff.

6 A. Wikgren, 'Patterns of Perfection in the Epistle to the Hebrews', *NTS* 6 (1959-60), 160. See also: R. N. Flew, *The Idea of Perfection in Christian Theology* (London, 1934), 75f; C. K. Barrett, 'The Eschatology of the Epistle to the Hebrews' in *The Background of the New Testament and Its Eschatology* (C. H. Dodd Festschrift), ed. W. D. Davies and D. Daube (Cambridge, 1956), 372.

7 *NTS* 14 (1967-8), 293-320.

8 Ibid. 314 (his italics).

9 Ibid. 317.

10 G. Delling, *TDNT* VIII, 72.

11 Similarly, P. J. du Plessis, ΤΕΛΕΙΩΣΙΣ, *The Idea of Perfection in the New Testament* (Kampen, n.d.), 229. O. Cullmann, *Christology*, 93, together with R. A. Stewart, 'The Sinless Highpriest', *NTS* 14 (1967-8), 135, and others include within the 'perfection' idea the letter's heavy stress on Jesus' sinlessness, but we should note also F. Büchsel's useful distinction between 'perfection' and the more negative concept 'sinlessness' (*Christologie*, 47ff and esp. 57f).

12 F. Brown, S. R. Driver and C. A. Briggs, *A Hebrew and English Lexicon of the Old Testament* (Oxford, 1906), s.v. מלא, pi'el.

13 See esp. Dibelius, 'Der himmlische Kultus', 166ff.

14 Delling, *TDNT* VIII, 83.

15 'Hebr 5.7-10', *ZNW* 44 (1952-3), 107ff.

16 F. Scheidweiler, 'ΚΑΙΠΕΡ nebst einem Exkurs zum Hebräerbrief', *Hermes* 83 (1955), 220-30; E. Brandenburger, 'Text und Vorlagen von Hebr 5.7-10', *NovT* 11 (1969), 190-224.

17 As is clear from Brandenburger's own study: 'Here [verses 8-10] is depicted the paradoxical story of the Son, that is, the freely obedient learning through suffering by the pre-existent one as the necessary presupposition of his saving function. The *obedience* of the humiliated which makes possible the *saving ability* of the exalted one, this . . . is the focal point of the whole passage' (p. 205, italics his; it is important to note that Brandenburger here has in mind only verses 8-10, which he regards as depending upon a source different to that of verse 7). See also C. Maurer, ' "Erhört wegen der Gottesfurcht", Hebr 5.7' in *Neues Testament und Geschichte* (O. Cullmann Festschrift), ed. H. Baltensweiler and B. Reicke (Tübingen, 1972), 275-84, esp. pp. 279ff.

18 I regret that I have not been able to consult the clearly important book by P.-G. Müller, ΧΡΙΣΤΟΣ ΑΡΧΗΓΟΣ (Bern, 1973).

19 See Michel, commentary, 145; A. Wikgren, *NTS* 6 (1959-60), 162; Flew, *Perfection*, 86f; Käsemann, *Gottesvolk*, 89.

20 Käsemann, *Gottesvolk*, 89.

Chapter 2. History

1 See Grässer, *ThR* n.s. 30 (1964-5), 204-14.

2 M. Barth, 'The Old Testament in Hebrews' in *Current Issues in New Testament Interpretation* (O. Piper Festschrift), ed. W. Klassen and G. F. Snyder (London, 1962), 59f; his italics. Similarly, see among others, Caird, *CanJTheol* 5 (1959),46; S. Kistemaker, *The Psalm Citations in the Epistle to the Hebrews* (Amsterdam, 1961), 151; and Westcott, commentary, 475.

3 Grässer, *ThR* n.s. 30 (1964-5), 213, concludes his ten-page survey of the literature on this theme citing the judgement of J. van der Ploeg: 'The last word on the theme "the Old Testament in Hebrews" is not yet spoken.'

4 It is fair to urge, I think, that the vast majority of the treatments of this theme in Hebrews have not attempted more than 'descriptive' studies, as of the Old Testament text used by the author, or of his relationship with other schools of exegetical tradition of his time (Philonic, Tannaitic or Qumran). Even the quite recent and detailed study of F. Schröger, *Der Verfasser des Hebräerbriefes als Schriftausleger*, in spite of the declared intention to show how the writer's exegetical methods can 'be of service to contemporary theological discussion' (p. 9), never moves far beyond the simple observation of the methods employed and their use in other comparable traditions (see the criticisms in J. Swetnam's review in *CBQ* 31 (1968), 131f).

The coincidence of very similar techniques in exegetical traditions which produce such fundamentally different results as Philo, Qumran, the Rabbis and Christians, raises the question whether it is to the techniques we should be looking, or not rather to the theologies of revelation which lie behind them and on which the divergent results really depend.

The writer of Hebrews' exegetical affinities with some features in Philo have, of course, frequently been documented (see esp. Büchel, *TSK* 79 (1906), 572-89; C. Spicq, *L'Epître aux Hébreux* I (Paris, 1952), 39-91 (though see also the wide-ranging criticisms of Williamson, *Philo, passim*); Sowers, *Hermeneutics*; Schröger, *Ausleger* 291-307).

But in 1875 Carl Siegfried had already demonstrated extensive parallels between the Philonic methods and certain features of Tannaitic exegesis (*Philo von Alexandria als Ausleger des Alten Testaments* (Jena, 1875); see esp. pp. 168-97), which similarities scholars have also been able to trace in Hebrews (see Schröger, *Ausleger*, 108, 113f, 119, 189, and cf. his reference to P. Pavda's work on p. 25; also Sowers, *Hermeneutics*, 124, 127ff). More recently D. Daube has argued plausibly that the rules developed for rabbinic exegesis really owe their origins to principles of Hellenistic rhetoric ('Rabbinic Methods of Interpretation and Hellenistic Rhetoric', *HUCA* 22 (1949), 239-64, and 'Alexandrian Methods of Interpretation and the Rabbis' in *Festchrift Hans Lewald* (Basel, 1953), 27-44). More recently still has been the epoch-making work of M. Hengel, *Judaism and Hellenism*, I and II (London, 1974) (cf., e.g., I, 81, 173f, and the references given in n. 438).

Nor have critics been slow to discern exegetical affinities between Hebrews and the Qumran *pesher* techniques (esp. Kistemaker, *Psalm Citations*, 64-70; see also F. F. Bruce, commentary, li, and *NTS* 9 (1962-3), 219-22; B. Gärtner, 'The Habakkuk Commentary and the Gospel of Matthew', *Studia Theologica* 8 (1954), 13. H. Kosmala, *Essener*, 16, actually appeals to these affinities to support his thesis that the letter is directed to Essenes).

In view of the extent to which the techniques of biblical exegesis appear to be more or less the common property of all the exegetical traditions known to us in the first century, yet with such divergent results, can we really be content simply to list the similarities and differences with these as shown in the author's *methods*, without first asking much more fundamental questions about his *theology* of scripture?

5　The earlier form of this work concluded with a chapter on the structures used by some contemporary theologians within which to speak of 'revelation'; namely, 'language' (E. Fuchs, G. Ebeling), 'history' (W. Pannenberg) and 'hope' (J. Moltmann).

6　See esp. J. Barr, 'Revelation through History', *Interpretation* 17 (1963), 198f, and *Old and New*, 69. Also see E. Fuchs, *Hermeneutik* (Bad Cannstatt, 1954), 162f, and J. McIntyre, *The Christian Doctrine of History* (Edinburgh, 1957), 5. For some remarks on how Christians first attempted to understand 'history' see E. Käsemann, *New Testament Questions of Today* (London, 1969), 96-8, and O. Piper, *New Testament Interpretation of History* (Princeton, 1963), esp. part II (Piper is mainly concerned with Luke and Acts).

7　Moule, *Birth*, 77ff, and see above, pp. 60f.

8　K. H. Miskotte, *When the Gods Are Silent* (London, 1967), 168.

9　H. Sasse, *TDNT* I, 198ff, esp. 201; also R. Bultmann, *TDNT* II, 842. Contrariwise see J. Barr, *Biblical Words for Time* (London, 1962), 63-78 *et al.*, in confrontation with (among others) O. Cullmann. On the Greek-Hebrew question see Barr, *The Semantics of Biblical Language* (London, 1961), ch. 2, and *Old and New*, ch. 2.

10　Barr, *Time*, 149.

11　For example, W. Pannenberg writes, 'The tension between promise and fulfilment makes history' in 'Redemptive Event and History' in *Essays on Old Testament Interpretation*, ed. C. Westermann (London, 1963), 318; also similarly and frequently in his *Jesus - God and Man* (London, 1968); cf. J. Moltmann: 'The promise which announces the *eschaton*, and in which the *eschaton* announces itself, is the motive power, the mainspring, the driving force, and the torture of history' (*Hope*, 165); and G. D. Kaufman: 'Purpose . . . is a concept that refers to man's capacity for and experience of "binding time", his power to connect together successive moments into an organic unity by instituting and carrying through a temporal plan of development. As such it is closely, perhaps inseparably, connected with our sense of time or history itself as a developing unity of past, present and future' (*Systematic Theology: A Historicist Perspective* (New York, 1968), 256f).

12　See Büchsel, *Christologie* 13f; Grässer, *Glaube*, 23; Michel, commentary, 120f; Montefiore, commentary, 48.

13　Michel, commentary, 120.

14　Here, as so often in exegesis of our letter, one is confronted with the decision as to whether, as C. K. Barrett sees it, 'The thought of Hebrews is consistent, and . . . in it the eschatological is the determining element' ('The Eschatology of the Epistle to the Hebrews', 366) or, as E. Grässer sees it, '[The author] accepts the traditions of primitive Christianity but he shapes them anew as a man of his own time [on the threshold of the post-apostolic period]' (*Glaube*, 184). If one is persuaded to follow Barrett (and on Grässer's handling, see above pp. 140f) then a great deal of movement and eschatological purposefulness is apparent in the letter.

15 Barr, *Old and New*, 70.

16 Cf. the importance attributed to the concept of the Creation for historical understanding by writers such as G. D. Kaufman, *Systematic Theology*, 274ff, and, much less penetratingly, E. C. Rust, *The Christian Understanding of History* (London, 1947), 209f. With reference to Hebrews, see the cautionary remarks of F. V. Filson, *Yesterday*, 58f.

17 Kaufman also sees in 'decision' an important historical or history-making concept (*Systematic Theology*, 333f and 336ff).

18 C. E. Carlston, 'Eschatology and Repentance in the Epistle to the Hebrews', *JBL* 78 (1959), 296–302.

19 Grässer, *Glaube*, 115ff.

20 Cf. the remarks of J. McIntyre, *History*, 22ff, on the irreversibility of time as one of the categories of Necessity in historical thinking.

21 Though this study differs at crucial points from that of F. J. Schierse, *Heilsvollendung* (see, for instance, pp. 42f, 45 above), attention must be drawn to the singularly clear way in which he has emphasised the antithesis between earthly and heavenly orders of existence in our epistle.

22 Hofius, *Katapausis*, 142.

23 Barrett, 'Eschatology', 376f.

24 Grässer, *Glaube*, 23, 31, 33, 40 *et al.*; see also Käsemann, *Gottesvolk*, 22, and Schierse, *Heilsvollendung*, 114, 171 *et al.*

25 Grässer has also drawn attention to this; *Glaube*, 22f.

26 So Michel, commentary, 252, and Grässer, *Glaube*, 31.

27 Cf. the title of part III of Schierse's book *Heilsvollendung*, 'Die himmlische Berufung'.

28 In distinction to most writers, O. Hofius denies that pilgrimage is a fundamental theme in the epistle. See *Katapausis*, section B, esp. pp. 116, 144–51.

29 The telic, promissory character of the Word of God in Hebrews is, of course, well known and comes to expression in the writers here mentioned (cf., e.g., E. Käsemann; 'That the εὐαγγέλιον is only ever grasped as ἐπαγγελία on earth is a fundamental assumption of our text': *Gottesvolk*, 6) to whom we may add B. Klappert, *Eschatologie* (esp. 27ff). Our interest here has been in showing how this is constituted by the particular relationship between the Word of God and history.

30 These remarks are directed especially toward the work of F. J. Schierse in his book *Heilsvollendung* and to some extent toward that of E. Käsemann in *Gottesvolk*. But similar patterns are reproduced over a wide range of studies of the epistle.

31 Schierse, *Heilsvollendung*, 39; see Michel, commentary, 136, 143.

32 Käsemann, *Gottesvolk*, 140.

33 As Schierse is obliged to acknowledge; *Heilsvollendung*, 37. See his further modifications and concessions, pp. 143, 165, 168.

34 *Gottesvolk*, 146f.

35 U. Luck, 'Himmlisches und irdisches Geschehen im Hebräerbrief', *NovT* 6 (1963), 210. See also E. Lohse, *Märtyrer und Gottesknecht* (Göttingen, 1955), 166, and Williamson, *Philo*, 191f. With respect to Schierse's

attempted antithesis between 'Gläubiger' and 'Menschen' (*Heilsvollendung*, 118f, 126), so that it is our humanity (i.e. corporeality) which distances us from heaven, one may simply observe that this is not a distinction made by the epistle. As Schierse knows (p. 142), Hebrews is wholly non-ʳ ᵐmittal concerning the position or fate of those beyond the influence of the Word of God. It is everywhere assumed that the readers and those of whom the letter speaks do stand before its diacritical authority and are therefore either orientated toward the future of which it speaks or else turn away to a fate specified only as 'death' (3.17). The main structures in the author's 'anthropology' are therefore not those of a flesh-spirit dualism but of obedience or disobedience before the Word of God. See, further, Williamson, *Philo*, 273–6, and esp. 404.

36 See Schierse, *Heilsvollendung*, 134f.
37 See esp. Hofius, *Katapausis*, 56f.
38 Schierse, *Heilsvollendung*, 134.
39 Käsemann, *Gottesvolk*, 12, 39.
40 So that A. Oepke, whose whole thesis is given to establishing the idea of Christians as the new people of God, can nevertheless say, 'One may speak meaningfully, from the point of view of the letter to the Hebrews, of an Old Testament church' (*Das neue Gottesvolk*, 71), and J. Moffatt, commentary, 39, has: 'ὁ λαός (τοῦ θεοῦ) is the writer's favourite biblical expression for the church, from the beginning to the end; he never distinguishes Jews and Gentiles'. See also R. Bultmann, 'History and Eschatology in the New Testament', *NTS* 1 (1954–5), 10f.
41 Faith as 'conviction of things not seen' (11.1) has been taken as one of the clearest examples of a Hellenistic, non-biblical, philosophical tendency in our author (so Grässer, *Glaube*, 51ff, 127). According to this interpretation, what we have to do with here is the Philonic conception of the pilgrimage of the soul from the phenomenal world to the world of heavenly reality. Certainly the possibility of a relationship with Philonic ideas cannot be ruled out, but if this is so then these have been so historicised (as E. Käsemann carefully points out, *Gottesvolk*, 94, 104, and see also G. Theissen, *Untersuchungen*, 102–6) that their basic presuppositions can hardly any longer be compared.

   Philo can certainly affirm the futurity of the transcendental world (*Migr. Abr.* 43) (though 'promise' is a term almost unknown to Philo, as indicated by Liesegang's concordance; moreover it is suggested to me by Dr A. J. M. Wedderburn that the extent to which Philo can speak of 'futurity' is in some ways a measure of his Judaism rather than his Hellenism). But that this is not a concrete future at the end of history in the apocalyptic sense is also clear (see Michel, commentary, 383, and Williamson, *Philo*, 9, 331ff, esp. 338, 363–72; cf. also Kosmala, *Essener*, 130).

   Many writers (e.g., Barrett, 'Eschatology', 374f; J. W. Doeve, *Jewish Hermeneutics in the Synoptic Gospels and Acts* (Assen, 1953), 110; G. Sauter, *Zukunft und Verheissung* (Zurich and Stuttgart, 1965), 53; and cf. Hofius, *Vorhang*, 4–27) have stressed the invisible or supravisible qualities attached to the object of Old Testament or apocalyptic hope. The overwhelming historical sense of the future in the wider context of Hebrews, not to speak of the immediate identification of the 'things not seen' as 'things hoped for' ensures that this is the operative idea here.

42 L. Goppelt, *Typos* (Gütersloh, 1939; Darmstadt, 1969), 209f.
43 J. W. Thompson, ' "That Which Cannot Be Shaken": Some Metaphysical
    Assumptions in Heb. 12.27', *JBL* 94 (1975), 580-7, proposes that the
    antithetical ordering of ψηλαφημένος/ἐπουράνιος (12.20, 22) and
    πεποιημένος/τὰ μὴ σαλευόμενα (12.27) implies 'metaphysical assumptions
    which show many affinities with Platonism and Gnosticism' (p. 587). It is
    difficult not to feel that this conclusion is stronger than the evidence
    permits. The ψηλαφημένος might quite well have been inspired by the
    πᾶς ὁ ἀψάμενος of Ex. 19.12f; and O. Hofius has given copious references
    for the 'immoveable' quality of God's place of abode, over against the
    transience of earth, in apocalyptic thought. See esp. *Katapausis*, 285; see
    also Hengel, *Judaism and Hellenism*, I, 205, 253.
44 Schierse, *Heilsvollendung*, 179.
45 See esp. Hofius, *Vorhang*, 72, and Williamson, *Philo*, 157f; indeed see the
    entire section in Williamson on 'Time, History and Eschatology', pp. 142-59.
46 So far as I can see, the fact that the two covenants stand as πρωτή to καινή
    is nowhere mentioned in Schierse's book. Certainly this fact is never
    raised for serious discussion.
47 So A. Cody, *Heavenly Sanctuary and Liturgy in the Epistle to the Hebrews*
    (St Meinrad, Ind., 1960), 1, 141. Note especially his attempt to distinguish
    between what he calls the 'axiological' and 'cosmological' heavens, p. 78.
    See also Luck, *NovT* 6 (1963), 207; R. Gyllenberg, 'Die Christologie des
    Hebräerbriefes', *ZSTh* 11 (1934), 665; Klappert, *Eschatologie*, 24f, 48, 50,
    59; and more generally, concerning the ambivalence which attaches to the
    term 'heaven' in the bible, K. Barth, *Church Dogmatics* III, part 1 (Edinburgh,
    1958), 101.
48 Caird, *CanJTheol* 5 (1959), 46.
49 Cf. F. Hesse, 'The Evaluation and the Authority of Old Testament Texts' in
    Essays in Old Testament Interpretation, ed. C. Westermann (London, 1963),
    307, and J. Bright, *The Authority of the Old Testament* (London, 1967), 206.
50 Käsemann, *Gottesvolk*, 39; see also references to J. Calvin and E. Grässer
    below, ch. 4 n. 8.
51 So Grässer, *Glaube*, 24 n. 64, and in *ThR* n.s. 30 (1964-5), 208; also
    Kosmala, *Essener*, 100; and Vielhauer, *VuF* (1951-2), 219.
52 '...the much more jejune conception of mere prediction and verification...'
    (C. F. D. Moule, *NTS* 14 (1967-8), 295).
53 The Alexandrian notions of inspiration are often appealed to as the con-
    stituent element in the 'contemporaneity' with which the Old Testament
    is used by the writer of Hebrews (H. Windisch, *Der Hebräerbrief* (Tübingen,
    1931²), 9f; Schierse, *Heilsvollendung*, 76; Schröger, *Ausleger*, 253f). Not
    only does this assumption lack evidence however (M. Barth, 'The Old
    Testament in Hebrews', 68, 77), but the historical perspectives of the
    author's theology of revelation stand in contrast to the flat, unhistorical
    conceptions where such theories of inspiration are operative (cf. J. D. Smart,
    The Interpretation of Scripture (London, 1961), 177-82). To posit such a
    view for Hebrews only exacerbates the problem under review in this
    chapter, namely how such a corpus of inspired material can contain so much
    that, from the writer's point of view, is now obsolete (see above, p. 35). Our
    point here is not to deny that the writer did believe in the inspiration of the

Old Testament scriptures, which would be equally to outrun the evidence, but to say simply that his interest is not so much in the documents as in the revelatory activity their existence implies.

54 Gyllenberg, *ZSTh* 11 (1934), 664.

55 Several writers have spoken of the passage as preparation for the λόγος τέλεως, i.e., the Christological passage beginning in chapter 7; Käsemann, *Gottesvolk*, 117ff; Köster, 'Die Abraham-Verheissung', 97f; and Klappert, *Eschatologie*, 27f.

56 So Grässer, *Glaube*, 28: 'νωθρός εἶναι means the same as ἄπιστος εἶναι'; similarly Michel, commentary, 235 and Montefiore, commentary, 102; see also O. Kuss, 'Der theologische Grundgedanke des Hebräerbriefes', *Auslegung und Verkündigung* (collected essays, vol. I) (Regensburg, 1963), 309f.

57 This is the meaning in the change in the psalm text at Heb. 3.10. By inserting a stop and the word διό after ἔτη the writer has associated the forty years with 'they saw my works' (i.e., they witnessed my gracious activities for forty years and still rebelled) rather than with 'I was wroth' as in the original. This is a tendentious change, as we can see from Heb. 3.17.

58 This is also suggested by the writer's identification of himself, in his regular use of the second person plural, with his readers in the task of 'encouragement' (παράκλησις); Michel, commentary, 247, and Kosmala, *Essener*, 1–4. See also Grässer, 'Das Heil als Wort', 269.

59 The Word of God is identified with the words of men at 13.7. Certainly at this place it was the function of a specialist group, the 'leaders', and not that of every member of the congregation to his fellows. It follows fairly simply, however, that the regular retelling of those words (in newer and deeper forms, as the present context indicates is necessary) is the way in which this Word continues to be present in the community. See Bornkamm, 'Bekenntnis', 192, and Schierse, *Heilsvollendung*, 161f.

60 διὰ τὸν χρόνον, 5.12, indicates that a natural (καὶ γὰρ ὀφείλοντες . . .) progression of Christians is envisaged with the passage of time. E. Grässer, *Glaube*, 137ff, sees here an indication of the theoretical nature of faith for the writer. But the real threat of apostasy in the readers' situation tells against this.

61 Can such a play on words be discerned in the writer's use of κλῆσις and παράκλησις at 3.1, 13?

62 E. Schweizer, *Church Order in the New Testament* (London, 1961), 10 b, c (pp. 114, 116).

63 The line of thought which runs between the apostasy language of 6.4ff and the lament that the writer's λόγος is for this congregation a λόγος δυσερμήνευτος is indicated in three ways. (a) The first is the puzzling διό of 6.1. As the commentators regularly notice, we should have expected something like 'Nevertheless let us press on . . .' In fact the διό indicates that for the Christian to remain without progress in theological reflection is not to remain at all. Contentment with 'elementary principles' already shows a marked degree of failure. There is no alternative (διό) but to press on to maturity. (b) The qualifying phrase ἐάνπερ ἐπιτρέπῃ ὁ θεός (6.3) indicates that the reversal of the presently deteriorating situation will be akin to a conversion. In that παράκλησις has the task of warding off

τὸ ἀποστῆναι ἀπὸ θεοῦ ξῶντος (3.12) it facilitates the same kind of effect as the original proclamation of the gospel: 'repentance from dead works and faith in God' (6.1). (c) The γάρ of ἀδύνατον γάρ clinches the point. Whether γάρ here refers back to τοῦτο (i.e., the whole intention to press on) or to the ἐάνπερ phrase does not materially affect the fact of the connection.

64 Comparing the use of this metaphor in Hebrews with that in Paul, O. Michel observes: 'Paul thinks of the Pneumatics, Hebrews of those who understand scripture' (commentary, 233).

65 J. W. Doeve, 'Some Notes with Reference to ΤΑ ΛΟΓΙΑ ΤΟΥ ΘΕΟΥ in Rom. 3.2' in *Studia Paulina* (J. de Zwaan Festschrift), ed. J. N. Sevenster and W. C. van Unnik (Haarlem, 1953), 115, comes to the conclusion that λόγιον means in Hellenistic writing 'always: divine utterance, oracle' and in the Jewish world (p. 121) 'A term indicating God's revelation in Holy Scripture'. G. Kittel writes of the LXX use: 'The term has become a vehicle for the biblical conception of revelation by word ('Wort-Offenbarungs-Gedankens')': *TDNT* IV, 138.

66 The precise meaning of the term is probably impossible to recover, not least because of the range of possible meanings for each of the constituent words. On the whole English-speaking interpreters have inclined to an ethical connotation and have seen overtones of Philo's ὀρθὸς λόγος (so, in their commentaries, F. F. Bruce, Moffatt, Montefiore, Nairne, T. H. Robinson (*The Epistle to the Hebrews* (The Moffat New Testament Commentary) (London, 1933¹, 1953⁷)); also H. P. Owen in *NTS* 3 (1956–7), 245). The difficulty is that it is not so much 'Christian ethics' in which these students are backward as 'dogmatics', so to speak; so Williamson, *Philo*, 291. Cf. also Kögel, 'Der Begriff τελειοῦν im Hebräerbrief', 44, 47; to the contrary, Grässer, *Glaube*, 139f.

A number of German commentators have suggested alternatively 'incapable of right speech', 'able only to speak baby-talk', (F. Delitzsch (*Commentar zum Brief an die Hebräer* (Leipzig, 1857)), Michel, Riggenbach, Strathmann; also G. Schrenk in *TDNT* II, 198). But that the phrase can mean this remains unsubstantiated (Windisch; also Käsemann in *Gottesvolk*, 120) and in any case is hardly to the point (Moffatt).

In this impasse we are perhaps justified in turning more to the Old Testament δικαιοσύνη– צֶדֶק group of ideas, where good evidence can be found for the sense 'authentic relationship', 'appropriate response' (W. Eichrodt, *Theology of the Old Testament* I (London, 1961), 240; G. von Rad, *Old Testament Theology* I (Edinburgh, 1965), 371–83 and esp. pp. 370, 378; D. Hill, *Greek Words and Hebrew Meanings* (Cambridge, 1967), 94ff; J. A. Ziesler, *The Meaning of Righteousness in Paul* (Cambridge, 1972), 38ff).

67 E. Riggenbach, commentary, 141, in fact urges on the basis of the parallelism that τὰ λόγια τοῦ θεοῦ at 5.12 must include the New Testament revelation (similarly Michel, commentary, 236, and J. Donovan, *The Logia in Ancient and Recent Literature* (Cambridge, 1924), 12). That there *is* a relationship is clear, but this does not necessitate an identification. The location of the whole passage indicates that the immediate problem is that of the Christian interpretation of the Old Testament, and the writer analyses this in terms of a low spirituality generally, as shown by the congregation's *equal* lethargy with respect to the 'Word of Christ'. See E. G. Selwyn, *The Oracles in the New Testament* (London, 1911), 399f.

68 The creative interaction of an author with the scriptural text, resulting
in a new form of revelation in which both the original scripture writer and
his later interpreter are equally agents under God, is found in all the
exegetical traditions at the time of our writer.

Philo speaks of himself as 'under the influence of the divine possession . . .
filled with corybantic frenzy' in which he 'obtained language, ideas, an
enjoyment of light, keenest vision, pellucid distinctness of objects, such as
might be received through the eyes as the result of clearest showing' (*de
Migr.* 34-5, Colson and Whitaker's translation). That this is directly associated with his exegetical work is seen at *de Cherub.* 27 (and see also *de Somn.*
1.164; 2.252; *de Mut. Nom.* 139 and the passages collected by C. H. Dodd
in *The Interpretation of the Fourth Gospel* (Cambridge, 1953), 191f, 221,
though these are not all with reference to biblical exegesis). S. G. Sowers,
Hermeneutics, 42, writes accordingly: 'We understand, then, that for
Philo . . . both writer and interpreter are seized with divine possession, in
one case writing, in another interpreting.'

The importance of the interpreter in securing a new and deeper meaning
is also well attested in the Qumran literature. See F. F. Bruce, *Biblical
Exegesis in the Qumran Texts* (London, 1960), 9; O. Betz, *Offenbarung
und Schriftforschung in der Qumransekte* (Tübingen, 1960), 16 and often; van
der Woude, *Vorstellungen*, 43f; W. H. Brownlee, 'Biblical Interpretation among
the Sectaries of the Dead Sea Scrolls', *BA* 14 (1951), 54-76; and K. Elliger,
Studien zum Habakuk-Kommentar (Tübingen, 1953), 118-64.

Moreover, even in rabbinic Judaism, the general truth of G. F. Moore's
famous axiom notwithstanding ('The characteristic thing in Judaism at the
beginning of our era is . . . that is conceived of itself as revealed religion':
Judaism I (Cambridge, Mass., 1927), 235), there were groups who regarded
the interpretative process itself as conducted under the direction of the
Holy Spirit and as the correlative of the inspiration of the biblical writer.
Even orthodox Judaism was bound to assert for the *middoth* (interpretational rules) an origin as equally authoritative as that of the scripture and
tradition; see Doeve, *Jewish Hermeneutics*, 56 n. 1.

Finally, for Christian prophets and scripture interpretation see
M. E. Boring, 'How May We Identify Oracles of Christian Prophets in the
Synoptic Tradition?' *JBL* 91 (1972), 516f.

69 See O. Glombitza, 'Erwägungen zum kunstvollen Ansatz der Paraenese im
Brief an die Hebräer 10.19-25', *NovT* 9 (1967), 148, and Michel, commentary, 550-2.

70 See, however, J. C. Adams, 'Exegesis of Hebrews 6.1f', *NTS* 13 (1966-7),
378-85, who argues, unsuccessfully I think, for ὁ τοῦ Χριστοῦ λόγος as a
subjective genitive and translates: 'Christ's original teaching' (p. 382). So
also do F. Büchsel, *Christologie*, 21 n. 1, and H. Kosmala, *Essener*, 30, who
translates, 'der Anfang des messianischen Lebens' to facilitate his thesis
that the epistle is directed to a nonbelieving, but messianically minded,
group of Essenes. In the subsequent pages he exploits the embarrassment
of more orthodox exegetes over the non-Christian character of the six
points of 6.1f and adduces many Qumran parallels to each.

71 See Kuss, 'Grundgedanke', 311.

72 This is seen especially clearly in the case of the kerygmatic formulae through

which these Christians first received the gospel, 6.1f. There was a time
when these elements did communicate the Word of God (6.5) and which
resulted in their 'turning away from dead works' (61.). But to say these
things over again can, *at this stage*, represent only a static orthodoxy or an
infantile 'laying again of foundations'.

73 M. Dibelius' claim on this ambivalence as evidence for his thesis that
Hebrews is not written to a single group of Christians but as a catholic
document is therefore not justified. The shift in perspective is as well
explained by the writer's different analysis of the readers' relation to the
Word of God. See his essay 'Der himmlische Kultus', 162.

74 The relationship between the two forms of the promise has been carefully
analysed by H. Köster in his study 'Die Abraham-Verheissung'.

75 Ibid. 107; also Barrett, 'Eschatology', 379. See, more generally, Cullmann,
Salvation in History, 124, 159; Moltmann, *Hope*, 106, 153; Schmitz, 'Das
Alte Testament im Neuen Testament', 65f; and Sauter, *Zukunft*, 156f.

76 See the discussion and references above, pp. 20ff.

77 For the same conception in Paul, see E. Käsemann, *Perspectives on Paul*
(London, 1971), 90.

78 Certainly there is involved what I should call 'an implicit polemic' (which
is why the position appears to me to be a mediating one). The fact that
the interrelationship between the covenants presents itself as a question –
or, stated in another way, that the historical elongation of revelation
should be seen as a problem – means that there have been doubts and
uncertainties which therefore demand satisfactory answers – hence the
monumental theological work of this thinker. But that this is a good deal
easier, and that more suppositions can be taken as read, in a *Christian*
situation, albeit a question-fraught one, seems obvious.

79 See, for instance, how C. F. D. Moule's 'polemical' interpretation in
JTS n.s. 1 (1950), 37f, issues in the problems raised in *The Birth of the
New Testament*, 76ff.

80 See Klappert, *Eschatologie*, 45 n. 96, 47; also Grässer, *Glaube*, 24 n. 64,
and his reference to W. G. Kümmel (writing in *RGG*³ V, cols. 1517ff).

81 As, for instance, F. Schröger, *Ausleger*, does with almost every citation he
discusses.

82 See n. 101 below for the statistics gathered by K. J. Thomas.

83 Of many possible examples, see the use made of Ps. 104.4 at Heb. 1.7. The
original context indicates that the poet wrote: 'He makes the winds to be
his messengers'. The theme 'nature at God's disposal' which ensures that
this is the intended meaning of the text is clear even in the LXX translation.

84 E.g., Ps. 95 and Gen. 2.2 in ch. 6 of Hebrews.

85 See the discussion above on Ps.8 (pp. 58f, 83f); there is a sense in which
this can be said of all the citations.

86 G. B. Caird has collected some of these opinions, *CanJTheol* 5 (1959), 44.

87 Caird, ibid. 47ff, shows that three (Ps. 95, Ps. 110, Jer. 31) of the four
central citations are handled explicitly in terms of the self-confessed in-
adequacies of the old order. See also Kosmala, *Essener*, 6.

88 Caird, *CanJTheol* 5 (1959), 44.

89 Because it is such a comprehensive theme, it does not seem to me that the
solution lies in finding explanations for individual citations (as, e.g., Moule,

Birth, 77f). Even if we accept B. W. Bacon's suggestion with respect to
Ps. 2.7 (see n. 109 below) as Moule suggests, we have still to find one for
Deut. 32.43 (Heb. 1.6) where the same exegetical methods are employed.
A more satisfactory answer seems to me to lie in the direction of the
author's wider understanding of the rule of the scriptures for the Christian.

90 J. Moffatt, commentary, xxvii, writes: 'Had the danger been a relapse into
Judaism of any kind, it would have implied a repudiation of Jesus as
Messiah and divine – the very truth which the writer can assume!' I hope it
is by now clear that the present essay distinguishes itself from Moffatt's
position on the 'apostasy' question, but the remark here cited serves at
least to show that the discussion must be an 'internal' one. See also
Manson, *The Epistle to the Hebrews*, 91, and Williamson, *Philo*, 536.

91 Strack and Billerbeck, *Kommentar* III, 675ff.

92 J. M. Allegro, 'Further Messianic References in Qumran Literature', *JBL* 75
(1956), 177.

93 J. M. Allegro, 'Fragments of a Qumran Scroll of Eschatological Midraŝim',
JBL 77 (1958), 350–4, and Y. Yadin, 'A Midrash on II Sam. 7 and Ps. 1–2
(4Q Florilegium)', *IEJ* 9 (1959), 95–8; see also Doeve, *Jewish Hermeneutics*, 172f.

94 Ps. 45 is understood messianically by the Targum on Psalms (Strack and
Billerbeck, *Kommentar* III, 679) which may be early enough to reflect
opinions going back to the time of our writer (see *Jewish Encyclopedia*
XII, 62).

95 Strack and Billerbeck, *Kommentar* IV, 457ff.

96 Westcott, commentary, 42.

97 Klappert, *Eschatologie*, 46.

98 βλέπομεν is not, of course, properly an imperative or an exhortation but
that it has this intention can be seen from the similar sentence at 12.1f:
'Therefore . . . let us run . . . looking to Jesus, who . . . is seated in glory at
the right hand of God.'

99 Kistemaker, *Psalm Citations*, 83. See also Buchanan, commentary, 38–51.

100 It is well known that the Hebrew poet's *parallelismus membrorum*:
וַתְּחַסְּרֵהוּ מְּעַט מֵאֱלֹהִים וְכָבוֹד וְהָדָר תְּעַטְּרֵהוּ is taken by Hebrews as a contrast!

101 In the present case this is limited to the excision of the superfluous line
καὶ κατέστησας αὐτὸν ἐπὶ τὰ ἔργα τῶν χειρῶν σου. Even if our author wrote
τίς ἐστιν ἄνθρωπος (see the critical apparatus) this is unlikely to have been
his own creation (as suggested by G. Zuntz, *The Text of the Epistles* (London,
1953), 48), since, as K. J. Thomas has shown fairly clearly ('The Use of the
Septuagint in the Epistle to the Hebrews', unpublished Ph.D. dissertation,
University of Manchester, 1959; see also his 'The Old Testament Citations
in Hebrews', *NTS* 11 (1964–5), 303–25, esp. pp. 320ff) in those instances
in which the A and B LXX texts differ, the author of Hebrews simply used
the text as he had it before him (which in this case would represent the A
text) (Thomas, 'Use of the Septuagint', 226). Thomas counts fifteen places
in seven citations where A is used over against B in direct citations and eight
places in five citations where B is preferred to A (p. 180).
  On the other hand Thomas' work also shows that in the majority of
cases where Hebrews differs from both LXX texts, the change has been
originated by this author. Thomas lists about (since it is not absolutely

clear in one or two cases which Old Testament passage is being cited) twenty-six places in thirteen citations where the text of Hebrews varies from both A and B without other MSS parallel; twenty-three places in thirteen citations where Hebrews is paralleled only by non-uncial MSS against A and B; and eight places in six citations where Hebrews is paralleled by uncials other than A and B. Thomas is able to adduce textual evidence to show that most of these parallels have been influenced by the text of Hebrews.

102   See the thirteen points enumerated by W. H. Brownlee for the exegetes at Qumran (*BA* 14 (1951), 60ff). For Philo see points 5, 7 and 11 in C. Siegfried's list of twenty-three Rules for Allegory, *Philo als Ausleger*, 168ff. In the case of the Rabbis, see J. W. Doeve, *Jewish Hermeneutics*, 109f, where he suggests Paul had good precedent for changing הגר into ההר at Gal. 4.25; the seven and the thirteen rules of rabbinic interpretation can also be found in J. Bowker, *The Targums and Rabbinic Literature* (Cambridge, 1969), 315ff.

103   Kistemaker, *Psalm Citations*, 103.

104   It is not easy to know whether the explanation frequently given by later Christian exegetes (i.e., that in Jesus all humanity is caught up and represented, so that ultimately every reference to humanity is a reference to Jesus; see Moule, *Phenomenon*, 32f, 92f; Westcott, commentary, 43; cf. also B. S. Childs, *Biblical Theology in Crisis* (Philadelphia, 1970), 162) was really the rationale adopted by the writer or does not rather represent the attempt to find a rationale for him. That he did think along these lines is suggested not so much by the equation αὐτῷ = Jesus (Heb. 2.8) but by the subsequent interest in Jesus' personal identification of himself with humanity (2.11ff). This would mean that the psalmist's υἱὸς ἀνθρώπου is in fact being taken at face value but that the event of Jesus' exaltation now gives to humanity as a whole a quite new perspective; so that the original meaning though not destroyed is given a new dimension not possible for the psalmist. If this is right, the process involved concurs closely with that we have observed in ch. 6 of the letter.

105   Goppelt, *Typos*, 205. For opinions against the 'scripture-proof' role of the citations, see Grässer, *ThR* n.s. 30 (1964–5), 207f.

106   It is fairly conclusively established that the language and construction of 1.3 represent an established formulaic expression around which the writer has built his highly wrought introduction (see above, pp. 6f). In light of this W. Manson in *The Epistle to the Hebrews*, 91f, has suggested that the following catena of scripture citations represents a kind of commentary on this confessional statement, point for point, and drawn from the Old Testament, chiefly from the psalms. If there is any merit in this suggestion it has an important bearing on the present discussion, for it would mean that all the citations of chapter 1 are already seen through the prism of, and are controlled by, a Christological confession. Whatever the merits or otherwise of Manson's suggestion, the practice it implies may be clearly discerned in other parts of the letter, as, for instance, in the Christological treatment of Ps. 110.4 in ch. 7 of Hebrews.

107   The importance to the writer of the concept 'worshipping angels' may be seen in the fact that he has especially constructed the citation from pre-

viously unconnected elements in Deut. 32.43. See Thomas, 'Use of the
Septuagint', 154ff.

108 Montefiore, commentary, 48.

109 Cf. O. Cullmann, *Christology*, 234, who regards κύριε as the linchpin by
which the citation is fastened in its place. See also T. F. Glasson, ' "Plurality
of Divine Persons" and the Quotations in Hebrews 1.6ff', *NTS* 12 (1965-6),
270-2, and B. W. Bacon, 'Hebrews 1.10-12 and the Septuagint Rendering
of Ps. 102.23', *ZNW* 3 (1902), 280-5.

110 Von Rad, *Old Testament Theology* II, 327.

111 See the list compiled by E. Grässer, *ThR* n.s. 30 (1964-5), 207. It is difficult
to understand how A. T. Hanson can begin his essay on the way Christ is
supposed to be found in the Old Testament in Hebrews by remarking,
'Apparently no one has ever suggested that the thought of the pre-existent
Christ active in Old Testament history is to be found in the Epistle to the
Hebrews' (*Jesus Christ in the Old Testament* 48).

112 So W. Manson, *The Epistle to the Hebrews*, 185-7, and M. Barth, 'The Old
Testament in Hebrews', 70. But see E. Grässer, *Glaube*, 29,and F. V. Filson,
Yesterday, 31ff, who have plausibly claimed that 'yesterday' at 13.8 refers
not to the time of the Old Testament but to that of the incarnate Jesus.

113 This is a fact which seems to me to warrant more attention than the casual
references often accorded it by the commentators; as, for instance, J. Moffatt,
commentary, 33, 138, and H. Montefiore, commentary, 63. See also, however, O. Michel, commentary, 158, and R. V. G. Tasker, *The Gospel in the
Epistle to the Hebrews* (London, 1950), 38.

114 Is it possible that the substitution at Heb. 2.12 of ἀπαγγελῶ for διηγήσομαι
of the LXX, apparently by our author (see Thomas, 'Use of the Septuagint',
39ff), reflects the influence of this tradition? Cf. the form known to Luke:
ἀπηγγέλη δὲ αὐτῷ, Ἡ μήτηρ σου καὶ ἀδελφοί σου . . . ὁ δὲ ἀποκριθεὶς εἶπεν
πρὸς αὐτούς, Μήτηρ μου καὶ ἀδελφοί μου . . . (Luke 8.20f).

115 For the Johannine version of this tradition see C. H. Dodd, *Historical Tradition in the Fourth Gospel* (Cambridge, 1963), 69. Cf. also E. Hoskyns and
N. Davey, *The Riddle of the New Testament* (London, 1931, 1958²), 173,
and Dodd, *The Interpretation of the Fourth Gospel*, 194.

116 See Grässer, *ThR* n.s. 30 (1964-5), 207f.

117 It is frequently noticed how the New Testament church has moved from an
understanding of Jesus' 'words', as communicating the Word of God, to an
identification of Jesus himself as the embodiment of that Word. See
Kittel, *TDNT*, IV,106f, 128f; Hoskyns and Davey, *The Fourth Gospel*
(London, 1940, 1947²), 161; A. Richardson, *Introduction to the Theology
of the New Testament* (London, 1958), 159. It is therefore an interesting
reflection of the 'salvation-historical' interests of the writer of Hebrews
that the words which for other New Testament authors are constituent
with Jesus' being himself the Word are, in this writer, expressed through
Old Testament words.

118 E.g., Büchel, *TSK* 79 (1906), 549, 551, 557.

119 G. von Rad, in his *Old Testament Theology* (II, 407, 409 and often) speaks
of the creative freedom with which the New Testament authors used the
Old Testament as 'charismatic'. In contrast, K. Schwarzwäller, *EvTh* 29
(1969), 290, speaks of the possibility of typological exegesis degenerating

into the mechanical pairing off of type and antitype. Similarly, B. S. Childs, *Crisis*, 158f, shows how the historical perspectives of the New Testament writers often have been flattened out into timeless, inspired 'truths' in later Christian exegesis. See G. Ebeling's essay 'The Meaning of "Biblical Theology" ' in *Word and Faith*, particularly 84ff, for post-Reformation examples.

120 See, e.g., R. W. Funk, *Language, Hermeneutic and Word of God* (New York, 1966), 199; Childs, *Crisis*, 120-2, and cf. pp. 174ff; Barr, *Old and New*, 28f.

121 To be included here are the significant number of texts which, though not speaking of the Messiah directly, had already been interpreted 'messianically' before the Christians took them up, precisely because it could be seen that the events of which they spoke were at most only inadequately achieved in their immediate historical context, thus creating an ever swelling sense of expectation. It has been the singular contribution of G. von Rad to discover and to present so effectively this conception of an ongoing movement to partial fulfilment in which 'Israel's history with God thrusts forward violently into the future' (*Old Testament Theology* II, 332). See also A. L. Moore, *The Parousia in the New Testament* (Leiden, 1966), 10.

122 See the reference above, n. 87, to G. B. Caird's work.

123 The degree to which this is so will be the subject for investigation in the subsequent chapter.

124 See, for example, Sowers, *Hermeneutics*, 29; Siegfried, *Philo als Ausleger*, 163; Williamson, *Philo*, 528.

125 So O. Michel, commentary, 92: 'Our epistle refers to the Address of God which has come to the community through history and from the most recent past. In distinction from Philo, the letter to the Hebrews thinks historically, messianically and eschatologically', and similarly in *TDNT* IV, 570 n. 9. See also J. R. Schaeffer, 'The Relationship between Priestly and Servant Messianism in the Epistle to the Hebrews', *CBQ* 30 (1968), 363; C. H. Dodd, *The Old Testament in the New* (Philadelphia, 1963), 6; Stanton, *Jesus of Nazareth*, 127; Williamson, *Philo*, 103 (citing W. Manson), 150f, 319, 530f; and, more generally, Barr, *Old and New*, 110.

126 Doeve, *Jewish Hermeneutics*, 54, and Hengel, *Judaism and Hellenism* I, 175.

127 E. E. Ellis, *Paul's Use of the Old Testament* (Edinburgh, 1957), 44f.

128 Betz, *Offenbarung und Schriftforschung*, 8ff.

129 The importance of Jesus as a figure of history in the establishing of relationships between the Old and New Testaments is reflected, again by way of contrast, in the Gnostics' discomfort with the concrete figure of Jesus: 'The Docetic concept of Christ was a necessary part of Marcion's teaching, for otherwise he would have been obliged to link Jesus with the Old Testament and with the Creator' (W. H. C. Frend, 'Marcion', *ExT* 80 (1968-9), 330).

130 We remarked above, ch. 1 n. 116, on the curious failure of O. Cullmann to appreciate the importance of Hebrews for his theme. The one brief mention Hebrews does receive is with respect to the writer's typological exegesis, which Cullmann claims, rightly I think, to presuppose a strongly historical concept of revelation (*Salvation in History*, 131f). See also the original Preface to Goppelt's *Typos* and Grässer, *ThR* n.s. 30 (1964-5), 210.

G. W. H. Lampe's judgement in *Essays on Typology* (London, 1957), 34, that the treatment of Melchizedek in Hebrews rests on 'sheer allegorizing' seems to me somewhat less than accurate. The thrust of the argument is that the levitical institutions *must* have been less than perfect because already in antiquity a more perfect one had already been conceived of and enunciated with respect to Melchizedek, 'priest for ever'. The details with which this is worked out are certainly imaginative but the exegetical principle, I should judge, falls short of 'sheer' allegory. See Sowers, *Hermeneutics*, 123–6, and R. P. C. Hanson, *Allegory and Event* (London, 1959), 86.

131   See C. H. Dodd, *History and the Gospel* (London, 1964), 25.

132   E. Käsemann, *Gottesvolk*, 27ff, has examined this passage carefully and has described it as of 'decisive importance' in Hebrews (p. 27); of the eschatological paradox involved, he writes: '[That the vision of Jerusalem comes in the form of a promise] confirms once again the recognition, already achieved, that the heavenly πατρίς is the singular goal of faith-pilgrimage. But at the same time it is to be noted that the unshakeable kingdom is . . . already revealed to the people of God' (p. 30).

133   This has been particularly well worked out by B. Klappert, *Eschatologie* (see esp. pp. 48f). G. Theissen, *Untersuchungen*, 93ff, has also perceived the distinction between paraenesis and theology in terms of eschatological perspectives, but seems to me not to have carried through his insights. He has been misled by his assumptions of a sacramentalist background for the epistle and by his preference for the questionable (for Hebrews) method of *Redaktionskritik* (pp. 96ff). F. Zimmermann's attempt, in *Die Hohepriester-Christologie des Hebräerbriefes* (Paderborn, 1964), 23f, to analyse the eschatological perspectives of Hebrews in terms of Christ's earthly and heavenly ministries (i.e., the death on the cross = future hope; the priesthood in heaven = present salvation) seems to me not to have been successful.

134   Isolated futurist–eschatological remarks may certainly be identified within the theological–Christological sections, as, for instance, at 9.14, καθαριεῖ τὴν συνείδησιν, and at 7.19 in the designation of Jesus' work as ἐπεισαγωγὴ κρείττονος ἐλπίδος which B. Klappert has correctly placed under the heading 'The Eschatological Event as Oath-Promise' (*Eschatologie*, 31, and see p. 27). Generally however it remains true that the theological parts of the epistle have as their subject the eschatological events that *have* happened, and the paraenetic parts are concerned that the readers should partake in the eschatological events that *will* happen.

135   The eschatological importance of the heavenly enthronisation scene of ch. 1 has often been noticed (see esp. Käsemann, *Gottesvolk*, 58ff, and Schierse, *Heilsvollendung*, 93ff). It has been the especial contribution of B. Klappert, however (*Eschatologie*, 22f), to draw attention to the revelatory significance of this eschatological event, as signified by the close conjunction of the enthronisation with the final form of God's Word (see also Schierse, *Heilsvollendung*, 197f).

136   In addition to the material gathered there we may now notice in finer detail the striking parallelism between 1.1f (the eschatological speaking through the Son) and 9.26 (the eschatological sacrifice of the Son). Both signify the end of the old aeon and distinguish themselves over against it by their finality in contrast to the partial, drawn-out qualities which characterised the institutions of that age, πολυμερῶς καὶ πολυτρόπως, 1.1; νυνὶ δὲ ἅπαξ, 9.26. See Grässer, *Glaube*, 36f.

137 See G. Stählin, *TDNT* I, 384; also W. Bieder, 'Pneumatologische Aspekte
     im Hebräerbrief' in *Neues Testament und Geschichte* (O. Cullmann
     Festschrift), ed. H. Baltensweiler and B. Reicke (Tübingen, 1972), 251.
138 The claim (made by R. Gyllenberg, *ZSTh* 11 (1934), 677ff, esp. p. 685,
     and continued by E. Lohse, *Märtyrer*, 163f, 167, and by E. Käsemann,
     Gottesvolk, 98–105, 143, and B. Klappert, *Eschatologie*, 54) that
     λύτρωσις and σωτηρία represent distinct aspects of Christ's eschatological
     accomplishments (i.e., λύτρωσις = he *has* overcome the power of death,
     2.14; σωτηρία = the salvation still to come) seems to me difficult to sustain.
     Apart from the disproportionate weight all these authors put on the single
     reference to Christ's overcoming of the Devil (2.14), their thesis seems to
     overlook the fact that *not* everything has been brought into subjection, so
     that mankind cannot yet be truly redeemed (2.8), and that part of the in-
     heritance for which the Son must wait is the putting of his enemies under
     his feet (1.13). In other words λύτρωσις is no more wholly *accomplished*
     than σωτηρία is wholly *future* (2.3). See especially the criticisms of
     A. Oepke, *Das neue Gottesvolk*, 63 n. 5.
139 That this cultic purity represents the eschatological state is to be seen in
     the reference back through σύν, 10.19, to the quotation from Jeremiah
     concerning the eschatological covenant of forgiveness, 10.16f.
140 C. E. Carlston, *JBL* 78 (1959), 300, notes that Hebrews nowhere specifically
     interprets the non-possibility of a second repentance 'horizontally', that is
     to say, because of the imminence of the second advent (though it might
     be deduced from statements like that at 10.25). Rather it belongs very
     clearly to the 'vertical' (or 'realised') part of the letter's eschatology. This
     implies a certain inconsistency with the general principle we have established
     about eschatological perspectives and the theology–paraenesis disjunctions,
     since all three 'sin' passages come in paraenetic contexts. In fact the dis-
     crepancy is more apparent than real, since the main interest in these
     passages is to show that *the* sin (of apostasy) is still possible and that salva-
     tion is still therefore a future entity. This also applies to the σωτηρία of
     2.3; the Word of Christ *is* a 'saving' Word (realised) but the possibility
     exists of neglecting it, making it clear that the salvation of which it speaks
     has not yet been attained by the Christians.
141 See ibid. 301; cf. also Schierse, *Heilsvollendung*, 146; Williamson, *Philo*,
     249f; F. M. Young, *Sacrifice and the Death of Christ* (London, 1975), 82.
142 K. Bornhäuser in his essay 'Die Versuchungen Jesu nach dem Hebräerbrief',
     72–86, advances very plausibly the thesis that 'temptation' in Hebrews
     always refers to the *Christian* temptation to fall away from faith and con-
     stancy rather than being a matter of ethical shortcomings. That Hebrews
     can consider day-to-day sins as distinct from *the* sin of apostasy is reflected
     in the insistence on the mercy and understanding of Jesus toward weaknesses
     (2.17f; 5.2, 7ff), not to mention the writer's demand (of Christians!) that
     they put off their sins (12.1). See E. Schweizer, *Lordship and Discipleship*
     (London, 1960), 72ff.
143 Schierse, *Heilsvollendung*, 145, 150.
144 Carlston, *JBL* 78 (1959), 300; Lohse, *Märtyrer*, 175, 180; Schierse,
     Heilsvollendung, 148, 151.
145 E. Grässer has drawn especial attention to the 'Old Testament character' of

Christian faith in Hebrews (see, e.g., the references above in Introduction, n. 5. Grässer is quite correct in his observations, as far as he goes. What I hope to show (pp. ■■■ff) is that this characterisation can only be maintained for the paraenetic sections of the letter and that Grässer's promotion of it into a generalised statement for the whole letter represents a methodological fault.

146 Cf. W. Bieder, 'Pneumatologische Aspekte', 255ff, on the significance of the 'eschatological' Spirit speaking through the LXX texts.

147 I refer again to the essay of G. B. Caird mentioned in n. 87 above.

148 See especially the criticisms directed toward the work of E. Grässer on pp. 137ff. More generally, however, one would have to include all those surveys of the eschatology of the letter which fasten on to one or the other aspect and attempt to make that regulative for the letter as a whole.

149 Perhaps the most valuable contribution of B. Klappert's small book is its insistence that the eschatological patterns in Hebrews have been dictated by the eschatological shape of the Christ-event itself (*Eschatologie*, 12 etc.). What seems to me confused and much less convincing is his attempt to show how an original 'Ιησοῦς-κοσμοκρατώρ confession has been modified in response to the delay of the parousia (p. 54 etc.).

150 Schierse, *Heilsvollendung*, 159; Moule, *JTS* n.s. 1 (1950), 37ff.

151 The exception perhaps is at 12.1f, where the 'surrounding cloud of witnesses' is not exactly a Christological theme. On the other hand exegetes have often suggested that Jesus is in fact seen as at the head of this list of faithful witnesses. See O. Michel, 'Zur Auslegung des Hebräerbriefes', *NovT* 6 (1963), 191.

152 ʼΕνεκαίνισεν (10.19) is probably suggested by the διαθήκη καινή of the Jeremiah quotation (cf. 8.8, 13).

153 It is often said that the resolution of the tension is found in the congregation's worship; e.g., see Grässer, *Glaube*, 182f, and Dibelius, 'Der himmlische Kultus', 176. This is a perfectly reasonable interpretation though, it should be stressed, an inferential one, usually dependent on the 'approach' language of 4.16, 7.25, 10.22 etc.

154 In a provocative article, J. Swetnam, 'Sacrifice and Revelation in the Epistle to the Hebrews', *CBQ* 30 (1968), 227-34, argues that πεφανέρωται of 9.26 should be construed with διὰ τῆς θυσίας αὐτοῦ and translated, 'once and for all, at the closing of the ages, for the annulling of sin, through his sacrifice, he [Christ] has been made manifest' (p. 228). Helpful as this would be for the thesis of this book, i.e., in its identification of the revelatory and sacrificial aspects of Jesus' death, the exegesis is not really convincing. (*a*) διὰ τῆς θυσίας αὐτοῦ really cannot be taken with πεφανέρωται in preference to εἰς ἀθέτησιν τῆς ἁμαρτίας (Swetnam claims this would not impair his thesis (p. 228), but that is more than open to question). (*b*) In the context, almost totally absorbed with Jesus' entry into *heaven*, πεφανέρωται must surely mean his appearance before *God* and thus be an extension of νῦν ἐμφανισθῆναι τῷ προσώπῳ τοῦ θεοῦ of verse 24.

155 O. Cullmann, *Christology*, 91f, says that 'the great significance of the Christological concept of Jesus the Highpriest' is that in its light 'the atoning death of Jesus demonstrates the true New Testament dialectic between deepest humiliation and highest majesty'. (Cullmann is thinking of the degrees of humiliation and exaltation which attend Jesus' person in Hebrews.)

But in that case the whole conception of Jesus *as one who intercedes* for his people would be a secondary development. However, the statement itself is open to question (see below, ch. 3 n. 79).

156 For a summary statement, A. H. McNeile, *An Introduction to the Study of the New Testament* (Oxford, 1953²), 224.

157 Cf. U. Luck, *NovT* 6 (1963), 200-3: 'The question which motivates the letter to the Hebrews seems to me to be: how can a community maintain a confession which acknowledges and proclaims Jesus as Son and as exalted Lord of the world, when in this world it is being persecuted and is under pressure precisely *as* the community of that Lord?' (p. 200).

Chapter 3. Jesus

1 E.g., R. Bultmann, *The History of the Synoptic Tradition* (Oxford, 1963), 303; R. H. Strachan, *The Historic Jesus in the New Testament* (London, 1931), 103; E. F. Scott, *The Epistle to the Hebrews*, 61; Hoskyns and Davey, *Riddle of the New Testament*, 166; Moffatt, commentary, xliv, li.

2 So E. Grässer in the closing remarks of his survey article, *ThR* n.s. 30 (1964-5), 236. See also his remarks on pp. 188ff on the relationship between Hebrews and the Synoptic gospels. Otherwise the only studies known to me addressed to the questions about Jesus – within the context of the modern debate – with respect to Hebrews are: Grässer's own article 'Der historische Jesus im Hebräerbrief', *ZNW* 56 (1965), 63-91, and that of U. Luck, 'Himmlisches und irdisches Geschehen im Hebräerbrief', *NovT* 6 (1963), 192-215; H. Anderson has a short but useful section on Hebrews in *Jesus and Christian Origins* (New York, 1964), 280-8. The studies of Strachan (mentioned above) and of A. M. Ramsay, 'The Gospel and the Gospels' in *Studia Evangelica* I, ed. K. Aland *et al.* (Berlin, 1959), 35-42, fall outside the modern debate; the lists of details of Jesus which they see as given by Hebrews include a number of aspects which, in terms of the modern discussion, cannot be regarded as historical but theological assertions. R. Williamson refers briefly to the possibilities offered by Hebrews in a footnote, 'Hebrews and Doctrine', *ExT* 81 (1969-70), 374 n. 4, and see his *Philo*, 154.

3 The course of this debate has been reviewed more often than to need repetition here. Full bibliographical details may be found in the two review articles by W. G. Kümmel, 'Jesusforschung seit 1950', *ThR* n.s. 31 (1965-6), 15-46, 289-315, and 'Ein Jahrzehnt Jesusforschung (1965-1975)', *ThR* n.s. 40 (1975), 289-336, and 41 (1976), 197-258. See also E. Grässer, 'Motive und Methoden der neueren Jesus-Literatur', *VuF* no. 2, 1973, 3-45.

4 So E. Trocmé, *Jesus and His Contemporaries* (London, 1973), 14: 'The other documents [beside the gospels] which tell us about Jesus are no more than subsidiary sources, which have nothing essential to offer.'

5 The *criteria* for this, of course, are infinitely more difficult to establish, so that in a way the 'quest for the historical Jesus' really means the 'quest for criteria for the historical Jesus'. See, among others, R. S. Barbour, *Traditio-Historical Criticism of the Gospels* (London, 1972), who refers to most of the more prominent essayists in this matter.

6 G. N. Stanton in his book *Jesus of Nazareth* presents a series of such cases; the speeches in Acts, Paul, Luke and the other Synoptic writers.

7 'If one wishes to speak of *discipleship*, one keeps running necessarily into the indivisibility of the name "Jesus Christ" which most of the books mentioned [Jewish and Marxist] do not willingly accept' (E. Grässer, *VuF* no. 2, 1973, 42; his italics).

8 Anderson, *Origins*, 262.

9 C. K. Barrett, *Jesus and the Gospel Tradition* (London, 1967), ix.

10 So Grässer, *ZNW* 56 (1965), 68, 71; cf. the method employed by C. H. Dodd in comparing the Johannine with the Synoptic traditions in *Historical Tradition in the Fourth Gospel* and, on a much smaller scale, by W. R. Farmer in 'An Historical Essay on the Humanity of Jesus Christ' in *Christian History and Interpretation* (J. Knox Festschrift), ed. W. R. Farmer, C. F. D. Moule and R. R. Niebuhr (Cambridge, 1967), 101-26.

11 Cf., for instance, the critical remarks of H. Windisch, commentary, 26: 'That the writer works from a full and concrete evangelical tradition cannot anywhere be shown convincingly. Rather, his knowledge of 'the life of Jesus' can perfectly satisfactorily be derived from the traditional Messiah-myth and from the LXX.'

12 Cf. G. A. Wells, *The Jesus of the Early Christians* (London, 1971), 157f.

13 Other New Testament references are at Acts 3.15, 5.31. See above, excursus 1 n. 18.

14 E. Grässer, *Glaube*, 59, and E. Käsemann, *Gottesvolk*, 81f, confidently assign to it gnostic, or at very least, Hellenistic, overtones. But O. Michel, commentary, 144, 433, suggests possible apocalyptic and rabbinic analogies, and the term is found in the LXX in both literal and figurative senses (Delling, *TDNT* I, 487).

15 E.g., Grässer, *Glaube*, 58. Also see ch. 2 n. 51 above.

16 Grässer, *Glaube*, 35, 39, 62f, 70, 117-25 *et al.*; see pp. 137ff above for more detailed references and discussion. H. Kosmala, *Essener,* 97ff, makes the same allegation.

17 Grässer, *Glaube*, 102.

18 An exception is the nicely ambivalent 'who leads us in our faith and brings it to perfection' of the Jerusalem Bible.

19 Commentary, 351.

20 R. Bultmann, for example, roundly declares that the gospels nowhere speak of Jesus' faith ('The Primitive Christian Kerygma and the Historical Jesus' in *The Historical Jesus and the Kerygmatic Christ*, ed. C. E. Braaten and R. A. Harrisville (Nashville, 1964), 34), a statement which has been disputed by E. Fuchs, *Studies of the Historical Jesus* (London, 1964), 28, 60ff, and especially by G. Ebeling, *The Nature of Faith* (London, 1961), 44-57, and *Word and Faith*, 234, 237, 297f and 301ff.

21 F. F. Bruce, commentary, 351: 'More probably we should recognise here the regular Greek usage of the article before an abstract noun, where English as regularly omits it'; and E. Grässer, *Glaube*, 58: 'The *nostrae* is eisegesis! There is nothing in this verse about our faith.'

22 Indeed the writer is not content even to leave it there, but goes on in the following verse: ἀναλογίσασθε γὰρ τὸν τοιαύτην ὑπομεμενηκότα . . . ἀντιλογίαν. And he has the same exemplary motif in mind: ἵνα μὴ κάμητε ταῖς ψυχαῖς ὑμῶν.

23 C. F. D. Moule, *An Idiom Book of New Testament Greek* (Cambridge, 1963), 204.

24 See esp. Westcott, commentary, 395.
25 Dautzenberg, *BZ* n.s. 15 (1973), 167f.
26 Cf. how E. Käsemann has seen here a reference, proleptically conceived, to the eschatological entry of the Son into his inheritance, at which the angels for the moment must represent the worshipping community (*Gottesvolk*, 58–60, 66–71); the point here, however, is that there is as yet *no* admission of the 'eschatological discrepancy' in the letter. All is cast in terms of a 'realised' eschatological present.
27 γάρ does not necessarily imply a continuity; it can as well signify a change of subject. Moffatt, commentary, 21.
28 This is reflected, not least, in the scripture citations. The exalted strains of Pss. 45 and 102 give way to the reflection on man 'for a short time made lower than the angels' and to the 'identification' passages quoted in 2.12f.
29 See Westcott, commentary, 57; Moffatt, commentary, 37, 39.
30 See ch. 2 n. 138 above.
31 Above, pp. 73f, and esp. p. 173 n. 157.
32 See esp. Michel, commentary, 139.
33 Westcott, commentary, 43; Moffatt, commentary, 23; Childs, *Crisis*, 155ff.
34 Cf. all the commentators; in addition, Childs, *Crisis*, esp. pp. 155–7; Moule, *Phenomenon*, 32f; and L. E. Keck, *A Future for the Historical Jesus* (Nashville, 1971), 115–17.
35 J. Moffatt makes the important point (commentary, 23), missed by some, that the identification between the 'man' of the psalm and Jesus should be seen to be less dependent on the αὐτῷ of verse 8 (which may quite well still mean 'mankind'); rather it is made in the recognition of τὸν ἠλαττωμένον as Jesus (verse 9).
36 Moffatt, commentary, 28: 'For the first time, the conception of suffering occurs, and the situation which gave rise to the author's handling of the subject arose out of what he felt to be his readers' attitude. "We are suffering hardships on account of our religion." But so did Jesus, the writer replies.'
37 Cf. Moffatt, commentary, 32.
38 O. Michel, commentary, 141, Cf. p. 148: 'The pre-existence conception ... speaks [in Hebrews] of God's action in the Word, of the association of the hidden Christ with the world and history.'
39 'The change of the verb [βλέπομεν in verse 9] from ὁρῶμεν in verse 8 cannot be without meaning. βλέπειν apparently expresses the particular exercise of the faculty of sight ...' (Westcott, commentary, 45).
40 In spite of the interchangeability of 'Jesus' with 'Christ' which we have already noticed (ch. 1 n. 104 above), many writers draw attention to the significance of Jesus' 'earthly' name here: J. C. Campbell, 'In a Son', *Interpretation* 10 (1956), 27; A. Nairne, *Epistle of Priesthood* (Edinburgh, 1913), 68; Moffatt, commentary, 23; Westcott, commentary, 45.
41 Cf. F. F. Bruce, commentary, 43. The term 'disclosure situation' is one borrowed by A. Richardson from I. T. Ramsey; see, e.g., Richardson's *History, Sacred and Profane* (London, 1964), 223ff. No commitment is intended, in the use of his phrase, to Richardson's views on history.
42 'God "brings" (ἀγαγεῖν) the many sons and Christ is their "leader" (ἀρχηγός)' (Westcott, commentary, 49).

43 The majority of commentators take ἐξ ἐνὸς πάντες as referring to our common spiritual origins, i.e., in God; O. Procksch, *TDNT* I, 112, sees in it a reference to Adam or Abraham; and J. C. Campbell, *Interpretation* 10 (1956), 32f (following W. Manson) takes it simply as 'they form a unity'.

44 J. Moffatt, commentary, 33, has: 'The fact that Jesus required to put faith in God proves that he was a human being like ourselves.' But F. Büchsel, *Christologie*, 45, sees that the point is not to establish Jesus' humanity but that it is his humanity which establishes his common lot with the Christians: 'As God's servant, Jesus believes just like his brothers.'

45 Campbell, *Interpretation* 10 (1956), 33.

46 See esp. Käsemann, *Gottesvolk*, 61-70, 98-105. It is important to note the Christian modifications which Käsemann sees as having taken place in the use of this scheme by the writer of Hebrews, as the kerygmatic declaration of Jesus' death as an event in history is brought to bear upon it (pp. 103ff and also 112f). See also Schierse, *Heilsvollendung*, 37, 82, 97-108, 118; it seems to me however that the admission by Schierse (p. 143) that death, in Hebrews, is not seen simply as a natural phenomenon ('nicht als naturhafte Gegebenheit') but as involving *guilt*, is a crucial one. Cf., alternatively, Lohse, *Märtyrer*, 165f; Luck, *NovT* 6 (1963), 210; and Michel, commentary, 161f.

47 Luck, *NovT* 6 (1963), 200f (cf. p. 173 n. 157 above).

48 For the exhortatory significance of 2.9, see above, ch. 2 n. 98.

49 Some hesitation may be felt in ascribing the quality of paraenesis to 2.5-18, which must seem to include a good deal of the writer's theology of incarnation. Certainly it is not so obviously exhortatory as some of the other paraenetic passages; but nor is it so clearly Christological as the 'comparisons' and functions rather more 'encouragingly' than 'dogmatically'.

50 Cf. the connection between Moses' stance and that of Jesus at 11.26; Childs, *Crisis*, 173f, 179.

51 See R. R. Niebuhr's essay 'Archegos' in *Christian History and Interpretation* (J. Knox Festschrift), ed. W. R. Farmer, C. F. D. Moule and R. R. Niebuhr (Cambridge, 1967), 84, 87ff etc.

52 This is reflected, for instance, in the implicit distinction between Jesus and the 'cloud of witnesses' of 12.1f. H. Anderson, *Origins*, 284f, 287, has rightly emphasised the importance of the ἐφάπαξ quality of Jesus' work in Hebrews in this respect, as eliminating the need or capacity of Christians to do over again what Christ has done once-for-all; similarly see Cullmann, *Christology*, 98ff, esp. p. 100; and, more generally, Grässer, *VuF* no. 2, 1973, 32.

53 See Lohse, *Märtyrer*, 164.

54 See W. L. Knox, 'The "Divine Hero" Christology in the New Testament', *HTR* 41 (1948), 245f.

55 Cf. J. D. G. Dunn, *Jesus and the Spirit* (London, 1975), 75; Fuchs, *Historical Jesus*, 60.

56 Keck, *A Future for the Historical Jesus*, 116, 183ff.

57 One is reminded here, as frequently in the Christology of Hebrews, of E. Schweizer's attractive anecdote about the small boy in the Swiss valleys who can walk home through the snow only because his father walks ahead, making the footsteps in which he can walk – the child must still walk, he is

not walked for, which would be for his father, alone, to go home 'in his stead'; but he does not imitate his father, which would be to break his own trail beside the father (*Lordship and Discipleship*, 11).

58 'οἱ πειραζόμενοι are people tempted to flinch and falter under the pressure of suffering . . . Courage, the writer cries, Jesus understands; he has been through it all, he knows how hard it is to bear suffering without being deflected from the will of God' (Moffatt, commentary, 39); see additionally pp. 37ff on ἐλεήμων καὶ πιστὸς ἀρχιερεύς. See also Büchsel, *Christologie*, 42, and D. G. Miller, 'Why God Became Man', *Interpretation* 23 (1969), 422f.

59 E.g., R. E. Omark, 'The Saving of the Saviour', *Interpretation* 12 (1958), 40.

60 Among the most recent investigations of this passage is that of E. Brandenburger, *NovT* 11 (1969), 190-224, who supplies detailed bibliographical information, p. 191 n. 1. Brandenburger's own suggestion is that verses 8ff are taken from a different liturgical or confessional source, and represent a rather different Christological point of view to that of verse 7, which accounts for the hiatus between them. See also, however, Maurer, ' "Erhört wegen der Gottesfurcht", Hebr 5.7', 278, 282 n. 24.

61 Brandenburger, *NovT* 11 (1969), 221; his italics.

62 See generally, M. Rissi, 'Die Menschlichkeit Jesu nach Hebr 5.7-9', *ThZ* 9 (1955), 28-45.

63 Any number of writers could be cited, but see, e.g., A. Snell, *A New and Living Way* (London, 1959), 165; Miller, *Interpretation* 23 (1969), 419; or D. E. Nineham, *New Testament Interpretation in an Historical Age* (London, 1976), 19. Cf. also T. C. G. Thornton, 'The Meaning of αἱματεκχυσία in Heb. 9.22', *JTS* n.s. 15 (1964), 63-5. Rather more surprising, in view of the fact that her interest is in the reinterpretation of sacrifice themes, is to find the same view in F. M. Young, *Sacrifice and the Death of Christ*, 70.

64 Young, *Sacrifice*, 31-46; see esp. the reference to Johanan ben Zakkai, p. 34. See also her forthcoming *Sacrificial Ideas in Greek Christian Writers* (Cambridge, Mass.).

65 W. von Loewenich, 'Zum Verständnis des Opfergedankens im Hebräerbrief', *ThBl* 12 (1933), cols. 167-72, has rightly called this a radicalising of the Old Testament blood regulation ('Blutkanon'), but his essay is unduly complicated by his failure to observe that 9.22 is not a definitive statement from the author himself.

66 It might be objected that the limitation placed on the efficacy of blood at 10.4 and other places refers only to the blood of 'bulls and goats' and that no such limitation is placed on blood as such (i.e., that the shedding of Jesus' blood was the necessary equivalent in the heavenly sanctuary; cf. 9.12ff). Here in chapter 10, however, where the discussion may be said to have reached its climax, the significance of Jesus' death is located unambiguously in the *obedience* of his offering.

67 See esp. Lohse, *Märtyrer*, 174f.

68 Though we have included this passage among the descriptions of Jesus the priest, there is indeed an element of 'inclusiveness' in his gathering up into this one offering the representative offering of each human will ('by this will have we been sanctified'), which belongs at least to the 'pioneer' or 'forerunner' category. See Moule, *Phenomenon*, 33.

69 See the reference to V. A. Harvey's strictures: n. 94 below.

70 See, for example, the essay by H. Köster on Heb. 13.9-14, *HTR* 55 (1962), 299-315.

71 The immediacy of the conjunction between Jesus as man and as exalted priest is regularly noticed by commentators; cf., for instance, Moffatt's opinion (commentary, xxxix) that the absence of the resurrection motif in Hebrews is to be accounted for by the continuity which the writer wished to establish between the earthly and exalted forms of Jesus' existence. See also W. F. M. Scott, 'Priesthood in the New Testament', *SJT* 10 (1957), 401-8; E. F. Scott, *The Epistle to the Hebrews*, 154; Luck, *NovT* 6 (1963), esp. pp. 198, 200ff.

72 Cf. the similar conception, though in a different context, of H. Berkhof, 'Über die Methode der Eschatologie' in *Diskussion über die 'Theologie der Hoffnung'*, ed. W.-D. Marsch (Munich, 1967), 178: 'Eschatology is indeed "projection" in the most positive sense of that word: projection in terms of magnification upon the screen of eternity of that which has already been [given] to us by God here and now.'

73 Grässer, *Glaube*, 29; Filson, *Yesterday*, 30-5.

74 O. Cullmann, *Christ and Time* (London, 1951), 50, and *Christology*, 9.

75 Anderson, *Origins*, 285.

76 O. Cullmann, *Christology*, 89-104, rightly describes three moments of Jesus' saving action in the letter – past, present, future. The last of these, however, while not unimportant as attesting the futurity of the things of salvation for the writer, is reduced – as far as Jesus' role is concerned – to his coming again, 9.28.

77 Kennedy, *The Theology of the Epistles*, 216f.

78 See below on the findings of E. Grässer in these respects, pp. 137ff.

79 Though the two ways of understanding Jesus' saving role, as pioneer and priest, do not exhaust all that the letter has to say about his 'humanity' and 'divinity' (for instance no mention has been made here of the dignity which attaches to his status as 'Son') it might be urged that these offer a more useful framework than the more traditional (humanity/divinity) antithesis, into which – one sometimes suspects – much later Christological concepts are being smuggled.

80 It is somewhat intriguing to notice how the subtlety of the issues eludes writers who really do know better. For example, L. E. Keck, who is very conversant with the whole Jesus discussion, properly sees the critical significance of historical research: '. . . the Christian stake in sound historiography . . .' 'The historical Jesus helps to keep the church honest through the constant pressure of having to do with a real human, historic figure' (*Future*, 127). And yet Keck can hardly be said to attend to the genuinely historical questions as to our *access* to this figure. In fact his argument depends so much on the post-Easter, Christian proclamation of Jesus ('[The Christian] knows that whatever happens to him cannot really separate him from God because nothing finally separated Jesus from God either', p. 240) that it is hard to know whether he has come very much further than Bultmann.

81 E. Grässer, 'Das Heil als Wort', 263-6, suggests that it is unclear whether the ἀρχή which is διὰ τοῦ κυρίου can be taken as a reference to the proclama-

tion of the earthly Jesus or to the kerygmatic Word of God 'in the Son' (1.2). However this is, it seems to him that 'the intention [of the reflection on the ἀρχή of salvation] is demonstrably to establish the *first* link in a chain of earthly witnesses' (p. 266).

82 Keck, *Future*, 127; Trocmé, *Contemporaries*, 68.

83 I.e., what is happening implicitly in Hebrews, and with reference to the traditions, is made explicit in Paul's appeal to the five hundred witnesses, 'most of whom are still alive' (1 Cor. 15.6).

84 See the references to Grässer and Filson above, ch. 2 n. 112; cf. also Moule, *Birth*, 76 n. 1.

85 Cf. the opposition to Docetism on the basis of the memories, 1 John 1.1–3.

86 See, for example, the judgements of O. Michel, commentary, 135, 138, 224, etc.

87 E. Grässer, *ZNW* 56 (1965), 63–91, makes the point frequently that interest in the humanity of Jesus in the letter is never separated from soteriological or Christological interests. But this can only become a critical matter if these Christological interests are found to be controlling the historical elements instead of the other way about.

88 This term is borrowed from V. A. Harvey, *The Historian and the Believer* (London, 1967), 51 etc., who in turn has borrowed it from S. Toulmin.

89 This is one of three references in the epistle which, according to E. Grässer, *ZNW* 56 (1965), 73ff, may be taken to indicate a knowledge by the writer of Synoptic traditions. The others are the allusion to Gethsemane at 5.7ff and Jesus' death outside the city, 13.12.

90 See his essay 'The Primitive Christian Kerygma and the Historical Jesus', esp. in this connection pp. 24ff.

91 So Grässer, *ZNW* 56 (1965), 76.

92 See the excursus on the historical Jesus in Windisch, commentary, 25f, and cf. Wells, *The Jesus of the Early Christians*, 158.

93 So formulated by V. A. Harvey, *The Historian*, 151: 'the issue is not whether the picture can be *verified* with certainty but whether historical research can *disconfirm* in principle any of the concrete traits' (his italics).

94 This kind of judgement provides the basis for Harvey's rejection of the work of the so-called 'new-questers', certain of the disciples of R. Bultmann who have resumed an interest in the historical Jesus and in finding lines of communication between the pre-Easter Jesus and the post-Easter Christ of Christian proclamation; see *The Historian*, 187ff. He claims that because it is notoriously difficult to establish motives from outward actions, the quest of Jesus' inner life 'tends to corrode the balance of judgement which is the *sine qua non* of critical history . . . by soliciting the heaviest possible assent to a historical judgement which, in this particular case, is most tenuous' (p. 193). Certainly it is true that a discrepancy between a person's outward actions and his inner motivation is always a possibility, so that at least in theory Jesus' outward stance might have concealed an inwardly rebellious spirit. But the rejection of this as a serious possibility is based precisely on that commonsense attitude to history, championed by Harvey himself (pp. 77ff and esp. p. 78), which accepts as a working hypothesis the assumption that a man's outward attitudes will cohere more or less with his inner disposition. See H. Anderson, 'Existential Hermeneutics', *Interpretation* 16 (1962), 140 n. 30, and n. 97 below.

95 'The indication of time at 10.5 is one of the few places in the letter where a concrete historical event in the life of Jesus is referred to (cf. 2.13, 5.7ff (?), 13.12)' (Schierse, *Heilsvollendung*, 54).

96 See esp. Barbour, *Traditio-Historical Criticism*, 19, 22, 24; see also the appreciative statements of W. G. Kümmel with respect to F. Mussner's essay 'Wege zum Selbstbewusstsein Jesu' (in *BZ* n.s. 12 (1968), 161-73): 'He deals in his essay with the idea - in my opinion correct, but controversial - that "Christology hangs in the air if it is not grounded in Jesus' own self-consciousness" ' (*ThR* n.s. 40 (1975), 319).

97 Such a possibility is not wholly theoretical, as the altogether serious (see Cullmann, *Christology*, 48 n. 1) attempt of A. Schweitzer to see Jesus as a desperate, disillusioned man indicates. See also the remark of R. Bultmann together with W. Pannenberg's rejoinder in Pannenberg, *Jesus - God and Man*, 349 n. 48. And see Farmer, 'An Historical Essay on the Humanity of Jesus Christ', 108.

98 See the survey by E. Grässer of Jewish studies of Jesus, *VuF* no. 2, 1973, 30-4, together with the essay by H. Maccoby, 'Is the Political Jesus Dead?', *Encounter* 46, 2 (February 1976), 80-9.

99 Cf. the observation, now somewhat dated but not without its point, made by D. M. Baillie in response to the then ascendant 'dialectical' theologies of K. Barth and R. Bultmann: 'Their position is quite a new one . . . and it might be given the new title of Logotheism, because it is so strictly a theology of the Word of God rather than of . . . the Word made flesh' (*God Was in Christ* (London, 1948, 1955²), 53.

100 F. Schröger, *Ausleger*, 120-7, gives a full and up-to-date (until 1968) survey, to which must be added, however, E. Brandenburger's essay, *NovT* 11 (1969), 190-224, who adduces several verbal echoes of Ps. 116 (LXX Ps. 114) in Heb. 5.7; similarly, C. Maurer, ' "Erhört wegen der Gottesfurcht" ', 279.

101 See, e.g., O. Cullmann, 'The Tradition' in *The Early Church* (London, 1956), 59-99; F. W. Beare, 'Sayings of the Risen Jesus in the Synoptic Tradition' in *Christian History and Interpretation* (J. Knox Festschrift), ed. W. R. Farmer, C. F. D. Moule and R. R. Niebuhr (Cambridge, 1967), 161-81; and Boring's article, already referred to, in *JBL* 91 (1972), 501-21; see also, however, D. Hill, 'On the Evidence for the Creative Role of Christian Prophets', *NTS* 20 (1973-4), 262-74.

102 This theme is too regularly traversed to permit or require detailed documentation here. Cf., among others, Downing, *The Church and Jesus*; H. Palmer, *The Logic of Gospel Criticism* (London, 1968); M. D. Hooker, 'On Using the Wrong Tool', *Theology* 75 (1972), 570-81 (almost the equivalent of 'Christology and Methodology', *NTS* 17 (1970-1), 480-7); D. G. A. Calvert, 'An Examination of Criteria for Distinguishing Authentic Words of Jesus', *NTS* 18 (1971-2), 209-19.

103 G. N. Stanton, *Jesus of Nazareth*, 70-8, has assembled cogent reasons for believing that underlying the speech of Peter in Cornelius' house (Acts 10.34-43) there are LXX references of which Luke himself is not aware, and which therefore attest the primitive rather than the novel quality of the traditions about Jesus which the speech contains.

104 See Dodd, *History and the Gospel*, 42ff, and *Historical Tradition in the Fourth Gospel*, 47-9.

105 'The question concerning the earthly Jesus is by no means forbidden, theologically, and "the historical scepticism toward the *entire* body of Jesus' words as mediated through the traditions never was, and is today even less, justified" ': W. G. Kümmel, *ThR* n.s. 40 (1975), 308, citing E. Grässer (Grässer's italics).

106 'To cleave firmly to history is one way of giving expression to the *extra nos* of salvation' (E. Käsemann, *Essays on New Testament Themes* (London, 1964), 33.

107 This is, clearly, rather too optimistic; in practice we are unlikely to get beyond Professor Hooker's 'from the more to the less probable' (*Theology* 75 (1972), 581). At the same time she acknowledges that 'there are no other [tools], and there are unlikely to be any better ones discovered' (pp. 580f). In view of what has been said above, one cannot but ponder with some uncertainty the opinion of C. F. Evans that 'the time has now come when "the historical method no longer suffices and the theologian has to look around for assistance from another quarter" ', cited by D. E. Nineham in 'A Partner for Cinderella?' in *What about the New Testament*? (Evans Festschrift), ed. M. D. Hooker and C. Hickling (London, 1975), 143. The citation is from Evans' *Queen or Cinderella*? (Durham, 1960), 22, which was unfortunately unavailable to me.

108 See R. S. Barbour's criticisms of J. Knox, whose statement that 'The historical Event to which all Christian faith returns is not an event antedating the Church, or in any sense or degree prior to it, but is the coming into existence of the Church itself' he describes as 'this plausible but disastrously dangerous doctrine' (*Traditio-Historical Criticism*, 42-6, citation from p. 44).

109 An attention to the historical lineaments of Jesus as he is remembered in the primitive traditions is also an indispensable controlling element in the ongoing 'indigenisation' of Christian understanding. Black (cf., e.g., J. H. Cone, *God of the Oppressed* (New York, 1975), known to me only through reviews), brown (i.e., in my own country, the call for a Maori Jesus), Aryan (see A. T. Davies, 'The Aryan Christ', *JES* 12 (1975), 569-79) or any other ethnically conceived Christologies disclose their invalidity to the extent that they lose sight of their origins in the Jesus of the earliest memories. Of perennial importance is H. J. Cadbury's *The Peril of Modernising Jesus* (London, 1962, 1937[1]); see esp. ch. 2, 'The Cause and Cure of Modernisation'.

110 This is generally agreed to have been initiated by E. Käsemann's essay 'The Problem of the Historical Jesus', now printed in *Essays on New Testament Themes*, 15-47.

111 Grässer, *VuF* no. 2, 1973, 12.

112 See the debate carried on between J. M. Robinson, *Kerygma und historischer Jesus* (Zurich, 1967), 8f, 16, 18, 35, 52, and V. A. Harvey and S. M. Ogden, 'How New Is the "New Quest of the Historical Jesus"?' in *The Historical Jesus and the Kerygmatic Christ*, ed. C. E. Braaten and R. A. Harrisville (Nashville, 1964), 197-242.

113 See his famous 'Heidelberg Reply', in which he defines himself as specifically as he can over against his erstwhile students, and in which he isolates the problem as that of speaking of Christian faith prior to Easter ('The Primitive Christian Kerygma and the Historical Jesus', 15-42; see esp. p. 33).

114 See Ebeling, *Word and Faith*, 223.

115 *Primitive Christianity in Its Contemporary Setting* (London, 1956), 71ff, and *Theology of the New Testament* I (London, 1952), 3.

116 'Prophecy and Fulfilment' in *Essays on Old Testament Interpretation*, ed. C. Westermann (London, 1963), 50–75, esp. pp. 72f.

117 The outlines of this have been presented more frequently than to need review here. Curiously, J. M. Robinson's *A New Quest of the Historical Jesus* (London, 1959; second edition in German as *Kerygma und historischer Jesus*, 1967) still provides a useful survey of the issues, tending to confirm E. Trocmé's sentiment that 'the advocates of "the new quest"' ... are marking time' (*Contemporaries*, 12).

118 D. Sölle, *Christ the Representative* (London, 1967), frequently but see esp. p. 113.

119 Grässer, *Glaube*, 45, 57 *et al.* Cf. Dautzenberg, *BZ* n.s. 15 (1973), 171f, 174ff.

120 Grässer organises his book, formally, on the basis that the faith-conception of an early Christian document will provide 'a clear index' of the 'centrality' or otherwise of its 'Christ proclamation' and other matters (*Glaube*, 2f). In effect this means a comparison with the faith-conception of Paul and the Synoptics (pp. 64–79); as for John, 'the difference is so clear that this would need a completely separate treatment' (p. 64). However, in his more recent publications - specifically, 'Zur Christologie des Hebräerbriefes' and 'Rechtfertigung im Hebräerbrief', in *Rechtfertigung* (E. Käsemann Festschrift), ed. J. Friederich, W. Pöhlmann and P. Stuhlmacher (Tübingen, 1976), 79–93 - Grässer has begun to present a considerably modified view of Hebrews' 'canonicity'. See further below, excursus 2 n. 22.

121 L. E. Keck, *A Future for the Historical Jesus*, 52: 'In [Luther, Kierkegaard, Herrmann and Bultmann] faith is understood as the crisis of the individual and of his capacity to believe, not as fidelity and trust, as in the Old Testament understanding of faith.' Keck goes on to explore the notion of 'trust' as a way of finding continuity between Jesus and Judaism on one hand (pp. 214ff) and Jesus and the church on the other (pp. 183ff etc.).

122 This is as finely expressed as anywhere in the essay by R. R. Niebuhr entitled, significantly, 'Archegos'. See esp. the section headed 'Faith before Faith' and also p. 98.

123 'History' is usually regarded in biblical–Christian traditions - as over against oriental or mystical traditions - as having positive connotations. But not always or necessarily. Cf. Käsemann, *Essays on New Testament Themes*, 18.

124 The image I have in mind is that of a photographer who attempts to find a 'frame' for his picture, perhaps an architectural one, or in the overhanging limb of a tree, etc. It is not that such objects are not 'there'. Nevertheless they have to be 'found'; they are not necessarily or immediately obvious. Having been found, however, they help to bring meaning and coherence to the subject as a whole. R. W. Funk in *Language*, 142, also uses the idea of frames, but in a rather different way.

125 D. O. Via, jun., *Kerygma and Comedy in the New Testament* (Philadelphia, 1975), 13, with reference to M. Merleau-Ponty.

126 Funk, *Language*, 194f. Cf. his detailed discussion of 'metaphor', ch. 5 and frequently.

127 B. S. Childs, *Crisis*, 140: 'Biblical interpretation as an art does not operate
     by a precise accumulation of scientific data, nor is its method so easily
     outlined. One rather tends to describe the product as illuminating, profound,
     or brilliant.'

Chapter 4. Hermeneutics

1 Cf. E. Flesseman-van Leer, 'Biblical Interpretation in the World Council of
   Churches', *Study Encounter* 8, 2 (1972), 1: 'Hermeneutics is the science
   which examines the conditions which allow the writer to express his
   intention in such a way that it can be recognised and understood by a
   contemporary audience.'
2 See *Truth and Method*, esp. pp. 269–74; see also R. E. Palmer, *Hermeneutics*
   (Evanston, 1969), 24f.
3 For the origins of this translation see ch. 1 n. 7 above.
4 According to Hesychius, the fifth-century-A.D. lexicographer, πολυμερῶς
   is the equivalent of πολυσχέδως; see J. H. Moulton and G. Milligan, *The
   Vocabulary of the Greek Testament* (London, 1914), s.v. πολυμερῶς.
5 Westcott, commentary, 4.
6 Barr, *Old and New*, 15, 23f.
7 Ibid. 25f. See also pp. 44, 46f above.
8 J. Calvin, *Commentary on Hebrews* (Grand Rapids, 1949), 32; also see
   Grässer, 'Hebräer 1.1–4', 74.
9 So J. Barr, *Old and New*, 150f: 'When we say that the God of Israel is the
   One God and Father of the Lord Jesus Christ, we are making an assertion
   which stands on the level of faith ... [so that] we do not claim that this
   statement can be validated or proved by historical, descriptive or structural
   studies of the two Testaments or their parts' (p. 150). And yet, 'though the
   statement is a faith-assertion in this respect, it cannot stand quite independent of historical, descriptive and structural studies ... Though the
   faith is not demonstrable by scholarly study ... [it] lives in awareness of such
   study and seeks to maintain consistency with it' (p. 151). Cf. also A. A. van
   Ruler, *The Christian Church and the Old Testament* (Grand Rapids, 1971),
   16f.
10 Cf. *The Bible Speaks Again* (a study commissioned by the Netherlands
    Reformed Church) (London, 1969), 153: 'This distance always demands a
    translation, an interpretation, a decision for today. We ourselves have to
    risk the application' (their italics). Similarly, p. 164. Cf. also Childs, *Crisis*,
    136.
11 Cf. the detailed attention given by H.-G. Gadamer to hermeneutical discus-
    sions in Plato and Aristotle, e.g., *Truth and Method*, 278ff, 367ff etc.
12 Ebeling, *Word and Faith*, 43.
13 See the early chapters of K. Scholder, *Ursprünge und Probleme der
    Bibelkritik im 17. Jahrhundert* (Munich, 1966).
14 Ibid. 132.
15 D. Bonhoeffer, *Letters and Papers from Prison* (London, 1959²), 122, 164;
    in fact E. Bethge, *Dietrich Bonhoeffer* (London, 1970), 757–92, makes it
    clear that only at the cost of distortion can this formula in Bonhoeffer
    signify radical (Godless) secularism.
16 Miskotte, *When the Gods Are Silent*, 1–7 and frequently.

17 G. D. Kaufman, 'What Shall We Do with the Bible?', *Interpretation* 25 (1971), 98ff.

18 In addition to books and essays otherwise mentioned in this chapter special mention might be made of G. Ebeling's article 'Hermeneutik' in *RGG*³ III, cols. 242–62 (including five columns of bibliography). In English see S. Neill, *The Interpretation of the New Testament 1861–1961* (London, 1964); W. Neil, 'The Criticism and Theological Use of the Bible, 1700–1950' in *The Cambridge History of the Bible – The West from the Reformation to the Present Day*, ed. S. L. Greenslade (Cambridge, 1963), 238–93; and in the same volume, A. Richardson, 'The Rise of Modern Biblical Scholarship and Recent Discussion of the Authority of the Bible', 294–338.

19 Harvey, *The Historian*, 33, 38 and frequently.

20 K. Barth, *The Humanity of God* (London, 1961), 41.

21 E. Fuchs begins his *Hermeneutik* with a consideration of Barth and 'the Text'; cf. also J. M. Robinson, 'Hermeneutic since Barth' in *The New Hermeneutic*, ed. J. M. Robinson and J. B. Cobb (New York, 1964), 1–77.

22 See *Lessing's Theological Writings*, ed. H. Chadwick (London, 1956), 53.

23 Cf. G. Ebeling in 1950, *Word and Faith*, 27, and B. S. Childs in 1970, *Crisis*, 102.

24 This is the now famous distinction made by K. Stendahl in his article 'Biblical Theology, Contemporary' in the *Interpreters' Dictionary of the Bible* I (Nashville, 1962), 419ff. Stendahl has frequently been sharply criticised for the distinction and his view that the task of biblical theology is purely 'descriptive'.

25 Cf. H. Thielicke, *The Evangelical Faith* I (Grand Rapids, 1974), 52: '[In the so-called 'Cartesian theologies'] it is clear how many questions crowd in upon us, all unleashed by the one fact that man has discovered and can no longer ignore himself in his adulthood . . . This is why there is such an expansion of introductory questions, as is most strikingly shown by the blossoming of hermeneutics . . . into a new theological discipline.'

26 This is one of the most sustained thrusts in Thielicke's book, both polemically against what he calls the 'Cartesian' theologies, and positively for his own understanding of 'a word which comes to man . . . by and in which God discloses himself' (p. 77). See chapters 7 and 8, 'Theological Starting Point in the Doctrine of the Holy Spirit' and 'The Holy Spirit as He who Creates Anew and Yet also Links to the Old'.

27 See the reference to J. Starobinski, n. 53 below.

28 Cf. K. H. Miskotte, *When the Gods Are Silent*, 199: 'For later generations than ours it will be almost incomprehensible that academic scholarship was capable of reducing the sacral narrative . . . to little stories which mean nothing whatsoever to us in our existence, which affect us less than the Greek or Teutonic myths and contain less wisdom than the Grimms' fairy tales.'

29 See the questions raised in perfect seriousness by J. Bowden at the commencement of the volume of essays for C. Evans ('Great Expectations? The New Testament Critic and His Audience' in *What about the New Testament?*, ed. M. D. Hooker and C. Hickling (London, 1975), 1–12), the questioning nature of which is reflected by many of the other essays.

30 Cf., for example, the essay by P. S. Minear, 'Christian Eschatology and

Historical Methodology' in *Neutestamentliche Studien für Rudolf Bultmann*,
ed. W. Eltester (Berlin, 1954), 15–23 (and see also the comments and
further references given by B. S. Childs in *Crisis*, 43f); one can find such
warning statements in J. D. Smart's *The Interpretation of Scripture*, e.g.,
'From within the Bible itself we meet more than once with the assertion
that faith is essential to understanding' (p. 30); B. S. Childs' call for a
recovery of 'the church's exegetical traditions' (*Crisis*, 147) is another
such protest against a swamping of the texts by the 'historicocritical
approach' (p. 138); we have already referred to H. Thielicke's urgent
summons for a 'non-Cartesian theology'; finally, see O. C. Edwards, jun.,
'Historical-Critical Method's Failure of Nerve and a Prescription for a
Tonic: A Review of Some Recent Literature', *AngTheolRev* 59 (1977),
115–34.

31 D. H. Kelsey, *The Uses of Scripture in Recent Theology* (Philadelphia,
1975), 135f, is critical of those who put the question: where does this
position begin? On the other hand we might be permitted to draw some
encouragement from the fact that Kelsey himself is inclined to start with
the 'single, synoptic, imaginative judgement' (p. 159) as fundamental in
any theologian, which imaginative judgement must then be subjected to
'controls' (pp. 170ff etc.).

32 H.-G. Gadamer speaks in places of the 'ideality' of words or of language as
a hermeneutical medium, e.g., *Truth and Method*, 352, 354, 356. In addition we can cite these key sentences: 'The experience of the world in
language is "absolute". It transcends all the relativities of the positing of
being, because it embraces all being-in-itself, in whatever relationships
(relativities) it appears' (p. 408), or, 'Our enquiry has been guided by the
basic idea that language is a central point where "I" and the world meet
or, rather, manifest their original unity' (p. 431).
       The same universalist elements appertain to structuralism: 'Structure . . .
is the hidden and unconscious system of presuppositions which accounts
for and holds together the visible, existing order, including its literary
texts' (D. O. Via, jun., *Kerygma and Comedy*, 13).
       It is not difficult to come to the conclusion that this Idealist element in
most, if not all, hermeneutical reflection, lies at the heart of German theological preoccupation with it and a corresponding lack of interest by
English theology; see H. W. Frei, *The Eclipse of Biblical Narrative*, 142ff,
155; cf. R. E. Palmer's observations on the meeting of Anglo-French
empirical realism and positivism, and German idealism, in the person of
W. Dilthey (*Hermeneutics*, 99); finally see E. Flesseman-van Leer's remarks
on the divergence of English and continental attitudes on hermeneutics in
'Dear Christopher . . .' in *What about the New Testament?* (C. Evans
Festschrift), ed. M. D. Hooker and C. Hickling (London, 1975), 234–42.

33 See the chapter on Fritz Buri in J. Macquarrie, *The Scope of Demythologizing*
(London, 1960), ch. 5; also the sections on P. van Buren and S. M. Ogden
in Funk, *Language*, 78–108; and Harvey, *The Historian*, 165–8.

34 Thielicke, *The Evangelical Faith* I, 102.

35 For example, J. D. Smart's criticism is representative of many: '[Bultmann]
insists that we are forbidden to consider anything true "which contradicts
the truths actually presupposed in the understanding I have of the world –

the understanding which is the guide for all my activity". Here the human self-understanding has become the final authority' (*The Interpretation of Scripture*, 52, quoting from Bultmann's 'The Problem of Hermeneutics', 261). See also J. Moltmann's criticism of what he terms 'The Theology of the Transcendental Subjectivity of Man' in *Hope*, 58ff.

36 The definitive discussions are contained in the five volumes of *Kerygma und Mythos*, ed. H.-W. Bartsch (Hamburg, 1948–55), selections from which have been translated as *Kerygma and Myth*, I and II (London, 1953, 1962). The most comprehensive survey of the literature known to me is G. Bornkamm's 'Die Theologie Rudolf Bultmanns in der neueren Diskussion', *ThR* n.s. 29 (1963), 33–141 (bibliography supplied by E. Brandenburger).

37 So, for example, R. E. Palmer, *Hermeneutics*, 124: 'In the phenomenology of Edmund Husserl, Heidegger found conceptual tools unavailable to Dilthey or Nietzsche.'

38 *Hermeneutik*, 126ff.

39 Ibid. 128.

40 Ibid. 126f.

41 Ibid. 131f.

42 Ibid. 130 (his italics).

43 Ibid. 131.

44 Ibid. 132 (his italics); similar statements will be found in the essay 'What Is a Language-Event?' now in *Studies of the Historical Jesus*, 207–12, e.g., 'The concrete word is what first raises being into being', and 'being without language is nothing; it is not even nature' (p. 209).

45 *Hermeneutik*, 133; we may also compare his statement in the earlier exposition of Heidegger, 'Man has not given birth to language, but is born of language' (ibid. 63).

46 'Proclamation and Speech Event', *Theology Today* 19 (1962–3), 347.

47 Ibid. 348; similarly in *Historical Jesus*, 221, 225f.

48 Cf. *Historical Jesus*, 46f: 'This is why the so-called existential interpretation denotes a corrective to the historical method. For existential interpretation examines the possibilities of existence not simply on the plane of succession but on the plane of the relation, and balances these two possible aspects of an event; and this is because it understands man primarily on the basis of language rather than of nature.'

49 Ibid. 196.

50 Ibid. 196.

51 Ibid. 197.

52 See the references to H. Thielicke in n. 26 above. In all fairness Fuchs does know about this: 'Therefore the Church prays for the Holy Spirit as the power of her word, too' (*Historical Jesus*, 227). The point is, however, that to recognise that language (without the Holy Spirit) may indeed be powerless implies that *in itself* language is not the means to understanding, but only language which is being made effective by the Spirit.

53 Cf. J. Starobinski: 'Everything happens as if the parabolic form was precisely chosen with the goal of creating a cleavage between those who *understand* the figurative meaning and those who cannot go beyond the literal meaning. The principle of election is therefore written at the same time in

the form of a *message* and in the listening ability of each of the *hearers'* ('The Gerasene Demoniac' in R. Barthes *et al.*, *Structural Analysis and Biblical Exegesis* (Pittsburgh, 1974), 77; his italics.

54 G. Ebeling, whose work in many ways closely parallels that of Fuchs, seems rather more conscious of this and similar problems; see *Word and Faith*, 323ff.

55 So D. H. Kelsey, *Uses of Scripture*, 177: 'What is decisive [about attempting to speak of the role of the bible] is a prior judgement about the "essence of Christianity" and the point of doing theology at all.' Similar statements are made on p. 159. See also D. Ritschl, 'A Plea for the Maxim: Scripture and Tradition', *Interpretation* 25 (1971), 115ff.

56 Cf. R. W. Funk on S. M. Ogden's attempt to translate for 'modern man': 'The response of Ogden's modern man to Ogden's own theological program can scarcely be anything other than an *existentiell* Ho-hum!' (*Language*, 107).

57 See references for these statements above, p. 100. Though we have attended mainly to the existence and language hermeneutical attempts, the same order of criticisms is likely to apply to the newer structuralist hermeneutics. For example, D. O. Via, jun., in *Kerygma and Comedy*, believes he can show structural similarities between the Christians' kerygma and the Greek comic plays. The conclusion follows: 'By showing that the New Testament kerygma belongs to the structure of comedy we can see why that which is most elemental in the Christian proclamation sets up reverberations in that rhythm of life which is most elemental in man as such' (p. 49). But the question for biblical hermeneutics is not the kinships the texts may share with other literary forms (though that is not unimportant), but how we may achieve an understanding of these texts in terms of their subject matter.

58 One of Bultmann's most crisp statements to this effect is found with reference to Paul (see Bultmann's *Theology of the New Testament* I, 191), but it is clear that however it is with Paul this is certainly the point of view of Bultmann. See W. Schmithals, *An Introduction to the Theology of Rudolf Bultmann* (London, 1968), 33ff.

59 See Grässer, 'Rechtfertigung im Hebräerbrief', 87.

60 Insofar as I can grasp the main thrusts of J. Barr's *The Bible in the Modern World*, my conceptions concur more or less with his. He too recognises that any attempt to handle 'the bible as literature' (for which he has considerable sympathy; see ch. 4) in the last analysis does not answer the theological questions raised: 'Is there really a God? Did Jesus come from him? Granted that the Resurrection is the central symbol of a Gospel, does it have existence only within the text of the Gospels... or does it also stand for something in the outside world?' (p. 74). For Barr (as for D. H. Kelsey), 'the status of the Bible is something implied in the structure of Christian (and of Jewish) faith' (p. 115). All other attempts to give an account of its status in the church must be seen in the end to be rationalisations which the evidence does not properly support (see his remarks on historical contingency, p. 156) and which must therefore either be abandoned, or continue to be affirmed but 'in an essentially irrational way' (p. 111). Barr is unambiguous in his choice of the latter: 'I have no faith in the vision of a Christianity which would emancipate itself more com-

pletely from biblical influence and go forward bravely, rejoicing in its own contemporary modernity' (p. 112) (though at the same time he does not feel 'anxious and unhappy by the fact that the status of the Bible is in question' p. 113). The chief interest of Barr's formulation for the present study is in his closing words: 'The profoundest unity is not a unity *within* the Bible, on the level of its common patterns of thought, or consisting in a balance we may discern between its different emphases, between its conflicting viewpoints; it is rather the unity of the one God ... Such a conviction, however, does not necessarily have to be comprehended now by us, or to be expressed in studies, in books and documents, as something we now perceive; its realization belongs rather to faith and hope' (p. 181, his italics).

61 See Ebeling, *Word and Faith*, 36f, 42 etc.; also W. Neil, 'The Criticism and Theological Use of the Bible, 1700-1950', 238, 271; and Käsemann, *Essays on New Testament Themes*, 56.

62 'This recourse [on Luther's part] to the literal sense was not "historical-critically" based, but was exclusively theological, namely, in the ... necessity to obtain unambiguous statements. The exegesis remained therewith basically within the compass of scripture; other than theological criteria were not to be admitted' (K. Scholder, *Ursprünge und Probleme*, 125, and cf. p. 74, where he suggests that the watershed between the middle ages and the modern period falls between Melanchthon and Galileo). See also Frei, *Eclipse*, 76, 90, and K. Frör, *Biblische Hermeneutik* (Munich, 1961), 48f.

63 Frei, *Eclipse*, chs. 3-7, gives a detailed survey of this period. Also helpful is B. Willey's *The Seventeenth Century Background* (Harmondsworth, 1962; Penguin edn).

64 Cf., for example, the conclusion to the report on 'Scripture and Tradition' (which included a section on hermeneutics) made to the Faith and Order Commission of the World Council of Churches in 1967: 'Though the general desire for a scientific method in the exegesis of Scripture is acknowledged, the *serious problems* facing theologians and the church cannot be ignored' (*New Directions in Faith and Order, Bristol 1967* (Geneva, 1968), 59; my italics). See Flesseman-van Leer, *Study Encounter* 8, 2 (1972), 5, and also 'Dear Christopher...', 235ff, on the unresolved differences behind this report.

65 See Nineham, *New Testament Interpretation in an Historical Age,* 16.

66 P. xii.

67 Some confusion may be felt in this claim upon Gadamer, who clearly belongs to the same traditions as the language and existence hermeneutical theorists who have already been criticised. The point is simply that Gadamer is not trying to tell us how we may discover an understanding of 'God' in the historically conditioned text forms.

68 I agree with E. D. Hirsch, *Validity in Interpretation* (New Haven, 1967), 8ff, that the distinction between 'meaning' and 'significance' is too often ignored. Even so, it seems to me clear that meanings of texts can change and not just their significance; see A. C. Thiselton, 'The Use of Philosophical Categories in New Testament Hermeneutics', *The Churchman* 87 (1973), 95ff.

69 F. D. E. Schleiermacher, *Hermeneutik*, ed. H. Kimmerle (Heidelberg, 1959), 87. See H.-G. Gadamer, *Truth and Method*, 171, for notes on the history of this expression.

70 See the reference to K. Stendahl in n. 24 above.

71 On the problem created for understanding biblical texts by modern rationalistic tendencies, see *The Bible Speaks Again*, 118f. Similarly Childs, *Crisis*, 141f.

72 See the long section on 'application' in Gadamer, *Truth and Method*, 274-305, esp. pp. 274-8. Cf. also the pejorative remarks about 'practical' or 'pastoral' theology directed toward K. Barth's commentary on Romans, now recorded in the second Preface of *The Epistle to the Romans* (London, 1933), 9. See K. Frör, *Biblische Hermeneutik*, 68, on preaching as an integral part of the hermeneutical process.

73 R. Descartes, 'Discourse on Method, Part II' in *Philosophical Writings*, ed. E. Anscombe and P. Geach (London, 1964), 20; see also Scholder's chapter on Cartesianism, *Ursprünge und Probleme*, ch. 6.

74 Harvey, *The Historian*, 103.

75 That which is seen by J. D. Smart and others as a serious, if not fatal, weakness in Bultmann's theology (see n. 35 above) is grasped by a writer such as S. M. Ogden as its strength. See Funk, *Language*, 89ff.

76 E.g., H. Lindsell, *The Battle for the Bible* (Grand Rapids, 1976).

77 This is the important truth which coheres in E. D. Hirsch's advocacy of a 'determinacy' in meanings (*Validity in Interpretation*, 44ff). Further, to see the task of 'boundary-setting' as a preliminary one is not, as D. E. Nineham infers, an 'essentially subordinate' one (see his *New Testament Interpretation in an Historical Age*, 15). To introduce value judgements of this kind only confuses the issue.

78 I am aware that Schleiermacher could define hermeneutics as 'the art of avoiding misunderstandings' (see Gadamer, *Truth and Method*, 163, for discussion and references). But I am not aware that I am dependent upon him for the formulations offered here.

79 As a matter of fact, once one has been alerted to it, examples of the 'double negation' are to be found quite frequently in discussions of the role of critical methods. One or two specimens from my collection are (my italics): J. Macquarrie, *The Scope of Demythologizing*, 93, 'a minimal core ... which *cannot* be reasonably *doubted*'; or W. Neil's 'the "assured results of criticism" have indeed *disposed* of a *wrong* approach', in his essay 'Criticism and Theological Use of the Bible', 293; or from A. Richardson in the same volume, 'no longer, for instance, could one find a scriptural basis for the doctrine of the Trinity in Isaiah's "Holy, holy, holy", or ... justify racial discrimination on the basis of the early chapters of Genesis' ('The Rise of Modern Biblical Scholarship', 301).

80 Cf. J. Barr, *Old and New*, 31: 'The validity of the claim that Jesus is the Christ depends on the validity of the claim that the speaking back in Old Testament times was real. The Old Testament brings out the lineaments of the Christ and so provides the forms in which he is understood; but conversely also Christ has meaning as one who came from God only if God was really behind that which was said as from God in the Old Testament.' See also p. 139: 'In the minds of the apostles ... the problem was not how to understand the Old Testament but how to understand Christ.' Similarly van Ruler, *The Christian Church and the Old Testament*, 75f, 80ff.

81 An example to which I have given some attention is the justification-by-

faith formula of Paul (see my article 'From Galatia to St Gyro's: "Justification by Faith" as a Cross-Cultural Problem', *South East Asia Journal for Theology* 17, 2 (1976), 23-31). Simply to *preserve* the Pauline formula in a setting in which virtually no one now knows what it would be like to have sought 'justification by the works of the Law' - or, for that matter, the 'cry for a gracious God' of Luther and his contemporaries (see K. Stendahl, 'The Apostle Paul and the Introspective Conscience of the West', *HTR* 56 (1963), 199-215) - is not to be faithful to the formula but to destroy it. Only in *interpreting* it for Western man, preoccupied with his own forms of 'self-justification', does the liberating power of the Pauline conception find its expression. So K. Frör, *Biblische Hermeneutik*, 16; 'An exposition which has understood the tradition is . . . only possible when it does not keep it in custody, but realises it afresh and therein interprets it anew.'

82   E. Schweizer, 'Scripture-Tradition-Modern Interpretation' in *Neotestamentica* (collected essays, 1951-63) (Zurich and Stuttgart, 1963), 203f. One of the most interesting things about Schweizer's essay, from our point of view, is his affirmation of the importance of the traditions for the New Testament church ('all New Testament authors emphasise that anyone who loses the connection with the original tradition will get lost like a child's balloon which is no longer held on its string', p. 204) together with their insistence that these be reinterpreted (they show 'at the same time how impossible it is to keep this tradition unaltered', p. 205).

83   C. Evans, *Is 'Holy Scripture' Christian?* (London, 1971), 2.

84   D. H. Kelsey, *Uses of Scripture*, 1 n. 2, gives a detailed discussion, with references, of the present situation in which the concept of biblical authority finds itself. In addition to the documents cited there, reference might be made to the report to the Faith and Order Commission, *Faith and Order, Louvain 1971* (Geneva, 1971), 9-23, and Barr, *The Bible in the Modern World*. See Kelsey's own discussion, pp. 97ff, 139ff, 207ff and otherwise frequently.

85   Kelsey, *Uses of Scripture*, 101, speaks of the modern theologian's appeal to 'patterns' in scripture which each 'takes to be authoritative'. Admittedly the variety in the kinds of pattern which have thus been selected makes it clear, as Kelsey shows, that the selection of the pattern depends rather more on the individual than has been suggested here. Nevertheless, to find the 'patterns' ('frames') and work within these is the interpreter's business. See especially the discussion, on pp. 192ff of Kelsey's book, on 'The Normativity of Patterns'. Cf. also the 'relational centres' of *Louvain 1971*, 17, and J. Barr's 'nodal points' (*Modern World*, 161).

86   H. Thielicke, *Evangelical Faith*, I, 129, draws attention to the once-for-all quality inherent in the ἐφάπαξ terminology of Hebrews (7.27, 9.12, 10.10). Cf. also Grässer, *VuF* no. 2, 1973, 32.

87   Ritschl, *Interpretation* 25 (1971), 126.

88   See esp. Käsemann, *Essays*, 54-8, 95-107. J. Barr, *Modern World*, 43, speaks of the 'accidental origins' of the canon, and describes its coming into being as 'a matter [which is] full of historical contingency and relativity' (p. 156). But he also sees that the decision to constitute the bible as scripture continues to 'make sense in relation to the basic nature of Christian faith' (p. 118). Similarly D. H. Kelsey claims that 'for a community to call itself

"church" is to say, *inter alia*, that it is a community whose continuing self-identity depends on the use . . . of just these writings' (*Uses of Scripture*, 105). See also *The Bible Speaks Again*, 107ff.

   C. Evans in *Is 'Holy Scripture' Christian?*, 24ff, feels that the 'fantasy' by which apostolic authorship was attributed to the New Testament writings has created endless problems for church and Christian life, among the more serious of which was the conception that 'truth lay in the past and the word "modern" was a pejorative term' (p. 31). However correct Professor Evans may be – and no doubt he is perfectly correct – about the 'historical and theological distortions involved in the emotive phrase "the death of the last apostle" ' (p. 17), the importance of the decision to 'draw a boundary line' between canonical and non-canonical writings (*Louvain 1971*, 19) lies not so much in its historical accuracy as in the theological instincts which that judgement reveals (see the comments of Kelsey, *Uses of Scripture*, 116f). See further K. Aland, *The Problem of the New Testament Canon* (London, 1962), H. von Campenhausen, *The Formation of the Christian Bible* (London, 1972), and Childs, *Crisis*, 99ff.

89   Ebeling, *Word and Faith*, 28f.
90   Christian faith, *fides qua creditur*, constantly struggles, as everyone knows, with the possibility of its inner transformation into 'the faith', *fides quae creditur*. In this respect there is a world of difference between the confession of the bible as the product of inspiration, and the formalisation of this into a dogmatic category. For recent discoveries of the former, see *Louvain 1971*, 20f; and cf. *The Bible Speaks Again*, 68f, 73; Barr, *Modern World*, 130f; and Childs, *Crisis*, 99f, 105.
91   The standard work is that of J. Jeremias, *The Parables of Jesus* (2nd rev. edn, London, 1963).
92   On multiplicity of 'kerygmata', see C. Evans, 'The Kerygma', *JTS* n.s. 7 (1956), 25–41, and *Is 'Holy Scripture' Christian?*, ch. 6; also W. G. Doty, *Contemporary New Testament Interpretation* (Englewood Cliffs, N.J., 1972), 135ff; and J. M. Robinson and H. Koester, *Trajectories through Early Christianity* (Philadelphia, 1971). For a cautionary statement on the idea of 'development', see G. B. Caird, 'The Development of the Doctrine of Christ in the New Testament' in *Christ for Us Today*, ed. N. Pittenger (London, 1968), 66–80.
93   Barr, *Modern World*, 161.
94   E. Schweizer, 'Scripture-Tradition–Modern Interpretation', 210, thinks that 'nobody is able to read the Scripture without choosing a centre in the light of which he reads all the other parts of the Bible'. Yet Schweizer himself on the preceding page seems to have offered several 'centres' from which to start, already within the New Testament. Cannot these 'centres' be mutually corrective, the selection of one of which is accomplished in the freedom of the interpreter, and in terms of whichever best suits momentarily the needs of his situation? See Kelsey, *Uses of Scripture*, 196, and also the statements on 'layers of meaning' in the 1967 report on hermeneutics to the Faith and Order Commission, *New Directions*, 35f.
95   Funk, *Language*, 122.
96   Cf. R. Schnackenburg, *The Will to Believe* (London, 1974), 56–61.
97   D. H. Kelsey, *Uses of Scripture*, 170ff, adduces three 'Controls on Imagina-

tion in Theology'; they are (*a*) the conditions which apply for intelligible human discourse (though this 'does not entail that the imaginative judgement itself should be arrived at through reasoned argument'; in fact exactly the opposite is the case) (p. 171); (*b*) the conditions applied by the prevailing culture in setting 'outside limits' for what is believable (p. 172); (*c*) the requirement of the theologian that he 'be responsible to the common structure' of the traditions (p. 174). A summary is given on p. 175.

98   For a brief survey of the exploration of 'parable' in recent New Testament hermeneutical reflection, see A. C. Thiselton, *The Churchman* 87 (1973), 89f.

99   *Louvain 1971*, 17.

100 See Kaufman, *Interpretation* 25 (1971), 111f.

101 Kelsey, *Uses of Scripture*, 6, and Funk, *Language*, 104.

102 See van Ruler, *The Christian Church and the Old Testament*, 93f.

103 Van Ruler, ibid. 11f, lists ten possible ways in which the Old Testament has been construed by Christians. Virtually all of these see the Old Testament as in some way or another subordinated to the New Testament.

104 K. H. Miskotte's *When the Gods Are Silent* represents a sustained attempt to approach issues of contemporary Christian living from an Old Testament vantage point. Of special interest here are these sentences from the translator's Preface: 'As far as I know, it is the first attempt in theological literature to use the Old Testament to provide an answer to the atheism and nihilism of our so-called "post-Christian era". It is interesting to see that Miskotte's frequent reference to Alfred Weber's "fourth man" has its parallel in Dietrich Bonhoeffer's "man come of age", and that Bonhoeffer, too, in his letters from prison recognised this importance of the Old Testament and stressed its relevance for our time and modern man's experience of life, because in the Old Testament man is seen in his total "this worldliness" and his alienation from God' (p. ix). Additionally see the references to F. Hesse and J. Bright, above, ch. 2 n. 49.

105 E.g., J. K. S. Reid, *The Authority of Scripture* (London, 1957), 238f.

106 Childs, *Crisis*, 180ff; Barr, *Modern World*, 167, and cf. *Old and New*, 139f; *The Bible Speaks Again*, 100f.

107 See the section in K. H. Miskotte, *When the Gods Are Silent*, on politics, pp. 271–82. It is, in fact, intriguing to note that when Christians have occasion to reflect on faith and politics or social issues they not infrequently turn (instinctively?) to the Old Testament. So that of the eight essays in the issue of *Interpretation* to commemorate the American bicentennial (January 1976; vol. 30, no. 1), five took their departure more or less specifically from Old Testament statements; further, it has been drawn to my attention (by Professor Moule) that J. V. Taylor in his *Enough Is Enough* (London, 1975) drew almost entirely upon the Old Testament (particularly the book of Deuteronomy) for his scriptural bases (see esp. ch. 3); finally, cf. H.-R. Weber, 'God and the Powerful – The Biblical Search for Wisdom', in press.

108 A. A. van Ruler, *The Christian Church and the Old Testament*, 42: ' "Insofar as the church is a shadow of the future, the *umbrae* of the Old Testament are true of it too." This insight is of incalculable importance. The church has again been set in an Old Testament situation . . . and thus the whole of the Old Testament, particularly its social and political aspects, becomes significant again' (citing H. W. Wolff); similarly, pp. 88f.

109 I. Greenberg, 'Judaism and Christianity after the Holocaust', *JES* 12 (1975),
534. See all the essays in this issue of *JES* (vol. 12, no. 4), which is especially
entitled 'Jews and Christians in Dialogue'; all the essays carry copious references to other literature.

110 Cf. additionally Dautzenberg, *BZ* n.s. 15 (1973), 177.

Excursus 2. Hebrews as interpretation for a late-apostolic church situation?

1 *Glaube*, 2.

2 Ibid. 1-4.

3 Ibid. 218f.

4 Ibid. 64-71, esp. p. 66.

5 Ibid. 77f.

6 Ibid. 56, 62, 77, 126-44, esp. pp. 136ff.

7 Ibid. 65f; cf. also pp. 78, 102, 146f.

8 Ibid. 35, 39, 62f, 70, 117-25.

9 Ibid. 27-9, 121ff.

10 Ibid. 174ff.

11 Ibid. 171: 'The eschatological paradox of the "already–not yet" has been resolved into a purely temporal scheme, that of "not yet but sometime (soon!)".'

12 Ibid. 62f, 67f, 117, 154ff.

13 Ibid. 44, 85, 105f, 144, 147, and cf. pp. 93f.

14 Ibid. 57, 102.

15 Ibid. 184. See the whole section: 'The development of internal Christian
problems as the motive for the particular faith-theme in Hebrews', pp. 198ff.

16 Ibid. 13.

17 Ibid. 13, also pp. 71, 147.

18 J. Barr, *The Semantics of Biblical Language*, 207: '... the difficult problem
of the relation of word and concept'. See specifically G. Dautzenberg, *BZ*
n.s. 15 (1973), 167 n. 19. A number of Dautzenberg's criticisms of Grässer
resemble those made here. The presence of this material in my 1971
Cambridge dissertation signifies that we have come to these independently.

19 Though see Dautzenberg, *BZ* n.s. 15 (1973), 174f.

20 I should say that Professor Grässer has noted in the margin of my manuscript
at this point that he is not concerned to contest this. Still, I think the assumption that the ways in which the πίστις words are used will provide in
themselves (i.e., without the need to attend at the same time to other lexical
and conceptual stocks in the letter) the indices for the major theological
issues mentioned at the outset, is one that runs throughout the book.

21 We might compare W. Pannenberg, *Jesus - God and Man*, 205: 'Having
community with Jesus is the basis of being Christian. How we can have
community with Jesus is the main problem not only of the church's doctrine, but also of her life.'

22 Two subsidiary and related criticisms of the oversharp cleavage which
Grässer sets up in *Der Glaube* between Hebrews and Paul (this has been
substantially modified in later essays, as we shall see) have to do with the
degree that 'faith' in Hebrews has been turned into a 'Christian ethic' and,
secondly, the degree to which faith has been 'historicised' as the result of
an increasing despair at the delay of the parousia (cf. ibid. 162: 'Christianity
has become, for the writer, an historical epoch in time').

With regard to the first, Grässer is bound to say that Paul's proclamation also entails an ethic: 'Paul, too, knows about the new life only as "in the testing circumstances of earthly existence" (G. Bornkamm)', but he insists that unlike Hebrews, 'in Paul the imperative never becomes an independent theme, but is always based on the indicative' (ibid. 152 n. 25). By way of contrast, what we find in Hebrews is that 'faith has less to do with the eschatological event, the καινὴ κτίσις, than with Christian behaviour ... From this conception it is but a short step to the incorporation of faith into a catalogue of ἀρεταί' (ibid. 144f).
Here, however, we have on one side to repeat (see above, ch. 1 n. 38; also p. 79) that the constancy to which Christians are called in Hebrews is never other than an outward presentation of their inner estimation of the veracity of the Word of God and therefore of God himself; and, on the other side we may note that for Paul πίστις *can* be listed, quite incidentally, along with other Christian virtues, including μακροθυμία Gal. 5.22)!
Secondly, Grässer's characterisation of Pauline eschatology as wholly 'realised' over against the wholly futuristic emphasis of Hebrews (*Glaube*, 64–8), so that Paul's 'now' of salvation has become in Hebrews a painful ἐπίλοιπος χρόνος (see ibid. 158–71, esp. pp. 161f), fails to do justice to what is universally recognised to be a most complex issue. See, for example, the treatments of Pauline eschatology in O. Cullmann, *Salvation in History*, 248–68; A. L. Moore, *The Parousia in the New Testament*, 61, 83f; and U. Wilckens, 'Die Rechtfertigung Abrahams nach Römer 4' in *Studien zur Theologie der alttestamentlichen Überlieferungen* (G. von Rad Festschrift), ed. R. Rendtorf and K. Koch (Neukirchen, 1961), 111–27, to name only a few writers who stress, to the contrary, the salvation-historical aspects of Paul's thought. It is not Hebrews but *Paul* who writes: 'For now is our salvation nearer than when we first believed. The night is far gone and the day is at hand' (Rom. 13.11f).
Over against these comments, however, we are certainly bound to make reference to more recent studies of Grässer, in which the recognition is quite clear that in spite of the formal differences between Paul and Hebrews there are strong *substantial* similarities. See particularly 'Zur Christologie des Hebräerbriefes', *passim* but esp. the concluding sentences, and 'Rechtfertigung im Hebräerbrief', esp. pp. 86, 88f, 93 etc.

23 In fact Grässer does devote himself to the theological structures of the letter – in four pages at the end of his book! (*Glaube*, 214–18). And there, we find, when one considers the theology of Hebrews, 'A suggestively gnostic terminology (κεκοινώνηκεν, μετέσχεν, ὁμοιωθῆναι, οὗ οἶκος ἐσμεν ἡμεῖς, μετριοπαθεῖν, τελειοῦν) takes the place of the otherwise regular πιστεύειν εἰς, in order to express the relationship, constitutive for salvation, between the bringer of salvation and its recipients. Hebrews does not by any means concede this basic structure; only the terminology is altered' (p. 216). With this we will certainly agree but it is not easy to see how these statements are to be reconciled to others such as: 'The vast distance between this alternative [περιποίησις or ἀπώλεια] and that of Paul [Law or gospel, faith or works, Jew or Gentile] corresponds to the great difference in meaning of this otherwise conceived πίστις in Hebrews: it does not bear a specifically Christian character' (ibid. 44f), or 'The specifically *Christian* ('Christological')

faith is not carried forward in Hebrews, either in the deliberate manner of the apostle Paul, or in the unreflecting style of the Synoptic writers' (ibid. 79; his italics). Similarly p. 35.

24 'The most probable date for the writing of Hebrews is in the ninth decade' (*ThR* n.s. 30 (1964-5), 152).

25 Grässer makes a good deal of the known second-generation origins of Hebrews (2.3). This in itself, of course, does not really establish a date so late as the ninth decade, since the church to which the writer belongs could perfectly well have been established in the first or second decade of the apostolic mission. A good deal of Grässer's argument also rests on the Hellenism which forms the obvious backdrop for this writer's thought. The implication is that the translation of the gospel into Hellenistic motifs points to a distance in time from the primitive church and the original missionary expansion. This is also unjustified. Not many scholars want to deny the Hellenistic flavour of much of the letter. But that this *in itself* involves a time-lag is false. The process would have begun immediately upon the author's conversion to Christianity, and on his entering into creative theological reflection, which may have involved only a very short space of time.

26 For example, C. K. Barrett is criticised: 'It is a decisive limitation in Barrett's study that the eschatological scheme of Hebrews is not seen from the point of view of the person who so conceives it, with respect to his situation in the history of the church. For only in connection with the development of the internal Christian problems can the elements which make up the eschatological picture be properly evaluated' (ibid. 172 n. 140). But the point is that it is precisely this theory of development in the church against which Barrett is protesting (see further n. 29 below).

So far as I can see, Grässer nowhere attempts to marshal more objective evidence for the late date he chooses. On the contrary he seems to suggest (*Glaube*, 8) that such objective methods are both useless and misconceived: 'In fact for the first time it [he is speaking here of Dibelius' study in *Geschichte der urchristlichen Literatur* (1926)] pointed to a way out of the cul-de-sac of the introductory questions in the more narrow sense: to understand Hebrews through its own exegesis, its time and its situation.' Even in his survey article in *ThR* n.s. 30 (1964-5), where he deals with 'Time and Place of Writing' (pp. 151f), consideration of a possible earlier date is confined to a dismissal of the argument from silence about the destruction of the Temple. Certainly, we may not be able to pin down the date of the letter's composition with much more certainty than this; but the dangers inherent in going on, without this certainty, to the massive kind of argument erected by Grässer need to be noted.

27 E.g., for the greater part of his book Grässer's analysis proceeds on the assumption that Hebrews is written under the influence of the parousia-delay despair. It has been this which has effected the author's removal of the events of salvation into an indefinite future with its consequent complete restructuring of the concept of faith. So (to take an example almost at random) we read: 'Theologically, the identification of πίστις and ἐλπίς in Hebrews signifies that salvation is ordered pre-eminently with reference to its still outstanding futurity ...' (*Glaube*, 117). But if one appeals

protestingly to the passages which seem to affirm the author's convincedness
of the 'already' aspect of Christian salvation, he does so in vain. For these,
no less than the other parts, confirm Grässer's thesis; only here they show
how the writer is *correcting* the misapprehensions of his readers: 'Unmis-
takeably the prologue introduction, 1.1-4, fastens immediately on to the
fundamental problem for the threatened community, that from which all
their other problems stem: this is the question as to the reality of the 'turn
of the ages'. Does the Christ-event really amount to an eschatological event?
Our writer answers affirmatively and gives as his reason: Christ is the Son.
That sets the tone for the theme of the first chapter. God has spoken
finally through the Son. That is the decisive signature for the time of the
End' (ibid. 206f).

28 So, e.g., ibid. 199.

29 C. K. Barrett, 'Eschatology', 366: 'The present essay proceeds on the . . .
belief . . . that the thought of Hebrews is consistent, and that in it the
eschatological is the determining element. Features which do not upon
the surface appear to be eschatological show, on closer examination,
traces of eschatological, even apocalyptic, origin and the thought of the
epistle . . . arises out of the eschatological faith of the primitive church.'

30 'It is important to note that the traditional early Christian apocalyptic
expectation, in the form of an imminent hope, is confined in Hebrews to
the paraenetic passages and is here clearly intended to stimulate the attitude
of the believers; whereas in the detailed soteriological and Christological
theses, the traditional eschatology either is present only as transposed into
a metaphysical dualism, or is divested of its temporally foreshortened perspectives, or else in central places is completely absent' (*Glaube*, 179f).

31 So B. Kappert comments: 'If we start out with the observation, really
formulated so clearly only by E. Grässer, "that the traditional, early
Christian apocalyptic expectation, in the form of an imminent hope, is
confined in Hebrews to the paraenetic passages . . .", we find there our own
observations confirmed with respect to a paraenesis which climaxes in a
future-eschatological declaration . . . The prevalence of the futuristic-apocalyptic
conceptualisation precisely in the paraenesis which provides the point for
the dogmatic, Christological sections, shows that the Alexandrian dualism . . .
stands *in the service of*. . .the establishing of a new basis for the futurist
eschatology' (*Eschatologie*, 49; italics mine; that Klappert shares with
Grässer, contrary to the view taken in this critique, the view that the so-
called 'parousia-delay' has been an important factor in the writer's understanding does not affect our agreement with the statement here cited).

32 G. Dautzenberg, *BZ* n.s. 15 (1973), 174ff, urges a further criticism toward
the postulate that Hebrews represents a deviation or devolution from an
originally unified faith-conception in the early church: 'The primitive
Christian faith-conception was not uniform from the beginning. The unity
in early Christianity was not based in a terminological and theological
uniformity in its faith-conception, perhaps not even in a terminological
uniformity in the kerygma, but in the Christ-event' (p. 175).

33 See W. Robinson, *The Eschatology of the Epistle to the Hebrews* (Birmingham,
1950), 15.

34 *Glaube*, 184.

BIBLIOGRAPHY OF WORKS REFERRED TO

(Figures in brackets at the end of each entry indicate pages in this book in which reference is made to the works listed.)

Adams, J. C., 'Exegesis of Hebrews 6.1f', *NTS* 13 (1966-7), 378-85. [164 n. 70]

Aland, K., *The Problem of the New Testament Canon* (London, 1962). [190 n. 88]

Allegro, J. M., 'Fragments of a Qumran Scroll of Eschatological *Midrašim*', *JBL* 77 (1958), 350-4. [166 n. 93]
'Further Messianic References in Qumran Literature', *JBL* 75 (1956), 174-87. [166 n. 92]

Allen, E. L., 'Jesus and Moses in the New Testament', *ExT* 67 (1955-6), 104-6. [147 n. 26]

Anderson, H., 'Existential Hermeneutics: Features of the New Quest', *Interpretation* 16 (1962), 131-55. [179 n. 94]
Jesus and Christian Origins (New York, 1964). [173 n. 2, 174 n. 8, 176 n. 52, 178 n. 75]

Baaker, A., 'Christ an Angel?', *ZNW* 32 (1933), 255-65. [146 n. 15]

Bacon, B. W., 'Hebrews 1.10-12 and the Septuagint Rendering of Ps. 102.23', *ZNW* 3 (1902), 280-5. [165 n. 89, 168 n. 109]

Baillie, D. M., *God Was in Christ* (London, 1948¹, 1955⁴). [180 n. 99]

Banks, R. J., 'The Eschatological Role of Law in Pre- and Post-Christian Jewish Thought' in *Reconciliation and Hope* (L. Morris Festschrift), ed. R. J. Banks (London, 1974), 173-85. [148 n. 35, 151 n. 55]
Jesus and the Law in the Synoptic Tradition (Cambridge, 1975). [148 n. 35, 151 n. 55]

Barbour, R. S., *Traditio-Historical Criticism of the Gospels* (London, 1972). [173 n. 5, 180 n. 96, 181 n. 108]

Barr, J., *The Bible in the Modern World* (London, 1973). [145 n. 17, 187 n. 60, 190 nn. 84, 85 & 88, 191 nn. 90 & 93, 192 n. 106]
Biblical Words for Time (London, 1962). [158 nn. 9 & 10]
Old and New in Interpretation (London, 1966). [145 n. 16, 158 nn. 6 & 9, 159 n. 15, 169 nn. 120 & 125, 183 nn. 6, 7 & 9, 189 n. 80, 192 n. 106]
'Revelation through History in the Old Testament and in Modern Theology', *Interpretation* 17 (1963), 193-205. [158 n. 6]
The Semantics of Biblical Language (London, 1961). [158 n. 9, 193 n. 18]

Barrett, C. K., 'The Eschatology of the Epistle to the Hebrews' in *The Background of the New Testament and Its Eschatology* (C. H. Dodd Festschrift), ed. W. D. Davies and D. Daube (Cambridge, 1956), 365–93. [156 n. 6, 158 n. 14, 159 n. 23, 160 n. 41, 165 n. 75, 195 n. 26, 196 n. 29]
  Jesus and the Gospel Tradition (London, 1967). [174 n. 9]
Barth, K., *The Epistle to the Romans* (London, 1933). [189 n. 72]
  The Humanity of God (London, 1961). [184 n. 20]
  Church Dogmatics, vol. III, pt 1 (Edinburgh, 1958). [161 n. 47]
Barth, M., 'The Old Testament in Hebrews' in *Current Issues in New Testament Interpretation* (O. Piper Festschrift), ed. W. Klassen and G. F. Snyder (London, 1962), 53–78. [157 n. 2, 161 n. 53, 168 n. 112]
Barthes, R., *et al.*, *Structural Analysis and Biblical Exegesis* (Pittsburgh, 1974). [144 n. 8, 186 n. 53]
Bartsch, H.-W. (ed.), *Kerygma and Myth*, vols. I and II (London, 1953, 1962). [186 n. 36]
  Kerygma und Mythos, vols. I–V (Hamburg, 1948–55). [186 n. 36]
Bauer, W., *A Greek–English Lexicon of the New Testament*, trans. and ed. W. F. Arndt and F. W. Gingrich (Chicago, 1957). [148 n. 30, 151 nn. 58 & 62]
Beare, F. W., 'Sayings of the Risen Jesus in the Synoptic Tradition' in *Christian History and Interpretation* (J. Knox Festschrift), ed. W. R. Farmer, C. F. D. Moule and R. R. Niebuhr (Cambridge, 1967), 161–81. [180 n. 101]
Beasley-Murray, G. R., 'The Two Messiahs in the Testaments of the Twelve Patriarchs', *JTS* 48 (1947), 1–12. [154 n. 99]
Behm, J., *Der Begriff ΔΙΑΘΗΚΗ im Neuen Testament* (Leipzig, 1912). [155 n. 118]
Berkhof, H., 'Über die Methode der Eschatologie' in *Diskussion über die 'Theologie der Hoffnung'*, ed. W.-D. Marsch (Munich, 1967), 168–80. [178 n. 72]
Bethge, E., *Dietrich Bonhoeffer* (London, 1970). [183 n. 15]
Betz, O., *Offenbarung und Schriftforschung in der Qumransekte* (Tübingen, 1960). [164 n. 68, 169 n. 128]
Bible Speaks Again, The, see under Netherlands Reformed Church.
Bieder, W., 'Pneumatologische Aspekte im Hebräerbrief' in *Neues Testament und Geschichte* (O. Cullmann Festschrift), ed. H. Baltensweiler and B. Reicke (Tübingen, 1972), 251–9. [171 n. 137, 172 n. 146]
Black, M., 'The Qumran Messiah and Related Beliefs' in *The Scrolls and Christian Origins* (London, 1961), 145–63. [154 n. 98]
Blass, F. and Debrunner, A., *A Greek Grammar of the New Testament* (Cambridge and Chicago, 1961). [151 n. 62]
Bonhoeffer, D., *Letters and Papers from Prison* (London, 1959[2]). [183 n. 15]
Boring, M. E., 'How May We Identify Oracles of Christian Prophets in the Synoptic Tradition?', *JBL* 91 (1972), 501–21. [164 n. 68, 180 n. 101]
Bornhäuser, K., 'Die Versuchungen Jesu nach dem Hebräerbrief' in *Theologische Studien Martin Kähler dargebracht* (Leipzig, 1905), 72–86. [148 n. 32, 171 n. 142]

Bornkamm, G., 'Das Bekenntnis im Hebräerbrief' in *Studien zu Antike und Urchristentum* (collected essays, vol. II) (Munich, 1959), 188–203. [146 n. 11, 148 n. 31, 162 n. 59]

'Die Theologie Rudolf Bultmanns in der neueren Diskussion', *ThR* n.s. 29 (1963), 33–141. [186 n. 36]

Bowden, J., 'Great Expectations? The New Testament Critic and His Audience' in *What about the New Testament?* (C. F. Evans Festschrift), ed. M. D. Hooker and C. Hickling (London, 1975), 1–12. [184 n. 29]

Bowker, J., *The Targums and Rabbinic Literature* (Cambridge, 1969). [167 n. 102]

Brandenburger, E., 'Text und Vorlagen von Hebr 5.7–10', *NovT* 11 (1969), 190–224. [156 nn. 16 & 17, 177 nn. 60 & 61, 180 n. 100]

Braun, H., 'Die Gewinnung der Gewissheit in dem Hebräerbrief', *ThLz* 96 (1971), cols. 321–30. [152 n. 75]

Bright, J., *The Authority of the Old Testament* (London, 1967). [161 n. 49, 192 n. 104]

Brown, F., Driver, S. R. and Briggs, C. A., *A Hebrew and English Lexicon of the Old Testament* (Oxford, 1906). [156 n. 12]

Brownlee, W. H., 'Biblical Interpretation among the Sectaries of the Dead Sea Scrolls', *BA* 14 (1951), 54–76. [164 n. 68, 167 n. 102]

Bruce, A. B., *The Epistle to the Hebrews* (Edinburgh, 1899). [149 n. 43]

Bruce, F. F., *Biblical Exegesis in the Qumran Texts* (London, 1960). [164 n. 68]

The Epistle to the Hebrews (The New London Commentary) (London, 1964). [143 n. 1, 149 n. 47, 157 n. 4, 163 n. 66, 174 nn. 19 & 21, 175 n. 41]

' "To the Hebrews" or "To the Essenes"?', *NTS* 9 (1962–3), 217–32. [147 n. 27, 157 n. 4]

Buchanan, G. W., *'To the Hebrews'* (Anchor Bible Commentary) (New York, 1972). [143 n. 4, 144 n. 11, 149 n. 46, 153 n. 92, 166 n. 99]

Büchel, C., 'Der Hebräerbrief und das Alte Testament', *TSK* 79 (1906), 508–91. [146 n. 17, 157 n. 4, 168 n. 118]

Büchsel, F., *Die Christologie des Hebräerbriefes* (Gütersloh, 1923). [154 n. 102, 156 n. 11, 158 n. 12, 164 n. 70, 176 n. 44, 177 n. 58]

Bultmann, R., 'History and Eschatology in the New Testament' *NTS* 1 (1954–5), 5–16. [160 n. 40]

The History of the Synoptic Tradition (Oxford, 1963). [173 n. 1]

'The Primitive Christian Kerygma and the Historical Jesus' in *The Historical Jesus and the Kerygmatic Christ*, ed. C. E. Braaten and R. A. Harrisville (Nashville, Tenn., 1964), 15–42. [174 n. 20, 179 n. 90, 181 n. 113]

Primitive Christianity in Its Contemporary Setting (London, 1956). [182 n. 115]

'The Problem of Hermeneutics' in *Essays Philosophical and Theological* (London, n.d.), 234–61. [152 n. 71, 185 n. 35]

'Prophecy and Fulfilment' in *Essays on Old Testament Interpretation*, ed. C. Westermann (London, 1963), 50–75. [182 n. 116]

Theology of the New Testament, vols. I and II (London, 1952, 1955). [182 n. 115, 187 n. 58]

Article on ζάω, *TDNT* II, 832–43. [158 n. 9]

Cadbury, H. J., *The Peril of Modernising Jesus* (London, 1962, 1937[1]). [181 n. 109]

Caird, G. B., 'The Development of the Doctrine of Christ in the New Testament' in *Christ for Us Today*, ed. N. Pittenger (London, 1968), 66–80. [191 n. 92]
'The Exegetical Method of the Epistle to the Hebrews', *CanJTheol* 5 (1959), 44–51. [155 n. 119, 157 n. 2, 161 n. 48, 165 nn. 86, 87 & 88, 169 n. 122, 172 n. 147]

Calvert, D. G. A., 'An Examination of Criteria for Distinguishing Authentic Words of Jesus', *NTS* 18 (1971-2), 209–19. [180 n. 102]

Calvin, J., *Commentary on Hebrews* (Grand Rapids, Mich., 1949). [183 n. 8]

Campbell, J. C., 'In a Son', *Interpretation* 10 (1956), 24–38. [175 n. 40, 176 nn. 43 & 45]

Campenhausen, H. von, *The Formation of the Christian Bible* (London, 1972). [190 n. 88]

Carlston, C. E., 'Eschatology and Repentance in the Epistle to the Hebrews', *JBL* 78 (1959), 296–302. [159 n. 18, 171 nn. 140, 141 & 144]

Chadwick, H. (ed.), *Lessing's Theological Writings* (London, 1956). [184 n. 22]

Charles, R. H., *The Book of Jubilees, with Introduction, Notes and Indices* (London, 1902). [147 n. 21]

Chavasse, C., 'Jesus: Christ and Moses', *Theology* 54 (1951), 244–50, 289–96. [148 n. 34]

Childs, B. S., *Biblical Theology in Crisis* (Philadelphia, 1970). [167 n. 104, 168 n. 119, 169 n. 120, 175 nn. 33 & 34, 176 n. 50, 183 nn. 127 & 10, 184 nn. 23 & 30, 189 n. 71, 190 n. 88, 191 n. 90, 192 n. 106]

Clarkson, M. E., 'The Antecedents of the High-Priest Theme in Hebrews', *AngTheolRev* 29 (1947), 89–95. [154 n. 113]

Clavier, H., 'ὁ λόγος τοῦ θεοῦ dans l'épitre aux Hébreux' in *New Testament Essays - Studies in Memory of T. W. Manson*, ed. A. J. B. Higgins (Manchester, 1959), 81–93. [145 n. 3]

Cody, A., *Heavenly Sanctuary and Liturgy in the Epistle to the Hebrews: The Achievement of Salvation in the Epistle's Perspectives* (St Meinrad, Ind., 1960). [161 n. 47]

Cone, J. H., *God of the Oppressed* (New York, 1975). [181 n. 109]

Culley, R. C., 'Structural Analysis: Is It Done with Mirrors?', *Interpretation* 28, 2 (1974), 165–81. [144 n. 8]

Cullmann, O., *Christ and Time* (London, 1951). [178 n. 74]
The Christology of the New Testament (London, 1963[2]). [154 n. 113, 156 n. 11, 168 n. 109, 172 n. 155, 176 n. 52, 178 nn. 74 & 76, 180 n. 97]
Salvation in History (London, 1967). [155 n. 116, 165 n. 75, 169 n. 130, 193 n. 22]
'The Tradition' in *The Early Church* (London, 1956), 59–99. [180 n. 101]

Daube, D., 'Alexandrian Methods of Interpretation and the Rabbis' in *Festschrift Hans Lewald* (Basel, 1953), 27–44. [157 n. 4]

'Rabbinic Methods of Interpretation and Hellenistic Rhetoric', *HUCA*
    22 (1949), 239–64. [157 n. 4]
Dautzenberg, G., 'Der Glaube im Hebräerbrief', *BZ* n.s. 15 (1973), 161–77.
    [148 n. 38, 175 n. 25, 182 n. 119, 193 nn. 110, 18 & 19, 196 n. 32]
Davies, A. T., 'The Aryan Christ', *JES* 12 (1975), 569–79. [181 n. 109]
Davies, W. D., 'A Note on Josephus, Antiquities 15.136', *HTR* 47 (1954),
    135–40. [147 n. 21]
    The Setting of the Sermon on the Mount (Cambridge, 1964). [156 n. 5]
Deichgräber, R., *Gotteshymnus und Christushymnus in der frühen
    Christenheit* (Göttingen, 1967). [158 nn. 10, 11 & 13, 161 n. 46]
Delitzsch, F., *Commentary on the Epistle to the Hebrews*, vols. I–II
    (Edinburgh, 1886). [149 n. 46, 163 n. 66]
Delling, G., article on ἀρχηγός, *TNDT* I, 487–8. [174 n. 14]
    Articles on τέλειος, τελειόω, τελείωσις, *TDNT* VIII, 67–78, 79–84,
    84–6. [156 nn. 10 & 14]
Descartes, R., *Philosophical Writings*, ed. E. Anscombe and P. Geach
    (London, 1964). [189 n. 73]
Dibelius, M., 'Der himmlische Kultus nach dem Hebräerbrief' in *Botschaft
    und Geschichte* (collected essays, vol. II) (Tübingen, 1956), 160–76.
    [153 n. 92, 156 n. 13, 165 n. 73, 172 n. 153]
Dodd, C. H., *Historical Tradition in the Fourth Gospel* (Cambridge, 1963).
    [168 n. 115, 174 n. 10, 180 n. 104]
    History and the Gospel (London, 1964). [170 n. 131, 180 n. 104]
    The Interpretation of the Fourth Gospel (Cambridge, 1953). [164 n. 68,
    168 n. 115]
    The Old Testament in the New (Philadelphia, 1963). [169 n. 125]
Doeve, J. W., *Jewish Hermeneutics in the Synoptic Gospels and Acts*
    (Assen, 1953). [160 n. 41, 164 n. 68, 166 n. 93, 167 n. 102, 169
    n. 126]
    'Some Notes with Reference to ΤΑ ΛΟΓΙΑ ΤΟΥ ΘΕΟΥ in Rom. 3.2'
    in *Studia Paulina* (J. de Zwaan Festschrift), ed. J. N. Sevenster and
    W. C. van Unnik (Haarlem, 1953), 111–23. [163 n. 65]
Donovan, J., *The Logia in Ancient and Recent Literature* (Cambridge,
    1924). [163 n. 67]
Doty, W. G., *Contemporary New Testament Interpretation* (Englewood
    Cliffs, N.J., 1972). [191 n. 92]
Downing, F. G., *The Church and Jesus* (London, 1968). [152 n. 71, 180
    n. 102]
Dunn, J. D. G., *Jesus and the Spirit* (London, 1975). [176 n. 55]
du Plessis, P. J., ΤΕΛΕΙΟΣΙΣ, *The Idea of Perfection in the New Testa-
    ment* (Kampen, n.d.). [156 n. 11]
Ebeling, G., article on 'Hermeneutik', *RGG*[3] III, cols. 242–62. [145 n. 16,
    184 n. 18]
    The Nature of Faith (London, 1961). [174 n. 20]
    Word and Faith (London, 1963). [145 nn. 15 & 16, 148 n. 38, 169
    n. 120, 174 n. 20, 182 n. 114, 183 n. 12, 184 n. 23, 187 n. 54, 188
    n. 61, 191 n. 89]
Edwards, O. C., jun., 'Historical-Critical Method's Failure of Nerve and a
    Prescription for a Tonic: A Review of Some Recent Literature',
    AngTheolRev 59 (1977), 115–34. [184 n. 30]

Eichrodt, W., *Theology of the Old Testament*, vol. I (London, 1961). [163 n. 66]

Elliger, K., *Studien zum Habakuk-Kommentar* (Tübingen, 1953). [164 n. 68]

Ellis, E. E., *Paul's Use of the Old Testament* (Edinburgh, 1957). [169 n. 127]

Evans, C. F., *Is 'Holy Scripture' Christian?* (London, 1971). [190 nn. 83 & 88, 191 n. 92]

   'The Kerygma', *JTS* n.s. 7 (1956), 25–41. [191 n. 92]

   Queen or Cinderella? (Durham, 1960). [181 n. 107]

Farmer, W. R., 'An Historical Essay on the Humanity of Jesus Christ' in *Christian History and Interpretation* (J. Knox Festschrift), ed. W. R. Farmer, C. F. D. Moule and R. R. Niebuhr (Cambridge, 1967), 101–26. [174 n. 10, 180 n. 97]

Filson, F. V., *Yesterday: A Study of Hebrews in the Light of Chapter 13* (London, 1967). [143 n. 4, 153 n. 87, 154 nn. 102 & 104, 159 n. 16, 168 n. 112, 178 n. 73, 179 n. 84]

Fitzmyer, J. A., ' "Now This Melchizedek . . .", Hebrews 7.1', in *Essays on the Semitic Background of the New Testament* (London, 1971), 221–43. [150 n. 50]

Flesseman-van Leer, E., 'Biblical Interpretation in the World Council of Churches', *Study Encounter* 8, 2 (1972), 1–8. [183 n. 1, 188 n. 64]

   'Dear Christopher . . .' in *What about the New Testament?* (C. F. Evans Festschrift), ed. M. D. Hooker and C. Hickling (London, 1975), 234–42. [185 n. 32, 188 n. 64]

Flew, R. N., *The Idea of Perfection in Christian Theology* (London, 1934). [156 nn. 6 & 19]

Frei, H. W., *The Eclipse of Biblical Narrative: A Study in Eighteenth and Nineteenth Century Hermeneutics* (New Haven, Conn., 1974). [145 n. 18, 185 n. 32, 188 nn. 62 & 63]

Frend, W. H. C., 'Marcion', *ExT* 80 (1968-9), 328-32. [169 n. 129]

Friedrich, G., 'Beobachtungen zur messianischen Hohepriestererwartung in den Synoptikern', *ZThK* 53 (1956), 265-311. [154 n. 113]

Frör, K., *Biblische Hermeneutik* (Munich, 1961). [188 n. 62, 189 nn. 72 & 81]

Fuchs, E., *Hermeneutik* (Bad Cannstatt, 1954). [158 n. 6, 184 n. 21, 186 nn. 38, 39, 40, 41, 42, 43, 44 & 45]

   'Proclamation and Speech Event', *Theology Today* 19 (1962-3), 341-54. [186 nn. 46 & 47]

   Studies of the Historical Jesus (London, 1964). [174 n. 20, 176 n. 55, 186 nn. 44, 47, 48, 49, 50, 51 & 52]

Funk, R. W., *Language, Hermeneutic and Word of God* (New York, 1966). [169 n. 120, 182 nn. 124 & 126, 185 n. 33, 187 n. 56, 189 n. 75, 191 n. 95, 192 n. 101]

Gadamer, H.-G., *Truth and Method* (London, 1975). [145 n. 18, 183 nn. 2 & 11, 185 n. 32, 188 nn. 66, 67 & 69, 189 nn. 72 & 78]

Gärtner, B., 'The Habakkuk Commentary and the Gospel of Matthew', *Studia Theologica* 8 (1954), 1-24. [157 n. 4]

Glasson, T. F., ' "Plurality of Divine Persons" and the Quotations in Hebrews 1.6ff', *NTS* 12 (1965-6), 270-2. [168 n. 109]

Glombitza, O., 'Erwägungen zum kunstvollen Ansatz der Paraenese im Brief an die Hebräer 10.19–25', *NovT* 9 (1967), 132–50. [164 n. 69]

Goppelt, L., *Typos* (Gütersloh, 1939; Darmstadt, 1969). [161 n. 42, 167 n. 105, 169 n. 130]

Grässer, E., 'Hebräer 1.1–4: ein exegetischer Versuch' in *Evangelisch-Katholischer Kommentar zum Neuen Testament*, pt 3 (Zurich and Neukirchen, 1971), 55–91. [145 n. 1, 146 nn. 5, 8, 11, 12, 14 & 15, 152 nn. 69 & 75, 153 n. 81]

'Der Hebräerbrief, 1938–63', *ThR* n.s. 30 (1964–5), 138–236. [144 nn. 9 & 10, 148 n. 37, 153 n. 78, 156 n. 1, 157 n. 3, 161 n. 51, 167 n. 105, 168 nn. 111 & 116, 169 n. 130, 173 n. 2, 195 nn. 24 & 26]

'Das Heil als Wort, Hebr. 2.1–4' in *Neues Testament und Geschichte* (O. Cullmann Festschrift), ed. H. Baltensweiler and B. Reicke (Tübingen, 1972), 261–74. [147 n. 22, 152 n. 69, 162 n. 58, 178 n. 81]

Der Glaube im Hebräerbrief (Marburg, 1965). [143 n. 5, 147 nn. 25 & 28, 148 n. 38, 152 n. 75, 153 nn. 81 & 82, 154 n. 97, 158 nn. 12 & 14, 159 nn. 19, 24, 25 & 26, 160 n. 41, 161 n. 51, 162 nn. 56 & 60, 163 n. 66, 165 n. 80, 168 n. 112, 170 n. 136, 171 n. 145, 172 n. 153, 174 nn. 14, 15, 16, 17 & 21, 178 n. 73, 182 nn. 119 & 120, 193 nn. 1–17 & 22, 194 n. 23, 195 nn. 26 & 27, 196 nn. 28, 30 & 34]

'Der historische Jesus im Hebräerbrief', *ZNW* 56 (1965), 63–91. [173 n. 2, 174 n. 10, 179 nn. 87, 89 & 91]

'Motive und Methoden der neueren Jesus-Literatur', *VuF*, no. 2 (1973), 3–45. [173 n. 3, 174 n. 7, 176 n. 52, 180 n. 98, 181 n. 111, 190 n. 86]

'Rechtfertigung im Hebräerbrief' in *Rechtfertigung* (E. Käsemann Festschrift), ed. J. Friederich, W. Pöhlmann and P. Stuhlmacher (Tübingen, 1976), 79–93. [182 n. 120, 187 n. 59, 193 n. 22]

Review of G. W. Buchanan's *'To the Hebrews'*, *ThLz* 100 (1975), cols. 752–5. [153 n. 92]

'Zur Christologie des Hebräerbriefes' in *Neues Testament und Christliche Existenz* (H. Braun Festschrift), ed. H. D. Betz and L. Schottroff (Tübingen, 1973), 195–206. [148 n. 38, 182 n. 120, 193 n. 22]

Greenberg, I., 'Judaism and Christianity after the Holocaust', *JES* 12 (1975), 521–51. [193 n. 109]

Greer, R. A., *The Captain of Our Salvation* (Tübingen, 1973). [143 n. 3]

Gutbrod, W., article on νόμος, *TDNT* IV, 1036–85. [150 n. 53, 151 n. 60]

Gyllenberg, R., 'Die Christologie des Hebräerbriefes', *ZSTh* 11 (1934), 662–90. [161 n. 47, 162 n. 54, 171 n. 138]

Hahn, F., *The Titles of Jesus in Christology* (London, 1969). [154 n. 108, 155 n. 114]

Hanson, A. T., *Jesus Christ in the Old Testament* (London, 1965). [149 n. 47, 168 n. 111]

Hanson, R. P. C., *Allegory and Event* (London, 1959). [169 n. 130]

Harvey, V. A., *The Historian and the Believer* (London, 1967). [178 n. 69, 179 nn. 88, 93 & 94, 184 n. 19, 185 n. 33, 189 n. 74]

Harvey, V. A. and Ogden, S. M., 'How New Is the "New Quest of the Historical Jesus"?' in *The Historical Jesus and the Kerygmatic Christ*, ed. C. E. Braaten and R. A. Harrisville (Nashville, Tenn., 1964), 197–242. [181 n. 112]

Hebert, A. G., *The Authority of the Old Testament* (London, 1947). [150 n. 50]

Hengel, M., *Judaism and Hellenism*, vols. I and II (London, 1974). [157 n. 4, 161 n. 43, 169 n. 126]

Héring, J., *Commentary on the Epistle to the Hebrews* (London, 1970). [143 n. 1, 146 n. 6]

Hesse, F., 'The Evaluation and the Authority of Old Testament Texts' in *Essays in Old Testament Interpretation*, ed. C. Westermann (London, 1963), 285-313. [161 n. 49, 192 n. 104]

Higgins, A. J. B., 'The Old Testament and Some Aspects of New Testament Christology' in *Promise and Fulfilment*, ed. F. F. Bruce (Edinburgh, 1963), 128-41. [154 n. 113]

'The Priestly Messiah', *NTS* 13 (1966-7), 211-39. [154 nn. 98 & 107]

Hill, D., *Greek Words and Hebrew Meanings* (Cambridge, 1967). [163 n. 66]

'On the Evidence for the Creative Role of Christian Prophets', *NTS* 20 (1973-4), 262-74. [180 n. 101]

Hirsch, E. D., *Validity in Interpretation* (New Haven, Conn., 1967). [188 n. 68, 189 n. 77]

Hofius, O., *Katapausis* (Tübingen, 1970). [143 n. 4, 148 n. 36, 149 nn. 39 & 41, 159 nn. 22 & 28, 160 n. 37, 161 n. 43]

Der Vorhang vor dem Thron Gottes (Tübingen, 1972). [143 n. 4, 152 n. 65, 153 n. 80, 160 n. 41, 161 n. 45]

Hooker, M. D., 'Christology and Methodology', *NTS* 17 (1970-1), 480-7. [180 n. 102]

'In His Own Image?' in *What about the New Testament?* (C. F. Evans Festschrift), ed. M. D. Hooker and C. Hickling (London, 1975), 28-44. [145 nn. 14 & 20]

'On Using the Wrong Tool', *Theology* 75 (1972), 570-81. [180 n. 102, 181 n. 107]

Hoskyns, E. and Davey, N., *The Fourth Gospel* (London, 1940, 1947²). [168 n. 117]

The Riddle of the New Testament (London, 1931, 1958²). [168 n. 115, 173 n. 1]

Hughes, G. R., 'From Galatia to St Gyro's: "Justification by Faith" as a Cross-Cultural Problem', *South East Asia Journal for Theology* 17, 2 (1976), 23-31. [181 n. 81]

Jacobson, R., 'The Structuralists and the Bible', *Interpretation* 28, 2 (1974), 146-64. [144 n. 8]

Jeremias, J., *The Eucharistic Words of Jesus* (London, 1966). [155 n. 120]

'Hebr 5.7-10', *ZNW* 44 (1952-3), 107-11. [156 n. 15]

Article on Μωυσῆς, *TDNT* IV, 848-73. [146 n. 19, 148 nn. 33 & 35]

The Parables of Jesus (London, 1963²). [191 n. 91]

The Jewish Encyclopedia, vols. I-XII, ed. C. Adler *et al.* (New York, 1901-6). [166 n. 94]

Johnson, M. D., *The Purpose of the Biblical Genealogies* (Cambridge, 1969). [150 n. 52, 154 n. 99]

Jonge, M. de, 'Christian Influences in the Testaments of the Twelve Patriarchs', *NovT* 4 (1960), 182-235. [154 n. 99]

Studies on the Testaments of the Twelve Patriarchs (Leiden, 1975).
   [154 n. 99]
The Testaments of the Twelve Patriarchs (Assen, 1953). [154 n. 99]
Jonge, M. de and van der Woude, A. S., '11Q Melchizedek and the New
   Testament', *NTS* 12 (1965–6), 301–26. [146 n. 15]
Käsemann, E., *Essays on New Testament Themes* (London, 1964). [181
   nn. 106 & 110, 182 n. 123, 188 n. 61, 190 n. 88]
New Testament Questions of Today (London, 1969). [158 n. 6]
Perspectives on Paul (London, 1971). [165 n. 77]
Das wandernde Gottesvolk (Göttingen, 1961[4]). [144 n. 13, 146 n. 16,
   152 n. 65, 153 nn. 76 & 77, 155 n. 2, 156 nn. 19 & 20, 159 nn. 24,
   29, 30, 32 & 34, 160 nn. 39 & 41, 161 n. 50, 162 n. 55, 163 n. 66,
   170 nn. 132 & 135, 171 n. 138, 174 n. 14, 175 n. 26, 176 n. 46]
Kaufman, G. D., *Systematic Theology: A Historicist Perspective* (New
   York, 1968). [158 n. 11, 159 nn. 16 & 17]
'What Shall We Do with the Bible?', *Interpretation* 25 (1971), 95–112.
   [184 n. 17, 192 n. 100]
Keck, L. E., *A Future for the Historical Jesus* (Nashville, Tenn., 1971).
   [175 n. 34, 176 n. 56, 178 n. 80, 179 n. 82, 182 n. 121]
Kelsey, D. H., *The Uses of Scripture in Recent Theology* (Philadelphia,
   1975). [185 n. 31, 187 n. 55, 190 nn. 84, 85 & 88, 191 nn. 94 & 97,
   192 n. 101]
Kennedy, H. A. A., *The Theology of the Epistles* (London, 1919). [149
   n. 44, 155 n. 120, 178 n. 77]
Kistemaker, S., *The Psalm Citations in the Epistle to the Hebrews*
   (Amsterdam, 1961). [157 nn. 2 & 4, 166 n. 99, 167 n. 103]
Kittel, G., articles on λέγω, λόγιον, *TDNT* IV, 91–136, 137–41. [163
   n. 65, 168 n. 117]
Klappert, B., *Die Eschatologie des Hebräerbriefes* (Munich, 1969). [143
   n. 4, 148 n. 31, 152 nn. 65 & 66, 159 n. 29, 161 n. 47, 162 n. 55,
   165 n. 80, 166 n. 97, 170 nn. 133, 134 & 135, 171 n. 138, 172
   n. 149, 196 n. 31]
Knox, W. L., 'The "Divine Hero" Christology in the New Testament', *HTR*
   41 (1948), 229–49. [176 n. 54]
Kögel, J., 'Der Begriff τελειοῦν im Hebräerbrief' in *Theologische Studien
   Martin Kähler dargebracht* (Leipzig, 1905), 35–68. [155 n. 1, 163
   n. 66]
Kosmala, H., *Hebräer–Essener–Christen* (Leiden, 1959). [154 nn. 100, 103
   & 108, 157 n. 4, 160 n. 41, 161 n. 51, 162 n. 58, 164 n. 70, 165
   n. 87, 174 n. 16]
Köster, H., 'Die Auslegung der Abraham-Verheissung in Hebräer 6' in
   Studien zur Theologie der alttestamentlichen Überlieferungen (G.
   von Rad Festschrift), ed. R. Rendtorf and K. Koch (Neukirchen,
   1961), 95–109. [152 n. 65, 162 n. 55, 165 nn. 74 & 75]
'Outside the Camp: Hebrews 13.9–14', *HTR* 55 (1962), 299–315. [153
   n. 88, 178 n. 170]
Kuhn, K. G., 'The Two Messiahs of Aaron and Israel' in *The Scrolls and
   the New Testament*, ed. K. Stendahl (New York, 1957), 54–64. [154
   n. 99]

Kümmel, W. G., article 'Schriftauslegung im Urchristentum', RGG^3 V, cols. 1517–20. [165 n. 80]

'Ein Jahrzehnt Jesusforschung (1965–1975)', *ThR* n.s. 40 (1975), 289–336; 41 (1976), 197–258. [180 n. 96, 181 n. 105]

'Jesusforschung seit 1950', *ThR* n.s. 30 (1965–6), 15–46, 289–315. [173 n. 3]

Kuss, O., 'Der theologische Grundgedanke des Hebräerbriefes – zur Deutung des Todes Jesu im neuen Testament' in *Auslegung und Verkündigung* (collected essays, vol. I) (Regensburg, 1963), 281–328. [162 n. 56, 164 n. 71]

'Der Verfasser des Hebräerbriefes als Seelsorger' in *Auslegung und Verkündigung* (collected essays, vol. I) (Regensburg, 1963), 329–58. [148 n. 38, 153 n. 93]

Lampe, G. W. H. and Woollcombe, K. J., *Essays on Typology* (London, 1957). [169 n. 130]

Leonard, W., *The Authorship of the Epistle to the Hebrews* (London, 1939). [149 n. 44]

Lessing, G. E., *Lessing's Theological Writings*, ed. H. Chadwick (London, 1956). [184 n. 22]

Lindsell, H., *The Battle for the Bible* (Grand Rapids, Mich., 1976). [189 n. 76]

Loewenich, W. von, 'Zum Verständnis des Opfergedankens im Hebräerbrief', *ThBl* 12 (1933), cols. 167–72. [177 n. 65]

Lohmeyer, E., *Diatheke – Ein Beitrag zur Erklärung des neutestamentlichen Begriffs* (Leipzig, 1913). [155 n. 118]

Lohse, E., *Märtyrer und Gottesknecht* (Göttingen, 1955). [159 n. 35, 171 nn. 138 & 144, 176 nn. 46 & 53, 177 n. 67]

Louvain 1971, see under World Council of Churches.

Luck, U., 'Himmlisches und irdisches Geschehen im Hebräerbrief', *NovT* 6 (1963), 192–215. [159 n. 35, 161 n. 47, 173 nn. 157 & 2, 176 nn. 46 & 47, 178 n. 71]

Maccoby, H., 'Is the Political Jesus Dead?', *Encounter* 46, 2 (February 1976), 80–9. [180 n. 98]

McIntyre, J., *The Christian Doctrine of History* (Edinburgh, 1957). [158 n. 6, 159 n. 20]

McNeile, A. H., *An Introduction to the Study of the New Testament* (Oxford, 1953^2). [173 n. 156]

Macquarrie, J., *The Scope of Demythologizing* (London, 1960). [185 n. 33, 189 n. 79]

Manson, W., *The Epistle to the Hebrews: An Historical and Theological Reconsideration* (London, 1951). [143 n. 2, 146 nn. 11, 14 & 20, 166 n. 90, 167 n. 106, 168 n. 112]

Maurer, C., ' "Erhört wegen der Gottesfurcht", Hebr 5.7' in *Neues Testament und Geschichte* (O. Cullmann Festschrift), ed. H. Baltensweiler and B. Reicke (Tübingen, 1972), 275–84. [156 n. 17, 177 n. 60, 180 n. 100]

Meeks, W. A., *The Prophet-King* (Leiden, 1967). [148 n. 35]

Michel, O., *Der Brief an die Hebräer* (Meyer Kommentar über das Neue Testament) (Göttingen, 1966^{12}). [146 nn. 6 & 11, 147 n. 24, 148

nn. 36 & 38, 149 n. 46, 150 n. 50, 151 nn. 55 & 59, 155 nn. 3 & 4,
156 n. 19, 158 nn. 12 & 13, 159 nn. 26 & 31, 160 n. 41, 162 nn. 56
& 58, 163 nn. 64, 66 & 67, 164 n. 69, 168 n. 113, 169 n. 125, 174
n. 14, 175 nn. 32 & 38, 176 n. 46, 179 n. 86]
Article on Μελχισεδέκ, *TDNT* IV, 568–71. [169 n. 125]
'Zur Auslegung des Hebräerbriefes', *NovT* 6 (1963), 189–91. [172
n. 151]
Miller, D. G., 'Why God Became Man', *Interpretation* 23 (1969), 408–24.
[177 nn. 58 & 63]
Minear, P. S., 'Christian Eschatology and Historical Methodology' in
Neutestamentliche Studien für Rudolf Bultmann, ed. W. Eltester
(Berlin, 1954), 15–23. [184 n. 30]
Miskotte, K. H., *When the Gods Are Silent* (London, 1967). [158 n. 8, 183
n. 16, 184 n. 28, 192 nn. 104 & 107]
Moe, O., 'Das Priestertum Christi im Neuen Testament ausserhalb des
Hebräerbriefes', *ThLz* 72 (1947), cols. 335–8. [154 n. 113]
Moffatt, J., *The Epistle to the Hebrews* (International Critical Commentary)
(Edinburgh, 1924). [143 n. 2, 144 n. 13, 150 n. 51, 151 nn. 54, 57,
59 & 60, 153 nn. 77, 82, 84 & 90, 154 n. 102, 160 n. 40, 163 n. 66,
166 n. 90, 168 n. 113, 173 n. 1, 175 nn. 27, 29, 33, 35, 36, 37 & 40,
176 n. 44, 177 n. 58, 178 n. 71]
Moltmann, J., *Theology of Hope* (London, 1967). [144 n. 6, 148 n. 38,
158 n. 11, 165 n. 75, 185 n. 35]
Montefiore, H. W., *A Commentary on the Epistle to the Hebrews* (Black's
New Testament Commentaries) (London, 1964). [158 n. 7, 159
n. 18, 161 n. 51, 162 nn. 56 & 61, 158 n. 12, 162 n. 56, 163 n. 66,
168 nn. 108 & 113]
Moore, A. L., *The Parousia in the New Testament* (Leiden, 1966). [169
n. 121, 193 n. 22]
Moore, G. F., *Judaism* I–III (Cambridge, Mass., 1927–30). [164 n. 68]
Morrice, W. G., 'Covenant', *ExT* 86 (1974–5), 132–6. [155 nn. 120 & 121]
Moule, C. F. D., *The Birth of the New Testament* (London, 1962). [144
nn. 7 & 12, 145 n. 2, 152 n. 65, 153 nn. 83 & 89, 158 n. 7, 165
nn. 79 & 89, 179 n. 84]
'Fulfilment Words in the New Testament: Use and Abuse', *NTS* 14
(1967–8), 293–320. [156 nn. 7, 8 & 9, 161 n. 52]
An Idiom Book of New Testament Greek (Cambridge, 1963). [174
n. 23]
The Phenomenon of the New Testament (London, 1967). [152 n. 68,
167 n. 104, 175 n. 34, 177 n. 68]
'Sanctuary and Sacrifice in the Church of the New Testament', *JTS* n.s.
1 (1950), 29–41. [144 n. 12, 153 nn. 85 & 86, 165 n. 79, 172 n. 150]
Moulton, J. H. and Milligan, G., *The Vocabulary of the Greek Testament*
(London, 1914). [183 n. 4]
Müller, P.-G., ΧΡΙΣΤΟΣ ΑΡΧΗΓΟΣ (Bern, 1973). [156 n. 18]
Mussner, F., 'Wege zum Selbstbewusstsein Jesu', *BZ* n.s. 12 (1968), 161–73.
[180 n. 96]
Nairne, A., *Epistle of Priesthood* (Edinburgh, 1913). [175 n. 40]
The Epistle to the Hebrews (The Cambridge Greek Testament for

Schools and Colleges) (Cambridge, 1922). [152 nn. 70 & 74, 163 n. 66]

Nauck, W., 'Zum Aufbau des Hebräerbriefes' in *Judentum, Urchristentum, Kirche* (J. Jeremias Festschrift), ed. W. Eltester (Berlin, 1960), 198-206. [144 n. 10, 145 n. 4]

Neil, W., 'The Criticism and Theological Use of the Bible, 1700-1950' in *The Cambridge History of the Bible – The West from the Reformation to the Present Day*, ed. S. L. Greenslade (Cambridge, 1963), 238-93. [184 n. 18, 188 n. 61, 189 n. 79]

Torch Commentary on Hebrews (London, 1955). [143 n. 1]

Neill, S., *The Interpretation of the New Testament 1861-1961* (London, 1964). [184 n. 18]

Netherlands Reformed Church, *The Bible Speaks Again* (London, 1969). [183 n. 10, 189 n. 71, 190 n. 88, 191 n. 90, 192 n. 106]

New Directions, see under World Council of Churches.

Niebuhr, R. R., 'Archegos: An Essay on the Relation between the Biblical Jesus and the Present Day Reader' in *Christian History and Interpretation* (J. Knox Festschrift), ed. H. R. Farmer, C. F. D. Moule and R. R. Niebuhr (Cambridge, 1967), 79-100. [176 n. 51, 182 n. 122]

Nineham, D. E., *New Testament Interpretation in an Historical Age* (London, 1976). [177 n. 63, 188 n. 65, 189 n. 77]

'A Partner for Cinderella?' in *What About the New Testament?* (C. F. Evans Festschrift), ed. M. D. Hooker and C. Hickling (London, 1975), 143-54. [181 n. 107]

Nomoto, S., 'Herkunft und Struktur der Hohenpriestervorstellung im Hebräerbrief', *NovT* 10 (1968), 10-25. [154 n. 113]

Oepke, A., *Das neue Gottesvolk* (Gütersloh, 1950). [154 n. 102, 160 n. 40, 171 n. 138]

Omark, R. E., 'The Saving of the Saviour', *Interpretation* 12 (1958), 39-51. [177 n. 59]

Owen, H. P., 'The "Stages of Ascent" in Hebrews 5.11-6.3', *NTS* 3 (1956-7), 243-53. [163 n. 66]

Palmer, H., *The Logic of Gospel Criticism* (London, 1968). [180 n. 102]

Palmer, R. E., *Hermeneutics* (Evanston, Ill., 1969). [183 n. 2, 185 n. 32, 186 n. 37]

Pannenberg, W., *Jesus – God and Man* (London, 1968). [158 n. 11, 180 n. 97, 193 n. 21]

'Redemptive Event and History' in *Essays on Old Testament Interpretation*, ed. C. Westermann (London, 1963), 314-35. [158 n. 11]

Piper, O., *New Testament Interpretation of History* (Princeton, N.J., 1963). [158 n. 6]

Polzin, R., 'The Framework of the Book of Job', *Interpretation* 28, 2 (1974), 182-200. [144 n. 8]

Procksch, O., article on ἁγιάζω, *TDNT* I, 111f. [176 n. 43]

Rad, G. von, *Old Testament Theology*, vols. I and II (Edinburgh, 1965). [163 n. 66, 168 nn. 110 & 119, 169 n. 121]

Ramsay, A. M., 'The Gospel and the Gospels', in *Studia Evangelica*, vol. I, ed. K. Aland *et al.* (Berlin, 1959), 35-42. [157 n. 2]

Reid, J. K. S., *The Authority of Scripture* (London, 1957). [192 n. 105]

Renner, F., '*An die Hebräer*' – *ein pseudepigraphischer Brief* (Münster-schwarzach, 1970). [143 n. 4]

Richardson, A., *History, Sacred and Profane* (London, 1964). [175 n. 41]

Introduction to the Theology of the New Testament (London, 1958). [168 n. 117]

'The Rise of Modern Biblical Scholarship and Recent Discussion of the Authority of the Bible' in *The Cambridge History of the Bible – The West from the Reformation to the Present Day*, ed. S. L. Greenslade (Cambridge, 1963), 294–338. [184 n. 18, 189 n. 79]

Ricoeur, P., 'Die Hermeneutik Rudolf Bultmanns', *EvTh* 33 (1973), 457–76. [145 n. 16]

Riggenbach, E., 'Der Begriff der ΔIAΘHKH im Hebräerbrief' in *Theologische Studien Theodor Zahn dargebracht* (Leipzig, 1908), 289–316. [155 n. 118]

Der Brief an die Hebräer (Leipzig, 1913). [148 n. 34, 150 n. 51, 151 n. 59, 163 nn. 66 & 67]

Rissi, M., 'Die Menschlichkeit Jesu nach Hebr 5.7–9', *ThZ* 9 (1955), 28–45. [177 n. 62]

Ritschl, D., 'A Plea for the Maxim: Scripture and Tradition', *Interpretation* 25 (1971), 113–28. [187 n. 55, 190 n. 87]

Robinson, J. M., 'Hermeneutic since Barth' in *The New Hermeneutic*, ed. J. M. Robinson and J. B. Cobb (New York, 1964), 1–77. [184 n. 21]

A New Quest of the Historical Jesus (London, 1959; 2nd rev. edn as *Kerygma und historische Jesus*, Zurich, 1967). [181 n. 112, 182 n. 117]

Robinson, J. M. and Koester, H., *Trajectories through Early Christianity* (Philadelphia, 1971). [191 n. 92]

Robinson, T. H., *The Epistle to the Hebrews* (The Moffat New Testament Commentary) (London, 1933[1], 1953[7]). [163 n. 66]

Robinson, W., *The Eschatology of the Epistle to the Hebrews* (Birmingham, 1950). [196 n. 33]

Ruler, A. A. van, *The Christian Church and the Old Testament* (Grand Rapids, Mich., 1971). [183 n. 9, 189 n. 80, 192 nn. 102, 103 & 108]

Rust, E. C., *The Christian Understanding of History* (London, 1947). [159 n. 16]

Sasse, H., article on αἰών, *TDNT* I, 197–208. [158 n. 9]

Sauter, G., *Zukunft und Verheissung* (Zurich and Stuttgart, 1965). [160 n. 41, 165 n. 75]

Schaeffer, J. R., 'The Relationship between Priestly and Servant Messianism in the Epistle to the Hebrews', *CBQ* 30 (1968), 359–85. [169 n. 125]

Scheidweiler, F., 'ΚΑΙΠΕΡ nebst einem Exkurs zum Hebräerbrief', *Hermes* 83 (1955), 220–30. [156 n. 16]

Schenke, H.-M. 'Erwägungen zum Rätsel des Hebräerbriefes' in *Neues Testament und christliche Existenz* (H. Braun Festschrift), ed. H. D. Betz and L. Schottroff (Tübingen, 1973), 421–37. [143 n. 1, 149 n. 48, 152 n. 74, 153 n. 80]

Schierse, F. J., *Verheissung und Heilsvollendung* (Munich, 1955). [145 n. 4, 147 n. 29, 151 n. 63, 159 nn. 21, 24, 27, 30, 31, 33 & 35, 160 nn. 36 & 38, 161 nn. 44, 46 & 53, 162 n. 59, 170 n. 135, 171 nn. 141, 143 & 144, 172 n. 150, 176 n. 46, 180 n. 95]

Schille, G., 'Erwägungen zur Hohepriesterlehre des Hebräerbriefes', *ZNW* 46 (1955), 81–109. [146 n. 10, 149 n. 46]

Schleiermacher, F. D. E., *Hermeneutik*, ed. H. Kimmerle (Heidelberg, 1959). [188 n. 69]

Schlier, H., 'Grundelemente des priesterlichen Amtes im Neuen Testament', *Theologie und Philosophie* 44 (1969), 161–80. [155 n. 114]

Schmithals, W., *An Introduction to the Theology of Rudolf Bultmann* (London, 1968). [187 n. 58]

Schmitz, O., 'Das Alte Testament im Neuen Testament', in *Wort und Geist* (K. Heim Festschrift), ed. A. Koberle and O. Schmitz (Berlin, 1934), 49–74. [155 n. 118, 165 n. 75]

Schnackenburg, R., *The Will to Believe* (London, 1974). [191 n. 96]

Schneider, J., *The Letter to the Hebrews* (Grand Rapids, Mich., 1957). [147 n. 24]

Scholder, K., *Ursprünge und Probleme der Bibelkritik im 17. Jahrhundert* (Munich, 1966). [183 nn. 13 & 14, 188 n. 62, 189 n. 73]

Schrenk, G., article on δικαιοσύνη, *TDNT* II, 192–210. [163 n. 66]

Schröger, F., *Der Verfasser des Hebräerbriefes als Schriftausleger* (Regensburg, 1968). [143 n. 4, 150 n. 53, 152 n. 65, 157 n. 4, 161 n. 53, 165 n. 81, 180 n. 100]

Schwarzwäller, K., 'Das Verhältnis Altes Testament–Neues Testament im Lichte der gegenwärtigen Bestimmungen', *EvTh* 29 (1969), 281–307. [145 n. 16, 168 n. 119]

Schweizer, E., *Church Order in the New Testament* (London, 1961). [162 n. 62]

Lordship and Discipleship (London, 1960). [171 n. 142, 176 n. 57]

'Scripture-Tradition–Modern Interpretation' in *Neotestamentica* (collected essays, 1951–63) (Zurich and Stuttgart, 1963), 203–35. [190 n. 82]

Scott, E. F., *The Epistle to the Hebrews: Its Doctrine and Significance* (Edinburgh, 1922). [143 nn. 1, 2 & 5, 144 nn. 12 & 13, 149 n. 43, 153 nn. 78, 81, 82 & 84, 154 n. 96, 173 n. 1, 178 n. 71]

The Literature of the New Testament (New York, 1932). [152 n. 70]

Scott, W. F. M., 'Priesthood in the New Testament', *SJT* 10 (1957), 399–415. [178 n. 71]

Selwyn, E. G., *The Oracles in the New Testament* (London, 1911). [163 n. 67]

Siegfried, C., *Philo von Alexandria als Ausleger des Alten Testaments* (Jena, 1875). [157 n. 4, 167 n. 102, 169 n. 124]

Simon, M., *St Stephen and the Hellenists in the Primitive Church* (New York, 1958). [146 n. 20]

Simpson, E. K., 'The Vocabulary of the Epistle to the Hebrews', *EQ* 18 (1946), 35–8, 187–90. [149 n. 40]

Smart, J. D., *The Interpretation of Scripture* (London, 1961). [161 n. 53, 184 n. 30, 185 n. 35]

Snell, A., *A New and Living Way* (London, 1959). [177 n. 63]

Sölle, D., *Christ the Representative* (London, 1967). [182 n. 118]

Sowers, S. G., *The Hermeneutics of Philo and Hebrews* (Zurich and Richmond, Va., 1965). [147 n. 22, 157 n. 4, 164 n. 68, 169 nn. 124 & 130]

Spicq, C., *L'Epître aux Hébreux*, vol. I (Paris, 1952). [157 n. 4]
Spivey, R. A., 'Structuralism and Biblical Studies: The Uninvited Guest',
    Interpretation 28, 2 (1974), 133–45. [144 n. 8]
Stählin, G., article on ἐφάπαξ, *TDNT* I, 383f. [171 n. 137]
Stanton, G. N., *Jesus of Nazareth in New Testament Preaching* (Cambridge,
    1974). [152 n. 72, 169 n. 125, 173 n. 6, 180 n. 103]
Starobinski, J., 'The Gerasene Demoniac' in *Structural Analysis and
    Biblical Exegesis*, R. Barthes *et al.* (Pittsburgh, 1974), 57–84. [184
    n. 27, 186 n. 53]
Stendahl, K., 'The Apostle Paul and the Introspective Conscience of the
    West', *HTR* 56 (1963), 199–215. [189 n. 81]
'Biblical Theology, Contemporary', *Interpreters' Dictionary of the
    Bible* (Nashville, Tenn., 1962), vol. I, 418–32. [184 n. 24, 189 n. 70]
Stewart, R. A., 'The Sinless Highpriest', *NTS* 14 (1967–8), 126–35. [156
    n. 11]
Strachan, R. H., *The Historic Jesus in the New Testament* (London, 1931).
    [173 nn. 1 & 2]
Strack, H. L. and Billerbeck, P., *Kommentar zum Neuen Testament aus
    Talmud und Midrasch*, vols. I–V (Munich, 1922–8). [146 n. 19, 154
    n. 111, 166 nn. 91, 94 & 95]
Strathmann, H., *Der Brief an die Hebräer* (Das Neue Testament Deutsch)
    (Göttingen, 1963[8]). [150 n. 53, 163 n. 66]
Swetnam, J., review of F. Schröger's *Der Verfasser des Hebräerbriefes als
    Schriftausleger, CBQ* 31 (1968), 130–2. [157 n. 4]
'Sacrifice and Revelation in the Epistle to the Hebrews: Observations
    and Surmises on Heb. 9.26', *CBQ* 30 (1968), 227–34. [172 n. 154]
Tasker, R. V. G., *The Gospel in the Epistle to the Hebrews* (London, 1950).
    [168 n. 113]
The Old Testament in the New Testament (London, 1946[1], 1954[2]).
    [146 n. 15]
Taylor, J. V., *Enough Is Enough* (London, 1975). [192 n. 107]
Theissen, G., *Untersuchungen zum Hebräerbrief* (Gütersloh, 1969). [143
    n. 4, 145 n. 3, 146 n. 10, 148 nn. 31 & 38, 149 nn. 42 & 46, 160
    n. 41, 170 n. 133]
Thielicke, H., *The Evangelical Faith*, vol. I (Grand Rapids, Mich., 1974).
    [184 nn. 25, 26 & 30, 185 n. 34, 186 n. 52, 190 n. 86]
Thiselton, A. C., 'The Use of Philosophical Categories in New Testament
    Hermeneutics', *The Churchman* 87 (1973), 87–100. [188 n. 68, 192
    n. 98]
Thomas, K. J., 'The Old Testament Citations in Hebrews', *NTS* 11 (1964–5),
    303–25. [166 n. 101]
'The Use of the Septuagint in the Epistle to the Hebrews', unpublished
    Ph.D. thesis, University of Manchester, 1959. [165 n. 82, 166 n. 101,
    167 n. 107, 168 n. 114]
Thompson, J. W., ' "That Which Cannot Be Shaken": Some Metaphysical
    Assumptions in Heb. 12.27', *JBL* 94 (1975), 580–7. [161 n. 43]
Thornton, T. C. G., 'The Meaning of αἱματεκχυσία in Heb. 9.22', *JTS* n.s.
    15 (1964), 63–5. [177 n. 63]
Thurén, J., *Das Lobopfer der Hebräer* (Åbo, 1973). [143 n. 4]

Trocmé, E., *Jesus and His Contemporaries* (London, 1973). [173 n. 4, 179 n. 82, 182 n. 117]

Tyrrell, G., *Christianity at the Crossroads* (London, 1909). [145 n. 20]

Vanhoye, A., *Structure littéraire de l'épître aux Hébreux* (Paris and Brussels, 1963). [144 n. 10]

Via, D. O., jun., *Kerygma and Comedy in the New Testament* (Philadelphia, 1975). [182 n. 125, 185 n. 32, 187 n. 57]

'A Structuralist Approach to Paul's Old Testament Hermeneutic', *Interpretation* 28, 2 (1974), 201-20. [144 n. 8]

Vielhauer, P., review of O. Michel's *Der Brief an die Hebräer*, *VuF* (1951-2), 213-19. [155 n. 3, 161 n. 51]

Weber, H.-R., 'God and the Powerful – the Biblical Search for Wisdom' (in press). [192 n. 107]

Welander, D. C. St V., 'Hebrews 1.1-3', *ExT* 65 (1953-4), 315. [145 n. 4]

Wells, G. A., *The Jesus of the Early Christians* (London, 1971). [174 n. 12, 179 n. 92]

Westcott, B. F., *The Epistle to the Hebrews* (London, 1889; repr. Grand Rapids, Mich., n.d.). [147 n. 24, 150 n. 51, 151 nn. 61 & 62, 157 n. 2, 166 n. 96, 167 n. 104, 175 nn. 24, 29, 33, 39, 40 & 42, 183 n. 5]

Westermann, C., 'The Interpretation of the Old Testament' in *Essays in Old Testament Interpretation*, ed. C. Westermann (London, 1965), 40-9. [152 n. 68]

Wieder, N. 'The "Law-Interpreter" of the Sect of the Dead Sea Scrolls: The Second Moses', *JJS* 4 (1953), 158-75. [148 n. 35]

Wikgren, A., 'Patterns of Perfection in the Epistle to the Hebrews', *NTS* 6 (1959-60), 159-67. [156 nn. 6 & 19]

Wilckens, U., 'Die Rechtfertigung Abrahams nach Römer 4' in *Studien zur Theologie der alttestamentlichen Überlieferungen* (G. von Rad Festschrift), ed. R. Rendtorf and K. Koch (Neukirchen, 1961), 111-27. [193 n. 22]

Willey, B., *The Seventeenth Century Background* (Harmondsworth, 1962; Penguin edition). [188 n. 63]

Williamson, R., 'Hebrews and Doctrine', *ExT* 81 (1969-70), 371-6. [173 n. 2]

Philo and the Epistle to the Hebrews (Leiden, 1970). [143 n. 4, 145 nn. 2 & 3, 149 n. 45, 153 nn. 94 & 95, 154 n. 112, 157 n. 4, 159 n. 35, 160 n. 41, 161 n. 45, 163 n. 66, 166 n. 90, 169 nn. 124 & 125, 171 n. 141, 173 n. 2]

Windisch, H., *Der Hebräerbrief* (Handbuch zum Neuen Testament) (Tübingen, 1931²). [161 n. 53, 163 n. 66, 174 n. 11, 179 n. 92]

Winter, P., 'Notes on Wieder's Observations on the דורש התורה in the Book of the New Covenanters of Damascus', *JQR* 45 (1954), 39-47. [148 n. 35]

World Council of Churches, *Faith and Order, Louvain 1971* (reports to the Faith and Order Commission of the World Council of Churches meeting in Louvain, 1971) (Geneva, 1971). [190 nn. 84, 85 & 88, 191 n. 90, 192 n. 99]

New Directions in Faith and Order, Bristol 1967 (reports to the Faith and Order Commission of the World Council of Churches meeting in Bristol, 1967) (Geneva, 1968). [188 n. 64, 191 n. 94]

Woude, A. S. van der, *Die messianische Vorstellungen der Gemeinde von Qumran* (Assen, 1957). [154 nn. 99 & 106, 164 n. 68]

Yadin, Y., 'The Dead Sea Scrolls and the Epistle to the Hebrews' in *Scripta Hierosolymitana*, vol. IV, ed. C. Rabin and Y. Yadin (Jerusalem, 1965), 36–55. [146 n. 15, 149 n. 44, 154 nn. 100, 101, 105, 109 & 110]

'A Midrash on II Sam. 7 and Ps. 1–2 (4Q Florilegium)', *IEJ* 9 (1959), 95–8. [166 n. 93]

Young, F. M., *Sacrifice and the Death of Christ* (London, 1975). [171 n. 141, 177 nn. 63 & 64]

Sacrificial Ideas in Greek Christian Writers (Cambridge, Mass.) (in press). [177 n. 64]

Ziesler, J. A., *The Meaning of Righteousness in Paul* (Cambridge, 1972). [163 n. 66]

Zimmermann, F., *Die Hohepriester-Christologie des Hebräerbriefes* (Paderborn, 1964). [170 n. 133]

Zuntz, G., *The Text of the Epistles* (London, 1953). [166 n. 101]

INDEX

Aaron, 13, 30, 80, 102
Abraham, 14, 16f, 20f, 42, 52, 58, 60, 86, 176 n. 43
access or approach: to heavenly realities, 13, 72f, 87, 90, 100, 103, 139, 172 n. 153, 193 n. 21; to Jesus of history, 75, 77, 178 n. 80, 179 n. 94, 181 n. 105
Alexandrian Judaism, dualism etc., 29, 42, 45, 66, 128, 151 n. 63, 160 n. 41, 161 n. 53, 195 n. 25, 196 n. 31
allegory, 65, 122, 169 n. 130
analogia entis, 117
angels, 6, 8f, 11, 13, 24, 54, 60f, 80, 102, 146 nn. 19 & 20, 147 n. 21, 167 n. 107; *see also under* servant
anonymity of Hebrews, 1, 25, 136, 152 n. 74
anthropology, 42, 118
apocalyptic ideas, 37, 41, 67, 141, 146 n. 9, 160 n. 41, 161 n. 43, 196 nn. 29f
apostasy (*includes references to despair*), 2, 46, 49f, 52, 58, 69, 77, 79f, 113, 131, 138, 142, 162 nn. 60 & 63, 171 nn. 140 & 142
apostle, Jesus as, *see under* Jesus
application, 73f, 108, 121, 125, 130, 134, 183 n. 10, 189 nn. 72 & 81
argument of the writer, 1f, 9, 11, 16-18, 22, 27f, 54-7, 94, 151 n. 61, 169 n. 130
atonement, 1, 30, 75, 89, 103, 118, 125
author of Hebrews, *see* writer
authority, 126-9, 190 n. 84

'boundaries', 119, 121f, 132, 189 n. 77

Canaan, 10, 43f
canon, 98, 126, 129f, 137, 182 n. 120, 190 n. 88

Cartesianism, 111, 121, 184 nn. 25f
church and Jesus, *see under* Jesus
city, heavenly, *see* heavenly city
comparison, threefold, of Jesus with Old Testament personages, 7, 9, 11-14, 16, 23f, 25, 28, 80f, 102, 145 n. 4, 149 n. 44
confession, maintenence of, 10, 38f, 56, 69f, 72, 74, 78f, 87, 173 n. 156
confidence, 48, 56, 72, 78, 84, 87f, 94, 100, 102, 109f, 131, 135, 142
continuity, between Old Testament and New Testament communities, institutions etc., 6, 11-13, 26, 41-4, 46f, 53, 66, 70, 86, 90, 98, 102f, 108, 126, 140, 160 n. 40, 189 n. 80
covenant, new, better etc., 9, 20f, 23, 25, 34, 42, 46, 67, 69
Creator, creation, 37, 39, 159 n. 16, 169 n. 129
critical historical method, the, 24f, 55f, 63, 105, 110-14, 119-24, 130f, 181 n. 107, 184 nn. 28 & 30, 189 n. 79

death, 15, 20, 69, 83f, 88, 104, 108, 176 n. 46
death of Jesus, *see under* Jesus
decision, 37, 39, 95, 113, 115, 159 n. 17
'definition', 16, 64f, 119, 130
Deist controversies, 111, 119
demonic forces (*includes references to the Devil*), 42, 83-5, 132, 171 n. 138
Deuteronomy, 59-61, 150 n. 51, 165 n. 89, 192 n. 107
'difficult word, the', 48f, 162 n. 63
'disclosure situation', 83, 94, 175 n. 41
distance, historical, of ancient texts, 1, 3f, 36, 39, 101, 110, 116, 118, 130, 183 n. 10
'double negation', 63, 105-7, 122f, 189 nn. 78f

214